THE AMERICANO

THE AMERICANO

Fighting with Castro
for Cuba's Freedom

Aran Shetterly

Algonquin Books of Chapel Hill
2007

Published by
Algonquin Books of Chapel Hill
Post Office Box 2225
Chapel Hill, North Carolina 27515-2225

a division of
Workman Publishing
225 Varick Street
New York, New York 10014

Library of Congress Cataloging-in-Publication Data
    Shetterly, Aran, 1970–
    The Americano : fighting with Castro for Cuba's freedom /
Aran Shetterly. — 1st ed.
        p. cm.
    Includes bibliographical references.
    ISBN-13: 978-1-56512-458-5
    1. Morgan, William, 1928–1961. 2. Cuba—History—
Revolution, 1959—Participation, American. 3. Revolutionaries—
Cuba—History—20th century. 4. Revolutionaries—United
States—History—20th century. I. Title.
F1788.22.M67S54 2007
972.9106'4—dc22   2006031640

10 9 8 7 6 5 4 3 2 1

First Edition

This book is for my family, whose love and support made the work
possible. It is also for the men and women of the Second National Front
of the Escambray, especially Eloy, Ramiro, Roger, Bibe, and Max,
in hopes that their stories will be remembered.

Contents

Cast of Characters

Second National Front of the Escambray (*Segundo Frente Nacional del Escambray*; SNFE)

William Alexander Morgan: Comandante. American from Toledo, Ohio; born April 19, 1928, in Cleveland; arrived in Cuba in early 1958; enlisted with SNFE and became Rebel hero

Eloy Gutiérrez Menoyo ("El Gallego"): Comandante. Born 1934 in Madrid, Spain; moved to Cuba as a boy; founded SNFE; Morgan's commander and close friend

Armando Fleites: Comandante. Doctor; ally of Menoyo

Lázaro Artola: Comandante. Affiliated with M-26-7

Miguelito de Camajuani: Close friend of Ramiro Lorenzo and Edel Montiel

Jesús Carreras: Comandante. Close friend of Morgan

Ramiro Lorenzo: Capitán. Close friend of Morgan and Menoyo; orginally affiliated with M-26-7 (*see below*)

Max Lesnik: Chief propaganda officer in Havana; close to Menoyo

Edel Montiel: Capitán. One of first SNFE rebels to turn against Castro; later sought Morgan's aid

Roger Redondo: Capitán. Confidant of Morgan and Menoyo

Roger Rodríguez: In charge of propaganda in Escambray; recruited Morgan to SNFE

Olga María Rodríguez Fariñas: Born in Santa Clara; student revolutionary, joined SNFE; married William Morgan

Felix "Bibe" Rafael Vázquez Robles: Young Rebel from Caunau; friend of Ramiro Lorenzo

26th of July Movement (*Movimiento 26 de Julio*; M-26-7)

Fidel Alejandro Castro Ruz: The Maximum leader of the Cuban Revolution; born Aug. 13, 1926, in Mayarí Oriente Province; has led Cuba since Jan. 1, 1959

Camilo Cienfuegos: Comandante. Beloved by the Cuban people; died in plane crash Oct. 28, 1959

Ernesto "Che" Guevara de la Serna: Comandante. Born June 14, 1928, in Rosario, Argentina; only foreigner with rank of comandante other than Morgan. Killed October 9, 1967, in Bolivia, where he was trying to start a rebel movement

Juan Almeida: Comandante. Became head of Revolutionary Armed Forces after Rebel victory

Revolutionary Student Directorate (*Directorio Revolucionario Estudiantil*; DRE)

José Antonio Echevarria: Leader of DRE; some say the only young Cuban to rival Castro in charisma; died in March 13, 1957, attack on Presidential Palace

Faure Chomón: Leader of DRE after March 13 attack; clashed with Menoyo and with Castro, but chose loyalty to Revolution

Raúl Nieves: Capitán. Loyal to Chomón and Castro

THE OLD GUARD

Carlos Prío Socarrás: President of Cuba 1948–52; left Cuba and presidency when Batista staged coup in 1952

Fulgencio Batista y Zaldívar: Born 1901; son of a poor laborer; rose to power through military ranks; elected president of Cuba (1940–44), retired, then took back presidency through army coup March 10, 1952; ruled until Jan. 1, 1959, when he left Cuba under pressure from Rebels and U.S. government; died in Spain Aug. 6, 1973

Manuel Benitez: Head of Havana police department under Batista; later an FBI informant

José Eleuterio Pedraza: Army general under Batista; led Cuban counterrevolutionary effort from Dominican Republic during Trujillo Conspiracy in effort to win Cuba back from Castro

Esteban Ventura Novo: Head of Batista's secret police

THE AMERICANS

Dominick Bartone: Associate of Jimmy Hoffa and Meyer Lansky

Laura Bergquist: Journalist for *Look* magazine; interviewed Morgan during summer 1960

Paul Bethel: Press attaché in U.S. Embassy in Havana; reported to CIA station chief Jim Noel

Philip Bonsal: The last American ambassador to Cuba

Michael Colin: Filmmaker, PR man, and opportunist in Cuba after Revolution; worked for Morgan and allegedly informed on him for CIA

Thomas Errion: FBI special agent; assigned to Morgan in Miami

James Haverty: Legal attaché in U.S. Embassy in Havana; kept FBI and State Department abreast of developments in Cuba

Gerry Patrick Hemming: Ex-marine involved with Fidel Castro and Rebel cause; stayed in Cuba, befriended Morgan; appears to have provided information to U.S. Army Intelligence

Ernest Hemingway: Famous American author; friend of Herbert Matthews; longtime resident of Cuba

J. Edgar Hoover: Director of FBI 1924–72

Herbert Matthews: Career employee of *New York Times* with later focus on Latin America; at age 57, broke story that Castro, though reported to be dead, was still alive in Cuba

Frank Nelson: Bagman; freelancer for Dominican government, associate of Myer Lansky; claimed to have worked for CIA

Westbrook Pegler: Columnist-cum-FBI-informant, associated with J. Edgar Hoover

Clete Roberts: Journalist for NBC; film and television actor; interviewed Morgan in fall 1959

Leman L. Stafford Jr.: FBI special agent; assigned to Morgan in Miami

THE DOMINICANS

Rafael Leónidas Trujillo Molina: Dominican dictator 1930–61

Johnny Abbes García: Head of Dominican Military Intelligence Service

Father Ricardo Velazco Ordóñez: Spanish priest; worked for Trujillo

OTHERS

Carlos Menoyo (brother): Brother of Eloy Gutiérrez Menoyo; died in attack on Presidential Palace, March 13, 1957

Carlos Menoyo (father): Father of Eloy Gutiérrez Menoyo; Spanish Republican; took his family to Cuba in 1940s

Ellen May "Theresa" Bethel: Married Morgan in 1954 or 1955, divorced him in 1958 while he was in Cuba; mother of his children Anne and William Jr.

Jorge Luís Carro: Morgan's defense attorney; later became dean of University of Cincinnati Law School

Alexander W. Morgan: William Morgan's father

Loretta Morgan: William Morgan's mother

ORGANIZATIONS AND HISTORICAL FIGURES

26th of July Movement (M-26-7): Revolutionary movement started by Fidel Castro and named for date of 1953 attack on Moncada barracks in Santiago, Cuba

Second National Front of the Escambray (SNFE): Rebel group, founded by Eloy Gutiérrez Menoyo, to help unseat Batista; most significant Rebel force after the M-26-7

Directorio Revolucionario Estudiantil (DRE): Radical opposition group, made up mostly of young people, with long history of influencing Cuban politics; SNFE broke off from an alliance with DRE

José Julián Martí y Pérez: Poet and writer (1853–95), the most important cultural and political figure in Cuban history; died fighting for Cuban independence from Spain

Henry Reeve ("El Inglecito"): American who fought for Cuban independence from Spain

Sir Henry Morgan: Welsh-born (1635–88) pirate and British privateer; government assigned him task of disrupting Spanish interests in Caribbean

Bohemia: Popular, liberal weekly magazine in Cuba; dissolved in August 1960 over differences with Fidel Castro's government

Revolución: Primary newspaper and journalistic voice of Revolutionary government in Cuba

Time Line

August 13, 1926: Fidel Castro Ruz is born in Mayarí, Cuba.

April 19, 1928: William Alexander Morgan is born in Cleveland, Ohio.

June 14, 1928: Che Guevara is born in Rosario, Argentina.

December 8, 1934: Eloy Gutiérrez Menoyo is born in Madrid, Spain.

March 10, 1952: Fulgencio Batista seizes power with a military coup, suspending Cuba's nascent democracy.

July 26, 1953: Fidel Castro leads an armed attack on the Moncada barracks in Santiago, Cuba, in an attempt to spark a revolt against Batista. He is captured and imprisoned. From now on, his revolutionary organization will be referred to as the 26th of July Movement.

May 13, 1955: Batista grants Fidel Castro amnesty and he is released from prison.

December 2, 1956: Fidel Castro, Che Guevara, and 80 other men land their boat, the *Granma*, on the southeastern Cuban coast with intention of overthrowing Batista; 18 of the 82 make it safely into the Sierra Maestra and begin the guerrilla war.

March 13, 1957: The Student Revolutionary Directorate (DRE) and Carlos Gutiérrez Menoyo attempt to assassinate Batista. Many of Cuba's promising young leaders are killed. Carlos's brother, Eloy, works behind the scenes.

November 10, 1957: Eloy Gutiérrez Menoyo forms a second guerrilla front (Castro's M-26-7 is the first) in the Escambray Mountains of central Cuba.

late January 1958: William Morgan joins Eloy Gutiérrez Menoyo and his Rebel army.

February 24, 1958: Morgan sends his statement of purpose, "Why am I here," to Herbert Matthews of the *New York Times*.

March 13, 1958: The United States withdraws military aid to Batista.

Spring 1958: William Morgan meets Olga Rodriguez Fariñas.

August 1958: Morgan's American wife, Ellen May Bethel, is granted a divorce.

September 1958: Morgan is reported dead by Cuban Army.

November 1958: William and Olga marry in the Escambray Mountains.

January 1, 1959: Fulgencio Batista leaves, turning Cuba over to Castro and the Rebels.

January 1, 1959: Morgan and the SNFE take control of the important port city of Cienfuegos.

January 16 and 22, 1959: Fidel Castro publicly denies that he's a Communist.

March 1959: Frank Nelson approaches Morgan with plan to overthrow Castro, thus beginning the so-called Trujillo Conspiracy.

April 15, 1959: Fidel Castro meets with Vice President Richard Nixon in Washington. Nixon suggests that Castro is either naïve or a Communist.

June 14, 1959: Failed invasion of Dominican Republic is launched from Cuba.

July 27 and 30, 1959: Morgan is interviewed by FBI special agents in Miami.

August 11, 1959: The Trujillo Conspiracy ends. Morgan becomes a Cuban hero.

August 20, 1959: Morgan calls the FBI to apologize for lying to them during his July interviews and states his loyalty to Cuba.

August 29, 1959: William and Olga's first daughter is born.

September 3, 1959: The story breaks in American press that Morgan's U.S. citizenship will be revoked.

October 28, 1959: Camilo Cienfuegos's plane disappears.

December 14, 1959: Huber Matos is charged with conspiring against Cuban government.

January 1960: The trial of those involved in the Trujillo Conspiracy takes place. Morgan is a witness.

February 1960: Soviet Deputy Premier Anastas Ivanovich Mikoyan visits Cuba and signs a trade agreement with Castro.

March 4, 1960: The Belgian cargo ship *La Coubre* explodes in Havana Harbor.

March 6, 1960: Morgan fires his PR man, Michael Colin, saying that he's "crazy."

March 7, 1960: In a *Miami Herald* article, Jack Lee Evans, who'd been staying with Colin in Havana, implicates Morgan in the *La Coubre* disaster.

March 1960: Eloy Gutiérrez Menoyo dissolves the SNFE in the interest of "national unity."

March 1960: Counterrevolutionaries make contact with Morgan.

May 23, 1960: Cuba asks U.S.-owned refineries in Cuba to process Russian crude oil. When the owners refuse, the refineries are nationalized.

June 19, 1960: Morgan and other members of SNFE, including Menoyo, agree that Fidel Castro is Communist.

July 6, 1960: President Eisenhower cuts U.S. commitment to purchase Cuban sugar by 700,000 tons.

August 1960: *Bohemia* editor Miguel Angel Quevedo leaves Cuba, announcing "a revolution betrayed."

September 5, 1960: Fidel Castro holds a meeting in Cienfuegos on strategy for clearing counterrevolutionaries out of the Escambray.

October 11, 1960: Siniseo Walsh and Plinio Prieto, former members of SNFE, are apprehended in Escambray, where they have been organizing counterrevolution.

October 21, 1960: Morgan, Jesús Carreras, and others are arrested and imprisoned in Cuban intelligence headquarters.

October 22, 1960: President Eisenhower withdraws Ambassador Philip Bonsal from Cuba.

October 25, 1960: All remaining U.S. corporate interests in Cuba are nationalized, including Coca-Cola.

January 3, 1961: U.S. officially breaks diplomatic relations with Cuba.

January 1961: Eloy Gutiérrez Menoyo, Max Lesnik, Armando Fleites, and others secretly leave Cuba by boat.

March 9, 1961: The trial of Morgan and Carreras begins.

March 11, 1961: Morgan and Carreras are sentenced to be executed.

March 11, 1961: Morgan and Carreras are executed at La Cabaña prison.

March 18, 1961: Olga Morgan is apprehended and jailed.

April 16, 1961: Fidel Castro declares Cuba a Socialist state.

April 17, 1961: U.S.-supported attack by Cuban exiles at Bay of Pigs begins and is defeated by Cuba's Revolutionary Armed Forces within 72 hours.

May 30, 1961: Rafael Leónidas Trujillo is assassinated in the Dominican Republic.

December 1964: Eloy Gutiérrez Menoyo returns to Cuba to start a counterrevolution.

January 1965: Menoyo is captured in eastern Cuba, where he spends 22 years in prison. His capture marks the demise of any significant counterrevolutionary activity inside Cuba, ending what Raúl Castro called a "civil war."

THE AMERICANO

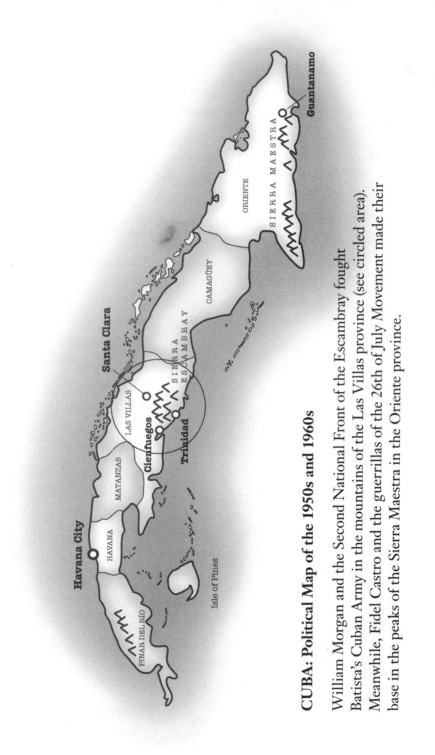

CUBA: Political Map of the 1950s and 1960s

William Morgan and the Second National Front of the Escambray fought Batista's Cuban Army in the mountains of the Las Villas province (see circled area). Meanwhile, Fidel Castro and the guerrillas of the 26th of July Movement made their base in the peaks of the Sierra Maestra in the Oriente province.

PROLOGUE

*. . . [I]t becomes harder and harder to know the truth
of many things which have occurred in Cuba [after the
Revolution]. . . . perhaps this is where History may be said
to have ended and contemporary politics begins.*
        Hugh Thomas, Cuba or the Pursuit of Freedom

"You should have come to see me before you went up to that
stupid little town. Now those old rebels think you are working for the CIA and the risk is greater for anybody who helps
you. You are lucky you aren't in jail," said the historian in Cuba
whom, for her sake, I will not identify.

The air in the library smelled like lost history, of mildew and
old, rotting paper. Sweat drizzled down my brow and tickled
my sides. Would I lose the access that I had so carefully culti-
vated? Access to people and to libraries that Americans don't
dream of, access that most Cubans aren't even allowed? This
was serious. I had not gone through proper channels before I'd
appeared in a small rural town and started nosing around its
thorny, forty-year-old Revolutionary history, and the Ministry
of the Interior, the Cuban equivalent of the FBI, acting on a
tip from the local Veterans Association, had told me to leave. I
couldn't just smile and charm my way around the country with
my Cuban expressions and gringo enthusiasm. Cubans who
mattered cared about what I was doing and how I did it.

I wasn't just researching a footnote of the Cuban Revolution; I was trying to tell the story of an American man referred to in official Cuban histories as a traitor. But he's also a man many Cubans inside and outside Cuba claim as a hero, and one who, some would go so far as to say, saved the Cuban Revolution from a quick and ignominious end before it was one year old. Other than this American, the only foreign Rebel to hold the rank of Comandante was Che Guevara, whose imposing stare animates billboards all around the country, challenging Cubans to think always of the nation first. William Morgan's name, however, elicits whispers and hushed tones. On anti-Fidel Castro Web sites, Morgan is listed as a martyr to the cause of ridding Cuba of its charismatic leader, though he's also considered one of the greatest Rebel guerrilla fighters of Fidel's own Revolution.

"Okay," I said to the historian, "tell me what I need to do."

"Come back tomorrow," she answered.

I sighed with relief. My mission to uncover the history of William Alexander Morgan's time in Cuba from 1958 to 1961 would continue.

≡ Little had I known that researching William Morgan's life would land me squarely in the middle of a struggle for historical hegemony: Who gets to tell Cuba's history? Whose version will be told and, more importantly, believed by Cubans, Cuban-Americans, Americans, and the world at large? The narratives that define the protagonists and antagonists in Cuban history are often tactics in the ongoing maneuvers for present and future control of the island. These manipulations themselves become part of the history. Sometimes, they are all that exist.

So how can the history be told? It must be recovered and cobbled together from the memories of those who participated, from the few recorded accounts, from declassified intelligence documents, and from often confusing and biased news reports.

The stories that are not told are at risk of being lost forever. The urgency of this problem cannot be exaggerated. Every day, pieces of history are lost. People die. Documents, newspapers, and letters crumble to dust or are destroyed.

William Morgan's Cuban story led me into the liminal space of unrecorded and unpublished history. For nearly every historical incident, there is an official version, in which the sides are clear—the Americans against the British, the Cubans against the Spanish, the United States against the Soviet Union. In each case, however, there is more than one story. There are more than two stories. The true stories of why and how events unfolded are always complex, and they come down to the fears, loves, angers, and hopes of the individual participants. William Morgan's story led me into gray, true, and unexplored aspects of the Cuban Revolution.

≣I first came across William Morgan's story in 2001. I was traveling in Cuba with a group, learning about Cuban art, before the Bush Administration made people-to-people contact between Americans and Cubans more difficult. Our itinerary included museums, galleries, and artists' studios, and we were also taken to places that highlighted the achievements of the Cuban government. We visited hospitals that practiced preventive medicine through outreach into the community. We toured a literacy museum where we learned how Cubans taught each other to read and became the most literate country in Latin America. And we met with a provincial secretary who argued (not convincingly) that Cuba's form of government was the most democratic in the world.

When he was done, I asked him if any Americans—particularly brigades of Americans—had come to Cuba to fight with Fidel against Batista. I had studied the Spanish Civil War and wondered if groups resembling the international brigades that fought fascism in Spain had joined Cuba's civil war.

"No," he said. Then he paused and added, "But there was one man. What was his name . . . ? William Morgan."

At that moment, I had an inchoate sensation that William Morgan's adventure in Cuba would lead me on my own. Who was he? Why had he gone to Cuba? What did he believe in? Beyond his personal story, I hoped that his rise and subsequent fall from favor in Cuba might help me, as an American, better understand some of the current tensions that exist today in Cuban–American relations.

I quickly learned that asking questions about William Morgan in either Cuba or Miami is like plugging directly into a current of emotion that runs as hot today as it did forty-five years ago, and offers lessons not only through what is said, but also through what goes unsaid, is unknown, and is withheld.

Before I illustrate this passion, however, I need to mention a couple of pieces of revolutionary history. First, Fidel Castro did not begin the guerrilla war in 1956 with overt Communist intentions. On the contrary, he said that among his goals were the removal of the dictator, Fulgencio Batista, the restoration of the democratic constitution of 1940, and alleviation of undue pressure from foreign governments, namely the United States. Second, Fidel Castro's Rebel organization, the 26th of July Movement, was not the only Rebel group fighting Batista's

Cuban Army. Two other significant groups were the Revolutionary Student Directorate (DRE) and the Second National Front of the Escambray (SNFE), the latter for which William Morgan fought as a Rebel soldier. The SNFE's contribution to the Rebel war has been edited out of official Cuban history.

≡ In July of 2004, I met Roger Redondo, who had been a Rebel soldier with William Morgan. He agreed to let me interview him about the Second National Front of the Escambray. We met on Eighth Street in Miami's Little Havana. He lives in Costa Rica, enjoying the ease that comes with being away from the political pressures of Cuban Miami, and was in town visiting his mother and his doctor, fellow SNFE veteran Armando Fleites. Redondo didn't want to be interviewed in any of the Cuban joints, so we met at McDonald's. We sat outside on the playground, surrounded by purple slides and green swings, a virtual jungle of American consumerism, and talked about Cuba.

Redondo's voice is naturally quiet, and as I leaned in to listen to his stories I felt like a spy—the unconventional meeting place; the hushed tones; the topic that still burns, after all these years, with an unresolved urgency. In the Otto Richter Library at the University of Miami, a librarian who was assisting me turned her back and walked away when I told her I'd interviewed Morgan's Rebel commander, Eloy Gutiérrez Menoyo. "My husband hates him," she hissed. "He's a Communist." Among the Miami Cuban Right, this is a common view of Menoyo and his friends in Miami and Washington, who, for the last ten to fifteen years, have favored dialogue with Castro as the best means for creating change on the Island. I could understand why Redondo, as an associate of Menoyo's, preferred to meet out of the public eye.

After we had spoken for a time, going over dates and events and the people involved, Redondo said, "We [the SNFE] just had no one at the level of Fidel Castro. He was always a couple of steps ahead of everyone else. He is so smart. He knew more than the rest of us and could see further ahead than we could." To hear a Cuban in Miami pay Fidel Castro a compliment is rare, to say the least. Most Miami Cubans, or certainly the most *outspoken* ones, would call Castro "evil," "ruthless," a "megalomaniac," or any number of descriptors delineating someone pathological, even satanic. You can hear tirades of this sort every day on Miami talk radio.

To hear Fidel called "smart" and "brave," on the other hand, gave me pause. Many of the veterans of the Second National Front of the Escambray who live in Miami, it turns out, would say similar things about Castro. These were men who had lost so much because their group had threatened Fidel's omnipotence. What pains them most is the exile, the fact that they are living away from friends and family, away from home. Yet Redondo and others spoke of Castro without bitterness and with a touch of awe, though not because they support or agree with the way he runs the Cuban government. They spent time on the same revolutionary playing field as Cuba's leader, and they recall him as would good baseball players who marvel at a great baseball player. They gave everything to the cause of a free Cuba. They put their lives on the line. In the end they were outmaneuvered, and they are willing to admit it.

After talking for more than two hours, Redondo began to tire. He has a heart condition that causes him pain and saps his energy.

Finally, he asked me a question: "Was Morgan with the CIA?"

I looked at this kind, smart man who had impressed me with both his memory and his persistence about getting things right, and I thought about what it must be to carry so many doubts about the facts of your own history. Redondo had met Morgan the day he arrived in the mountains. He fought with Morgan, partied with Morgan, worked with Morgan, and yet he, like so many others, remains unsure of his friend's motivations. Back in 1958 it would never have occurred to him that Morgan was an intelligence agent, but now he wondered.

During the summer of 2002, Comandante Raúl Nieves invited me to his duplex apartment across from the Malecón seawall and promenade in Havana to talk about the Escambray and the Revolution.

Nieves, in his seventies now, is a little hard of hearing, which may account in part for his revolutionary shout, a tone I encountered often among Cubans who find comfort in parroting reams of official history. It's like listening to a quarreling spouse who wants his entire argument to be heard uninterrupted, hoping that some incantatory power will make what he says unquestionable.

It's also like Fidel Castro's impassioned discourses, which are ubiquitous on Cuban television. He's not just standing there, he's always talking, delivering long lectures that, for the most part, sound nothing like the "reasonable" political speeches to which we are accustomed in the United States. Fidel argues and defends, rants and chides. He pauses to fiddle with the microphones, collects himself for a particularly salient barb aimed at some aspect of U.S. policy. Then he bounces up onto his toes, cocks his head, rolls his *R*s, points his finger, accusing and justifying. Regardless of what he's saying, his passion is impressive. The modulation of his voice and his body language persuade before the ideas have come to rest in the listeners' minds. It's great drama and it's on almost every day.

The revolutionary shout of other Cubans seems to imitate the tone of Fidel's conviction, often repeating something *el Comandante en Jefe* has said. Sometimes the speakers even reference their source, saying, for example, "As Fidel said about the French Revolution, . . ." While the imitators can reproduce the volume, they have trouble reflecting the passion and, since they are merely sourcing their information, when they finish what they can remember they often start over from the beginning.

Nieves gnawed on an unlit cigar and listened to the quick synopsis of my research. Then he disappeared upstairs and brought back his personal archive of photos, documents, and notes on the Revolution. He was planning a book, he said, one that would tell the true story of the Escambray.

As he shuffled his papers, Nieves ignored or didn't hear my first questions about the Second National Front of the Escambray. A rooster walked through the laundry room beyond the kitchen. The Comandante laid out black-and-white photographs from 1958, '59, '60, and '61. Photographs of the Rebel Nieves showed a man who looked like a young Robert De Niro, wiry, tough, and clearly loving the adventure of rebellion and revolution. "Faure Chomón," he said, identifying his commander and the leader of the DRE. "But who's that?" I asked, pointing at an unnamed man beside Chomón. At first, Nieves ignored me, and I thought maybe he'd forgotten the man's name. I tried again. Finally, exasperated, he bellowed in a pitch-perfect revolutionary shout, "*Traidor!*—Traitor!"

It soon became evident that only two categories of people

existed: heroes and traitors. The heroes had names. The traitors didn't. "Who's that?" I'd ask. "Traitor!" he'd bellow. Misguided. Nothing good about them—ever. Even the things they'd done in support of the Revolution before they became traitors were erased! They mattered only as a category of people to be eliminated, and as a foil to those who had remained loyal to Castro's Revolution.

Our conversation went on from there, question and deflection, parry and riposte, like a fencing match, each of us daring the other to expose a little more of what he knew.

"The Second National Front of the Escambray never fought in a single battle. When Faure Chomón arrived in the Escambray, he realized immediately that Menoyo and his companions were traitors. He denounced them and expelled them from the DRE."

"All they did," he continued in the loud monotone, "was eat the peasants' cows, chase the peasant women, and get fat."

That was it, the entire history of the SNFE according to Raúl Nieves. Over the course of our two hours, I heard this version several times.

As Nieves told me about "traitors" and "*comevacas*—cow eaters," I peered over his shoulder at the notes he flipped through as we talked. When he noticed my gaze, he turned slightly, as if to block my view, but he did not put the papers away. In the documents, I caught brief glimpses of lists of men who fought with the SNFE and charts detailing the SNFE's battles with the Cuban Army, battles that Nieves was telling me had never happened. The notes on Nieves's dining-room table, the ones he was allowing me to catch bits and pieces of, contradicted nearly everything he was telling me. On one list, next to almost every Rebel victory in the Escambray was written the name of Morgan or Menoyo. I saw location names: La Diana, Charco Azul, Michilena, Linares, Hanabanilla, Río Negro. The list went on.

Was he trying to protect himself and give me information at the same time? Or was he careless? Nieves never strayed from the official talking point, that the SNFE were traitors and agents of the imperialists. I had nothing on tape that would compromise him.

When we finished the interview Nieves and his wife insisted on taking me to lunch. We went to an outdoor restaurant that catered to the Cuban elite and foreign diplomats. The three of us were whisked into a mobile, aluminum storage building that had been outfitted as a dining room for special parties. There were no windows. The air conditioning whirred and I shivered as the three of us ate alone in the room. Nieves had a glass of rum, his mood darkened, and I wondered at the personal toll his distortions had exacted.

≡ This book tells stories kept quiet both in Cuba and in Miami. There's the story of the people who fought to rid Cuba of a dictator and to improve the lot of the Cuban people and then lost the struggle for democracy at the hands of Fidel Castro. Some, like Redondo, managed to flee Cuba; others, like William Morgan, died on the island; and still others, and perhaps Nieves was one of these, stayed and conformed.

And then there's William Morgan's personal story, which helps set straight distortions generated by the clash of right and left and reminds us that there existed a middle ground: that of the reformists. It gives voice to people, like Roger Redondo, whose words and thoughts have been drowned out by the extremes. I have stitched William Morgan's story together using fragments pulled from a gray world of contested history, a world I stumbled into and couldn't leave until I understood what had happened to this young American man. Morgan's story opens a door to unknown aspects of the Cuban Revolution. His life is filled in by the people who knew him and by the Rebels who, in Cuba, loved him.

Part I

REBELLION

LIMBO

In the life of a man, his time is but a moment, his being an incessant flux, his senses a dim rushlight, his body a prey of worms, his soul an unquiet eddy, his fortune dark, and his fame doubtful. In short, all that is of the body is as coursing waters, all that is of the soul as dreams and vapors, life a warfare, a brief sojourning in an alien land; and after repute, oblivion.

Marcus Aurelius, Meditations, *Book 2, no. 17*

"Why do I fight here in this land so foreign to my own . . . Is it because I seek adventure? No, . . . I am here because I belive [sic] that the most important thing for free men to do is to protect the freedom of others . . . I cannot say I have always been a good citizen but . . . [o]ver the years we as Americans have found that dictators, and communist[s] are bad people with whom to do business yet here is a dictator who has been supported by the communist[s] and he would fall from power tomorrow if it were not for the American aid. And I ask myself why do we support those who would destroy in other lands the ideals which we hold so dearly?"

With these words, a young American named William A. Morgan defended his decision to join the Cuban Rebels in their struggle against the dictator Fulgencio Batista. He set his thoughts down in a letter, dated February 24, 1958, and sent them to the *New York Times.*

Three years later, on March 15, 1961, Herbert Matthews, the *New York Times* reporter who received the letter, himself something of a legend with a storied and controversial career, sent a note to his friend Ernest Hemingway, whom he had met more than twenty years earlier while covering the Spanish Civil War. That letter outlined the story of the young Morgan, who had just been executed in Havana by the Cuban authorities. William Morgan had, in Matthews's words, "got himself shot" for conspiring against Cuba's government. After suggesting that Morgan's story reminded him of a Hemingway tale, Matthews went on to summarize Morgan's remarkable time in Cuba as a Rebel hero, ending with the thought that "unfortunately for him, he continued to believe in freedom and to disapprove of Communism." Matthews believed that the young man's resistance to compromise on this point had, in the end, marked his path to the firing squad. "From all accounts," wrote Matthews, "he died bravely."

Three years prior to his execution, Morgan had been fighting on the same side as Fidel Castro. Morgan had helped the young Cuban leader come to power, and had done so believing that he was fighting not only against the tyranny of Batista's dictatorship but for democracy and freedom. Today, after more than two generations of a Castro-run Cuba, it's difficult to remember that in the 1950s one could be for revolution in Cuba, consider Fidel Castro a beacon of democratic justice, *and* hold the line against Communism. Indeed, even Che Guevara, the Argentine Marxist, said that the original intention was "bourgeois reform" but that a series of factors, including violent opposition to the Rebels' early policies, forced the Revolutionaries into a more radical position.

In 1961, as Matthews approached retirement, the legacy of his own career was being called into question. Near the close of his letter to Hemingway, he half-jokingly refers to "what I have to put up with these days" and mentions that demonstrators had picketed the New York Times Building to protest his views on Cuba, specifically his early, enthusiastic support of Fidel Castro. Matthews believed that Fidel's intentions had been democratic, but diplomatic clumsiness and heavy-handedness on the part of the United States, in combination with the inexperience and defensive pride of the young Cuban revolutionaries, had forced an outcome that would be undesirable to both sides, namely an incipient relationship between Cuba and the Soviet Union.

Within the context of the Cold War, only a few years past the height of red baiting and McCarthyism, there was little, if any, room in the United States for a nuanced position with respect to Communism. Either Fidel Castro was a Communist or he wasn't.

Mix into this indigenous political culture an angry and influential community of dispossessed exiles—the wealthy and well-connected Cubans who had fled Castro's ever more radical reforms—and discussions about sharing blame for Castro's politics sank like leaky boats caught in the strong Gulf currents. Castro, to them, was a violent thief who had taken what they believed to be theirs.

The Cuban and American businessmen whose interests had been circumscribed by the Revolution knew that crying "Communism!" would elicit a Cold War response from the American government. And so they did, early and often. There was to be no talk about Castro's *becoming* a Communist. By 1960 the issue had settled, officially, into a starkly contrasting black-and-white binary. Castro—and with him Cuba, as far as the U.S. was concerned—was playing on the wrong side.

In a 1961 review of Matthews's book, *The Cuban Story*, published in the *Nation* magazine, Warren Miller wrote that "Matthews must feel, as does anyone who tries to make himself heard on Cuba, that no one wants to listen; or if any do, most are determined to go away unviolated by a new idea." It could be argued that this has changed only in degree over the last forty-four years. The biggest difference may be that fewer people now have any real opinion on the subject and those who do know what they think defend their opinions like dogs guarding meaty bones.

By refusing to relinquish his more nuanced analysis, Matthews found himself marginalized as a popular figure and also at the *New York Times* itself. Both colleagues and superiors believed that Matthews led with his heart, eschewing the dispassionate role of the reporter, and in so doing had damaged the paper's reputation. There is something to this: when Matthews first journeyed into the Sierra Maestra in 1957 to meet Castro and his guerrilla army, it was clear from his articles that Matthews (like the majority of Americans, among them William Morgan) was rooting for the young revolutionary. It seemed that, in Castro, Matthews saw the Great Latin American Hope. Following their meeting, Matthews wrote that Castro "is a political mind rather than a military one. He has strong ideas of liberty, democracy, social justice, the need to restore the Constitution, to hold elections."

Matthews's coverage of the Cuban rebellion would prompt a mocking cartoon, published in the conservative *National Re-*

view. It showed Fidel Castro astride his country like a cowboy upon his pony with the tag line, "I got my job through the *New York Times.*"

It is little surprise, therefore, that Matthews's tone in the letter to Hemingway reveals some sympathy for Morgan and the younger man's unwillingness to compromise his hope for a democratic outcome in Cuba. Like Morgan, Matthews maintained optimism long after it became fashionable to do so, and he suffered for it. Unlike Morgan, he did not pay the ultimate price.

≣ When the Cuban government executed Morgan, not everyone in the United States was sympathetic to his cause. Even opponents of Fidel Castro, who might have used the American's death to rally anti-Castro sentiment, stayed clear of Morgan's complex story.

Perhaps Morgan's most outspoken public critic was a syndicated columnist named Westbrook Pegler, who also happened to be a friend of the FBI director, J. Edgar Hoover. In his columns, Pegler projected gritty common sense guided by unquestioning patriotism. The caricature that accompanied his column presents a man past middle age with the lined face of a smoker set in a head shaped like a bow tie turned on end.

Pegler expressed intense distaste for Morgan. He pegged Morgan as someone with no moral foundation, who determined his allegiance not by the quality of a political ideal but by the size of the possible paycheck. In a column for the *New York Journal-American* shortly after Morgan's death, Pegler quoted the opinion of an American judge "angrily deplor[ing] the glamorous publicity which some of our press had accorded to William Morgan merely because, in the end, he faced the firing squad with the flippant courage of the traditional Latin American filibuster. When he finally looked death in the eye he did not flinch." However, the judge, concluded: "I had no respect for him [Morgan]. He had no loyalty."

The William Morgan that Pegler described was a "nasty fellow," a brutal soldier of fortune, unconcerned with the cost of winning fame and wealth. In Pegler's opinion, Morgan had "ruined the lives of his respectable mother and father and, in the end, he betrayed first the United States to the Communist regime of Cuba and then betrayed Castro."

Despite his virulent and long-held anti-Castro views, Pegler resisted any temptation to exploit Morgan's execution, to canonize the American as a martyr to the cause of removing Castro from power. Morgan's early support of Castro was an indelible stain. Or was it his opposition to Batista? More important than this, however, was the conviction on the part of Hoover and his friend Pegler that individual Americans should be discouraged from playing a part in any Latin American revolution. The only loyalty that counted was allegiance to the United States and its interests; the dirty work was to be left in the hands of the professionals.

≡A third impression of Morgan arises from an article written by Laura Bergquist. Bergquist was the only one of these three journalists who had met and interviewed Morgan and the only one who believed that he might not have actually turned against Castro at all. (Surprisingly, for all the time he'd spent in Cuba, Matthews had not met Morgan, though his wife, Nancie, had.)

On a rainy day in August of 1960, more than a year and a half after the Rebel victory, Bergquist was "caroming around Cuba for a *Look* [magazine] study of Castroland" when she roamed west of Havana to visit an American who was raising frogs.

Bergquist barely noticed the frogs. The "guns and bearded bodyguards" distracted her from the aquaculture. After all, the topic that preoccupied most American journalists beating around Cuba during this period was Communism. More specifically, she wanted to know what this American-turned-Rebel soldier-turned-frog-farmer, William A. Morgan, thought of the government installed by Fidel Castro. She wanted to know if Morgan believed that Fidel was creating a Communist government just ninety miles from the United States.

When Bergquist interviewed Morgan and one of his Cuban assistants, each was outfitted in the olive green uniform of the Cuban Revolutionary Armed Forces, .38-caliber sidearm belted to his waist. In a photo from her visit, Morgan, short haired, clean shaven, the top two buttons of his military shirt unbuttoned, smiles a broad, relaxed smile.

To an American journalist in Cuba, talking with Morgan must have offered a sense of common ground and easy communication. Surely, with Morgan, Bergquist experienced a feeling common to so many travelers in a foreign land: the instinctual understanding, even trust, of a compatriot. These moments of the familiar in an unfamiliar context lend brief comfort and respite from the struggle to understand the new place.

A series of three photographs that accompany the article capture Morgan's expressive face. The cameraman caught him listening intently in one, raising his eyebrows to convince his audience in the next, and appearing to crack a wry joke from the side of his mouth in the last. This was a man of many expressions . . . or masks.

When the military tribunal leveled its charges against Morgan, several months later, Bergquist, obviously charmed by the American Rebel, wrote, "I tend to believe Morgan's innocence, for a number of reasons. Among them was the fact that the Cuban intelligence . . . kept a hawk-eye watch on Morgan. . . . His 'counterrevolutionary' activities supposedly took place in September. Yet, late in August, Morgan was a man bursting with future plans. . . ."

In Cuba, one does not find a diversity of opinions about Morgan. The official history is brief and to the point: Morgan worked for the CIA. He was a pawn of the imperialists. He had no real agency of his own. He represents nothing more than a small, shadowy episode in the David and Goliath narrative that pits Cuba against the United States.

In Toledo, Ohio, Morgan's family and the men and women with whom he'd grown up didn't know what to make of the native son who had ended up so far from home. They couldn't get past the transgressions of his youth. He'd dropped out of high school, spent time in jail, and left his young family behind when he embarked on his Cuban adventure. Surprisingly, given the fact that the *Toledo Blade* kept close track of Morgan's activities in Cuba, many of his high school classmates continued to believe that Morgan had been a Communist. While this idea might not be consistent with the facts, it, like Pegler's version, fits with a story of wrong choices made and the rejection of all things familiar.

Each version of Morgan's story suits the agenda or interests of the teller. Indeed, the retelling becomes a kind of morality tale, meant to teach a lesson to those who will listen. For

Matthews, Morgan supports the belief that Cuba might have become a democracy; Pegler uses him to suggest that only cruel, dangerous people support Latin American revolutions; Bergquist shows that earnest idealists were betrayed by the Revolution. The Cuban government bolsters the argument that they are in a life-and-death battle with an amoral and insidious superpower. Morgan's contemporaries in Toledo emphasize the danger of turning away from solid, Midwestern values.

Since 1961 Morgan's story has rested in an uncomfortable limbo. In the ongoing Cold War between the U.S. and Cuba, it froze. One historian has suggested that if John F. Kennedy hadn't been assassinated, we would know more about Morgan, that those interested in figuring out Morgan's story turned their attention to the mystery of who shot the President. However, the primary reason we might know more about Morgan if Kennedy hadn't been killed in 1963 is that the president was working on a possible rapprochement with Cuba. If the political air between Havana and Washington had grown warmer, Morgan's story would, undoubtedly, be told differently.

Beyond its obvious point, the *National Review* cartoon attacking Matthews suggests that a single person can affect or alter the flow of a historical moment. William Morgan, a curious but by no means successful man in his life prior to the Cuban Revolution, inserted himself into a pivotal moment in the history of the island and became a leader in one of the most important revolutions in the Western Hemisphere, a figure who had to be taken into account by the governments of both the United States and Cuba. He left behind friends, lovers, and enemies in two countries. He began this journey with little more than chutzpah and a dream of reinventing himself.

REBEL

After peaceful elections in 1944 and 1948, Cuba seemed poised to become a reasonably stable—if corrupt—democracy supported by a large middle class. But in March of 1952, Fulgencio Batista snatched power with a military coup and declared himself president. Many Cubans, especially students and young professionals such as Fidel Castro, who had been running for an elected office in 1952, immediately defied the new regime. By the mid-1950s, robust resistance networks existed throughout the country. In December of 1956, Fidel took a boat from Mexico, where he'd been plotting in exile, and landed with eighty-two guerrillas on the southeastern coast of Cuba. He had returned, as promised, to rid the country of Batista and corruption and to restore democracy. By the end of 1957, Fidel and his followers in the 26th of July Movement had been fighting for almost a year. Other opposition groups, such as the Second National Front of the Escambray, encouraged by the success of the 26th of July Movement, formed rebel units and made their way into the hills to join the armed struggle. The overriding mission shared by all such groups—to force Batista from the country—masked political and ideological differences that would emerge later.

• • •

Late January, 1958

Below his sentry post, Ramiro Lorenzo saw a trail of dust float into the air where a path emerged from the trees. He was expecting Faustinito, a peasant farmer who spent his life cultivating and scavenging the hills of central Cuba. Today, Faustinito was due to deliver a recruit to the Rebel camp. Only two weeks before, Faustinito had led Ramiro himself from the city of Sancti Spíritus to this Rebel camp in the woods, picking his way along the game trails and streambeds as if he had made them.

The newest and youngest member of this small guerrilla group had very soon become known as Ramirito, a nickname that reflected both his youth and his diminutive stature. As the junior member of the group, he was expected to pass long hours standing sentry with a borrowed gun. Ramirito raised the rifle he'd fired only a handful of times in practice, sighted along the barrel, and pointed it toward the spot where the visitors would come into view. Just in case.

Behind Ramirito, up the mountain, about thirty men were busy plotting a strategy for challenging Fulgencio Batista's dictatorship of Cuba while they awaited a shipment of weapons from Miami. The arms and munitions would not only increase their firepower but would allow them to recruit more men into the struggle. With these weapons, they believed, their guerrilla war would begin.

For just over two months this core group had been at the camp not far from the highway outside of the town of Banao. Some had been there longer than that as fugitives wanted by Batista's police for agitating against the regime. Though these young men were planning a rural campaign, many of them were city boys becoming acclimated to a life of hammocks and campfires, and to moving lightly through a landscape of forests, coffee plantations, and small subsistence farms.

At night they crouched around a campfire, inspecting and cleaning the few old guns they possessed. After weeks in the mountains, their bodies were lean and hard from nearly constant movement and the adjustment to the harsh life of a guerrilla soldier. During the day they walked for hours at a time, hacked trails up and down steep slopes through dense underbrush, scavenged food, dug up malanga roots to boil, and hunted. They bought beans, bananas, and the occasional chicken from local sharecroppers whose trust they had gained.

Some were dressed in olive-colored pants and shirts, make-shift army clothes, others in whatever they had worn into the mountains. Most of the men in the group were in their twenties. Many of them had been students striving for the middle-class lives of businessmen, doctors, and lawyers before they dropped everything to take action against Batista. They were far from the comforts they'd known in Havana, Cienfuegos, Sancti Spíritus, and Trinidad. Others were rural kids and cattle rustlers, more accustomed to roughing it, to living off the land. All were wary, learning to read the forest sounds. So far, luck was with them and the Cuban Army had not detected their presence.

Ramirito heard the soft trilling whistle of a friendly visitor and responded in kind with a low *woooo* that resembled the eerie call of the Cuban trogon, a beautiful red, blue and white bird that looks like it's cloaked in the Cuban flag. He heard the signal again, then footsteps from the path. As Faustinito came into view, Ramirito echoed the signal call one more time.

Behind the wiry, barefoot farmer were two men, one thin

and one heavy. The heavy man labored to keep up. Even from a distance, Ramirito could tell he was not Cuban. He wore city clothes, a white shirt, matching slacks, and city shoes. But it was the man's carriage that gave the young Cuban pause; in spite of his clothes and bulk, he walked with a dogged purpose, as if he belonged in these hills. There was nothing tentative in the way he pushed himself to mark pace with the guide.

Ramirito lowered his gun and watched the men approach. As they passed by, Faustinito offered an "*Hola*" and a nod in salutation. The light-haired American—Ramirito was sure of it now, though he'd seen only a few Americans in his life—nodded at the boy, flashed a conspiratorial smile, and winked one blue-gray eye.

What is he doing here? Ramirito wondered. This question, he knew, was not his worry. *El Gallego* and the others would know what to make of this *americano*.

After an exhausting journey, William Morgan had arrived at the Rebel camp. He had left Havana three days earlier. Back in the capital, the party went on despite the civil war that encroached each day on the country's daily business. For the American tourist, Havana was notorious as the pleasure capital of the hemisphere. The historian Hugh Thomas wrote that "the traveler's first sight of Havana on arrival by sea remained what it had always been: a broad harbour, commanding buildings on either side, a multitude of ships, his views overlaid no doubt by the sentiment that Havana had been for longer than any city in the New World a center for pleasure."

Tourists, traders, and politicians came for Cuba's cigars, coffee, sugar, rum, the casinos with a Caribbean beat, and the women. Havana was a place geographically close to home where Americans could explore their appetites. One such American who played the party circuit in Havana was a junior senator from Massachusetts, John F. Kennedy, who traveled there with his friend George Smathers, the Florida senator and an intimate of Batista's.

By 1957, however, thousands of police prowled Havana to keep the city safe for tourists or, perhaps more precisely, to obscure the intensity of the civil war. As much as Batista wanted to crush the Rebels militarily, he also struggled to maintain the country's laissez-faire image by controlling all news of the Rebel intransigence. Batista's utility to the United States would diminish rapidly if he could no longer protect the American interests that controlled as much as 70 percent of Cuban business.

So, Havana's mob-run casinos and hotels stayed open. There were incidents: bombs exploded, gunfire popped in the distance, police cars raced to apprehend men and women who moved carefully between professional jobs and covert sabotage against the government. To a surprising degree, life in Havana proceeded apace and the active urban insurgency remained largely invisible to tourists.

However, the scene changed dramatically when one attempted to travel beyond the city limits. There the national schizophrenia revealed itself at checkpoints; it was nearly impossible to enter Cuba's interior without encountering the police, rural guard, or army along the way.

The driver from Havana who took Morgan as far as Sancti Spíritus told him not to say anything if army patrols stopped them. The driver and Morgan's Rebel chaperone, Roger Rodríguez, would tell the soldiers that they were taking an American businessman to Sancti Spíritus and then into the country to see the coffee plantations. They drove and smoked cigarettes, flicking the ashes out the window into the warm air. Morgan watched the landscape and dozed. Army patrols stopped them twice, and the driver related the prepared story. The soldiers looked at the driver's identification, at the American's passport and fancy suit, and let the men pass.

In Sancti Spíritus, Morgan was hustled into the Suarez house, a stop on an underground railroad that delivered men and supplies to the Rebels. Two days later, Rodríguez whisked Morgan from the house and they drove south along the highway, back toward Trinidad. At an appointed spot, the car stopped, a man whistled from the trees, and Rodríguez and Morgan got out of the car and followed Faustinito through the heat of the day, into the woods and up toward the hills of Banao.

The Escambray Mountains run through the center of the old Las Villas province. They aren't particularly tall mountains—none surpasses four thousand feet above sea level—but they look bigger because of how sharply they angle into the air. On a sunny day, when framed by blue sky, they look like purple-and-green triangles drawn by a child with a quick zig-zag, nearly archetypal.

Now, as the sun fell toward the horizon, the valley and slopes below were bathed in the clear afternoon light. From this elevated vantage, what had seemed, as they had walked through it, like a dense forest looked like a neat patchwork of commercial crops, kitchen gardens, and woods. Under the shade of the forest, Morgan could make out the dark green coffee bushes stretching up the slopes. Stands of banana palms with their large yellow-green leaves marked the edges of tenant farmers' yards and gardens. Smoke rose from behind one of these stands where a sharecropper's wife cooked the evening meal over an outdoor fire. Keeping to the shadows, the guide had led him within sight of one of the thatched huts, a *bohío*, the guide called it.

Morgan could hardly believe he was here, that the scene before him was real, not a dream or a Hollywood set. Soon enough all this—the trees, trails, fruits, the men, women, and children who inhabited the *bohíos*—would be familiar. But not yet.

Moments later Morgan walked into the Rebel camp. His light clothes glowed in the dwindling light, making the American stranger appear even bigger than he was. Most of the assembled Cubans were slight and stood at five foot eight or less. Morgan, at nearly six feet tall and weighing well over two hundred pounds, strong but out of shape, arrived in the gloaming like a white elephant, a huge Anglo-Saxon whose presence seemed, for some reason, to raise the spirits of this largely inexperienced and unproved group.

The man who stood before them had light hair and eyes, jutting ears, and a sharp nose. He was handsome, not in a seductive way but with no-nonsense good looks that exuded confidence and practical intelligence. The lines in his face and his weight made him look older than his twenty-nine years, but there was also a less tangible quality, a playful, open demeanor suggesting that he was going to tease you or tell you something about himself.

A number of the men approached the new recruit. Roger Rodríguez proudly let people know that he had brought an American with U.S. military experience. "World War II?" asked one in strongly accented English. Morgan only shrugged, not wanting to complicate matters with the history of his military service. His past, he suspected, wouldn't count for all that much here in the mountains. This was part of the reason he had come: the chance for a fresh start. What would matter was his willingness to live in caves and walk for miles over rough mountain trails, risking death to knock Batista off his perch in the Presidential Palace.

Morgan removed his shirt, which was soaked through with sweat, and revealed a broad expanse of chest and back and stomach. He looked soft to the men before him, but that was tempered by the nine-inch knife scar that sliced across the *americano*'s chest, the marks of old burns on his right arm, and the scar that dimpled the tip of his chin. He told the assembled Cubans that a friend of his, an old Army buddy, had been running guns from the States to the Rebels. The man had gone missing and Morgan, suspecting that his friend had been caught by Batista's police, had come to investigate.

"What I found out in Havana," Morgan told his audience, "was that my friend was murdered by Ventura and his men. They threw his body into the harbor."

Someone who knew English relayed this story. All of them had had their own run-ins with Colonel Esteban Ventura and his men, or knew people who had been harassed or tortured by Batista's secret police, the dictator's primary agents for repression and control of the people.

In fact, Lázaro Artola and a small group of men had fled Havana and Ventura that past summer, hoping to make it to the eastern end of the island, where they could join Fidel in the Sierra Maestra. Getting all the way across the country proved too difficult, and so they settled down in the hills of Banao to wait, to see what would happen, and to avoid the Cuban Army and police. So far they had remained undiscovered.

Artola regarded this chunky *yanqui*, skeptical about whether he could stick it out under the harsh conditions of mountain life. How much food would a man like that need? When Morgan needed to go to the bathroom, Artola pointed him right through a patch of *chichicate*, a bush with small, painful spines that can cause prickly discomfort for hours. An early test. When Morgan returned, his back and chest were turning red from the stings. "Shit! Fuck!" he cursed in English. Some of the men snickered—everyone knew a few words of English.

Roger Redondo had gone to gather food. He didn't like to cook and so volunteered for hunting and gathering instead. When he returned from his excursion, sweaty from digging malanga tubers out of a streambed, his backpack heavy and wet with his success, he noticed his companions milling about the camp clearing. In one hand, he carried a gun in case he should stumble across an army patrol and for the lucky chance to take a shot at one of the cat-size rodents, the *jutía*, that ran around these woods. Roasted on a spit over an open fire, a *jutía* was a chewy source of protein and a pleasant respite from a vegetarian diet of plantains, malanga, beans, and rice.

As Redondo drew nearer he caught a flash through the trees. A little closer and he realized that what he had seen was a wide back that expanded and folded as it approached the waist of the man's pants. It was the whitest skin he'd ever seen.

"We've got a new recruit, an American, brought in by Roger Rodríguez," someone said to the skinny and coolly handsome Redondo as he came into camp. Rodríguez was a neighbor of Redondo's from Sancti Spíritus. Redondo, a twenty year old who favored aviator glasses and cowboy hats, looked at the American and wondered how he would make it up and down the hills during the long, daily treks they employed to keep track of army movements.

Not in the least deterred by his newly acquired rash, Morgan smoked and gestured and argued his reasons for staying with the Rebels, explaining what he could do to help them. Even those who could not understand his words enjoyed watching his animated, expressive face. He asked for a knife, and when he was presented with one of adequate size, he picked out a tree a good twenty yards away. The Cubans watched as Morgan took a step and flicked the knife. There was a blur, a thud, and the knife shivered as the blade held in the tree trunk.

"*Coño!*—Damn!" murmured Eloy Gutiérrez Menoyo, the skinny, reserved leader of the group. Though he had lived in Cuba since he was a boy, El Gallego spoke Spanish with the hard edge and touch of a lisp that came from Spain, different from the soft, percussive Spanish spoken by the Cubans under his command.

Menoyo appeared even younger than his twenty-three years. After more than two months in the mountains, only the slightest wisps of beard grew from his chin, like the first dusky ribbons of smoke from a fire that has yet to catch. His authority at this early stage was less earned than inherited from a history of family conviction, courage, and loss.

As he did with any man who wished to join his Rebel force, Eloy Gutiérrez Menoyo interviewed William Morgan to discover the man's purpose and to let him know what would be expected of him. Every recruit was carefully screened to ensure that his intentions were aligned with those of the group and that he was not an infiltrator sent by Batista. But clearly Morgan wasn't that; he didn't speak a word of Spanish. How hard would it be to communicate with the American? At least he would only understand exactly what they wanted him to . . . until he learned *castellano*. And that would take a while. Could he cope with the strenuous life in the mountains, with the scarcity of food and cigarettes? Would the

American care enough to stick around after the first couple of weeks?

The question of why Morgan would have joined the Rebels is still being asked forty-eight years later. Many people, inside and outside Cuba, find it difficult to believe that the choice was purely personal. Did someone, they wonder, send Morgan to Cuba in an effort to influence the Rebels or to collect information?

"Why do you want to fight with us?" Menoyo asked Morgan through Artola, who was translating.

"I was in Miami a couple of years ago," said Morgan. "I learned about Batista then. I've been following your revolution in the papers and admire your fight for freedom. Before I came here I worked with some people to help supply the Rebels with guns from the United States. And now my friend's been killed."

"How do you think you can help us?"

"Well, I've had some military training. I can probably help train up some of your men in basic skills: how to use a weapon, execute an ambush, approach a target, fight hand-to-hand combat, set up a rescue mission for a downed man. That sort of thing. From what I understand they aren't the most experienced when it comes to fighting against an army. It's not the same as putting a bomb through a window at night and running away."

"Are you a Communist?"

This was a startling question for an American who was, generally speaking, patriotic, one who merely believed, like much of the American public, that the U.S. government had made a mistake in supporting a dictator like Batista.

"No. Is that a good or a bad thing?"

Menoyo had two reasons for asking this question of every potential recruit. He took off his horn-rimmed glasses with their Coke-bottle lenses and rubbed his eyes.

"Batista," he explained, "is supported by the American government, which gives him planes, tanks, artillery . . . all the latest machines. Technically, these weapons are given to fight Communism whether it develops internally or threatens from abroad. These weapons are not to be used to suppress movements advocating democratic reform. That's one reason no opposition group, with the exception of the Partido Socialista Popular—People's Socialist Party—will say they support Communism. Batista will still say we are Communists and use the damn weapons your country gives him, but when he does, he loses what little moral authority he might have had with the Cuban people or with world opinion.

"This is not a political group," he continued. "We are the military group supported by the Directoria Revolucionario Estudiantil—Revolutionary Student Directorate—a second guerrilla front in the fight against Batista. Fidel Castro opened the first Rebel front. Men who fight with him become part of the Movimiento de Julio—the 26th of July Movement. Fidel is a political leader. I am not a political leader. My only goal is to overthrow Batista. Any man who wants to fight with us, regardless of his affiliation with a political party or revolutionary group, can fight with the Segunda Frente—Second Front—as long as he is willing to accept my command.

"I am the Chief of Military Action for the DRE. Artola"—he gestured toward Lázaro Artola—"is a member of the 26th of July Movement. So is Ramirito. There are others. We can all work together."

Menoyo's father had taught him that political differences

between the factions fighting Franco in Spain weakened the resistance against the Nationalists. The Communists, for example, imposed rules that alienated many within the Republican Army. While the civil war was being fought, those opposed to Franco spent too much energy jockeying among themselves for control of Spain's political future. Their unity fractured. Franco and his disciplined army won.

In Cuba, Menoyo had seen infighting hinder the opposition to Batista: "Politics is why Batista is still alive. When the political people get involved, they get drunk and fight with each other and tell secrets, and by the time you spring your trap everyone knows what is happening. Batista doesn't show up. Everyone gets caught. We almost got him in Havana last March, though.

"The only people who are not allowed to participate in this group are political Communists who feel it is their duty to convert others to Communism," Menoyo told Morgan. Morgan nodded, following Artola's translation.

The apolitical nature of Menoyo's organization appealed to Morgan, who'd witnessed government corruption firsthand when he was growing up in Toledo, Ohio, and later, he felt, when he was in the U.S. Army. In Toledo, it wasn't always easy to tell where the organized crime ended and the government or the workers' unions began. Things were not so different in Cuba from what he understood. This second front could focus on an immediate goal, the freedom and liberty of the Cuban people, without getting mixed up in the details of what would follow.

"So," Morgan wanted to know, "is Fidel Castro a Communist? There's been a lot written about him in the States ever since Herbert Matthews interviewed him. Most people, like Matthews, think he's for democracy, but some are worried."

"No," Menoyo laughed. "He's *un hijo 'e puta*—a son of a bitch—but he's no Communist. The only ones who say that are friends of Batista, like some of those senators in your government. Fidel's the leader of this insurrection. For the Cuban people, and now for the world, he's the symbol of the fight against Batista. He's fighting for the Cuban Constitution, the same way we are. We can't afford to be Communists, not ninety miles from the United States with a cold war on."

That first night, Morgan lay on a hammock under a stretched tarpaulin. He smelled the rich smoke from the Cuban cigarettes. Mingling with it were the sweet, pungent odors of the forest, the tang of the kitchen fires from the distant *bohíos*, and the scent of men who had carved out a life in the woods. He listened to the men's whispering, then to the piercing squeaks of the bats that flew out of nearby caves to dart after insects in the night sky. He tried to remember everything Menoyo had said.

Over the weeks and months that followed, from the stories of his fellow fighters, Morgan would come to understand more clearly what it was he was doing in Cuba. Through them, his choice to climb into the mountains would gather meaning far greater than simply avenging the death of a friend.

MENOYO

In our revolution there are elements of the gunman and of St. Francis.

Carlos Franqui, Cuban writer and historian

Eloy Gutiérrez Menoyo's earliest memories were of hunger and war. He was born in Madrid on December 8, 1934, at the doorstep of the civil war in Spain. When the fighting began in 1936, his father, one of the founding members of the Socialist Worker's Party, signed on as a medic with the Republican army and went off to the front to fight the fascist troops of Generalissimo Francisco Franco.

There were six Menoyo siblings, three brothers and three sisters. Eloy was the second to youngest. His eldest brother, José Antonio, lied about his age and at sixteen reached the front as a soldier. The boy was still sixteen when a Falangist bullet pierced his neck and killed him. Eloy's sister Mercedes smuggled supplies to the Republican soldiers and, near the end of the struggle, the second son, Carlos, took up arms against the Fascists.

During the last days of the civil war and afterward under the oppressive poverty of Franco's dictatorship, Eloy would dash to the rail yards with a knife and a bowl, sneak up beside the offloaded burlap sacks of beans, make a quick stab, fill a bowl with garbanzos, and run home. Overwhelmed by a world in which her youngest son had become a thief, Eloy's mother would weep. Then she would cook the garbanzos he had brought home, and the family would eat them for dinner.

After the Spanish Civil War ended, at the start of the Second World War, Carlos Menoyo slipped across the Pyrenees and joined the struggle against Fascism in France. Liberty, it seemed, or the hope of liberty, was the only nation to which the Menoyos would pledge allegiance.

Carlos Menoyo would end World War II alive and victorious under the command of the American general George Patton. There was no sign that Franco would lose his grip on power in Spain, so the Menoyos looked for a place to live where they could take a break from the decade of poverty and violence they had endured.

Mercedes established contact with an uncle in Cuba. The uncle invited the family to join him on the island, which fifty years earlier had been a Spanish colony. Here, the *tío* said, there is some kind of democracy. It might not be perfect, but individual freedoms are respected. One can live in peace.

The family made their way to Cuba. On the big, lively island that Christopher Columbus described as a "country . . . of such marvelous beauty that it surpasses all others in charms and graces as the day doth the night in luster," the Gutiérrez Menoyos began to lead normal lives.

For Eloy, it was the first time he'd gone to school without warnings from his parents telling him what he should and shouldn't say. He could speak his mind in Cuba. The government might be run by corrupt politicians, who lined their pockets with funds from government contracts, but, as his uncle had said, the constitution ratified in 1940 for the most part protected individual freedoms. He found the balmy climate luxurious, and there were plenty of jobs for a smart, young man whose primary ambition was to achieve a comfortable middle-class life.

How things had changed since Eloy arrived in Cuba! Twelve years of constitutional democracy ended suddenly on March 10, 1952, when the former general and president, Fulgencio Batista, retook power with a military coup. Under Batista's leadership, Cuba became an even more hedonistic paradise for moneyed tourists, a comfortable place for men with little or no interest in social equality to do business, and a repressive and dangerous hell for anyone who actively opposed the president. The elections Batista had promised never happened.

The Menoyos, who thought they had left political trouble on the other side of the Atlantic Ocean, now faced the problems of their adopted home. Once again, Eloy had to be careful about what he said. And Eloy's father, a firm believer in democratic socialism, continued to stoke the fire of political idealism in his children.

In his initial conversation with Morgan, Eloy made reference to the DRE's attack on the Presidential Palace in March of 1957. The assassination attempt had failed, but it catalyzed a series of events that sent many young men into exile. In the ensuing power vacuum, Menoyo assumed the leadership role, which eventually led him into the Escambray. Fidel Castro had disapproved of the assassination attempt, believing that the Cuban people were not yet ready for Batista's removal and the change that should follow it.

Morgan knew something of this story of the assault on the palace. Just days earlier, when he arrived in Havana to find out what had happened to his friend, a trail of clues and contacts led him to people who had been involved in the same coup attempt. It was suggested that Morgan's buddy, who he claimed was killed by Batista's police, had supplied some of the weapons used in that attack on Batista. An American named Peter Korenda had in fact been shot as he looked out at the attack on the Presidential Palace from room 501 of the Regis Hotel, though it's not clear whether he was shot intentionally or if he had any connection to Morgan. Morgan would later give the name of his friend as Jack Turner. As Morgan suggested, there is no official mention or record of the death of anyone named Jack Turner in Havana. This connection, however tenuous, was what Morgan claimed had carried him to the mountains and to Menoyo.

Shortly after Batista seized power, Eloy's brother Carlos became involved in the resistance. Carlos's history in Spain and France gave him more military experience than almost anyone else in the Cuban opposition. He worked with various groups to plan Batista's assassination, believing that by killing the man at the top they could shift the whole system back to the constitutional democracy that had been in place between 1940 and 1952—that it was only Batista's charisma, Batista's American contacts, Batista's friends in the Cuban Army that kept him in power.

Time after time, however, the best-laid plans to kill or capture the dictator were foiled. Carlos believed that too many people were involved. Word of a developing plot reached Batista or the secret police every time. Once, a group Carlos was working with planned to blow up Batista in his car as he passed through a tunnel under Havana Harbor. The bombs were in place and the snipers in position to ensure that the job got done. But only the police made an appearance. Someone had talked.

Each time something upset Batista's regime, Ventura and his men responded with brutal tactics. *New York Times* journalist Herbert Matthews reported in 1957, "As a desperate measure of counter-terrorism . . . the police kill someone virtually every time a bomb is exploded in Havana, riddle his body with bullets, put a bomb in his hand and call the press photographers to come and take photographs. This macabre procedure is sardonically called by Habaneros, 'Batista's classified advertisement.'"

Batista kept his office in the ornate Presidential Palace just east of Paseo Martí, the lovely pedestrian boulevard lined by plane trees and bronze lions. The Prado, as Paseo Martí was more commonly known, runs from the Parque Central to the seawall that protects Havana from surging waves. This marble promenade to the sea was a monument to Cuba's wealth, and it seemed to symbolize both Cuba's historical reliance on shipping and its long-standing dependence on the United States, just ninety miles due north from the end of the promenade.

While the majority of Cubans were poor and a large number desperately so, living in shanty towns in run-down sections of Havana or in dirt-floored, palm-thatched shacks in the country, the surging economy of the 1950s had broadened the island's middle class. During the period, sugar exports grew and investment by foreigners brought fancy hotels and casinos. Cubans owned more TVs and American cars than the people of any other Latin American country. In 1956 more Cadillacs were sold in Havana than in any other city in the world. The rich and the tourists lived the high life, and the middle class lived in comfort. There were Cubans who traveled almost weekly by ferry or by plane to Miami for shopping, visits with friends and family, and to stay in the art deco hotels along the beach. Many Cubans sent their children to prep schools and colleges in the United States.

But the increasing wealth was not enough for many among Cuba's middle-class youth who, like the Menoyos and Castro, were hungry for democracy and a more equitable society.

The stronger the opposition to Batista grew within Cuba, the harder he worked to shore up support among his American political and business allies. By the late 1950s, many Cubans were of the opinion that if it weren't for U.S. support, Batista would have been gone long ago.

Carlos and his men hoped to surprise the dictator where he least expected it—not in his car or at his beach home, Kukin, but inside the Presidential Palace itself.

About one and a half miles west of the palace, in the comfortable, tree-lined neighborhood of Vedado, across from the Menoyo family's home, Menoyo had established a popular little bar called Eloy's Club. He had a regular clientele that included both Cubans and tourists from the Capri, the Nacional, the Presidente, and other nearby hotels. He prided himself that either he or his bartenders could mix any known drink. They were never at a loss when a tourist placed an exotic order, say, for a Sazerac, the popular New Orleans bourbon cocktail. Sometimes Eloy would step from behind the bar, taking a turn with the house band to croon the latest Cuban hits in a competent tenor.

Carlos trusted his brother more than he trusted anyone, but he did not want Eloy connected too closely to the assassination plans. He hoped to protect his sibling from reprisals if the attempt were to fail. Eloy was charged with organization and communication, making sure that the coup would transpire according to plan, that backup forces would arrive in time to support the front lines of the attack. He was, for the most part, an invisible presence, orchestrating movements from behind the scenes while he maintained a visible presence at the bar.

As the plans developed, Carlos decided to include a student political group called the Directorio Revolucionario Estudiantil in the plot. The Student Revolutionary Directorate was led by José Antonio Echevarria, one of the few young men in the country who could rival Fidel Castro's energy and charisma.

El Gordo—The Fat One, as Echevarria was known—had built an aggressive organization that disrupted daily life in Havana with explosions and power outages. He dodged and ducked the police, popping up to launch pointed verbal tirades against the Batista regime. While Carlos designed the military element of the plot, El Gordo planned for the political aftermath. There was no doubt that Batista had lost the youth generation in Cuba and that there was no getting them back. The question was what they would do with power if they ever were to get it.

On March 13, 1957, Carlos and about forty men raced to the entrance of the Presidential Palace in a red Fast Delivery truck. They leaped from the truck and rushed into the palace and up the stairs toward Batista's living quarters. A few blocks away, El Gordo took over the offices of Radio Reloj, where, in a fiery speech, he broadcast news of Batista's death and the return of a free Cuba.

Carlos died in the Palace. No one reached the third-floor apartment where Batista was hidden away. When El Gordo left the Radio Reloj offices, he was shot dead on the street.

Batista's guards were prepared and the plan became a mad, suicidal dash that left many of Havana's most promising young leaders dead.

That day, *el trece de marzo*, Menoyo had lost his second, and last, brother. While some might have chosen this moment to withdraw from the fracas, Eloy believed his only choice was to continue in the spirit of his brothers, to pick up the fight for freedom and become even more involved in the struggle against Batista.

Many of the survivors of *el trece de marzo*, including the DRE's secretary general, Faure Chomón, exiled themselves in Miami, hoping to evade Ventura's manhunt. Eloy, instead, returned to work at the family bar in Vedado. The remnants of the DRE and Carlos's military action group requested that Eloy follow in the footsteps of his brother and become the organization's Chief of Action. He accepted the charge, knowing that the infrastructure of the DRE would be necessary to supply him with the resources to plan armed resistance against Batista. However, with his wariness of political ideology in the context of an insurrection, he never fully committed to the DRE as a political organization.

Eloy dreamed of opening a second guerrilla front in the mountains, one that would complement the band of guerrillas fighting with Fidel Castro on the eastern end of the island. After the tragedy at the Presidential Palace, Eloy believed that the strategy should shift from one of assassination to a grinding guerrilla war, which would gradually win over the Cuban people and wear down the will of the young men in the Cuban Army.

Just three months before the attack of *el trece de marzo*, in December of 1956, Fidel Castro ran the yacht carrying his invasion force into the mud a few hundred yards off Cuba's southeastern coast. They were spotted by soldiers and as they waded to shore, lifting their guns over their heads to keep them dry, the men came under fire. The Rebel group scattered, taking refuge in a sugarcane field. Many were killed. Others were captured. In the end, only eighteen men, including Castro and the Argentine, Che Guevara, emerged from amid the sweet stalks. Limping and famished, they stumbled uphill to the safety of the peaks of the Sierra Maestra. This small band formed the high-profile guerrilla nucleus that would continue to harass Batista politically and militarily.

A second front, Eloy believed, would dilute the Cuban Army's ability to combat the armed opposition. In addition, he wanted to open his front in the mountain range at the center of the country, closer to Havana, a region more populous and trafficked than the isolated Sierra Maestra.

Eloy traveled to the Escambray Mountains and began scouting. At five feet eight inches, with slender build and sleepy eyes set wide apart in a sharp face, Menoyo, as he would now be known, did not offer the same imposing physique or verbal charisma as Fidel. However, he came from a tradition of resistance fighters. His brother was freshly martyred. Men would follow him.

In the hills above Banao, he discovered Lázaro Artola and his small group hiding out. Menoyo was encouraged by their having survived in the hills for a few months undetected by the army. This, he thought, will be where we will start. Artola, a representative of Fidel's 26th of July Movement, agreed that if Eloy could supply the weapons to arm a guerrilla force, he would hand over his command to the Spaniard.

In early November, after seven months spent planning and

gathering what arms remained from the attack on the Presidential Palace, Menoyo led a small group of men into the mountains of the Escambray. Fidel and his followers in the 26th of July Movement had been fighting for almost a year.

The founding members of the Second National Front of the Escambray signed a simple document that marked their membership in the new Rebel group:

> Today, November 10 of 1957, is founded the Second Front Revolutionary Army. It is created in the hills of the province of Las Villas and all its members will sign, swearing to fight and defend with their lives this little piece of free territory that we will deliver to all of Cuba. Each of us swears the following: First: Not to argue with orders but to comply with them. Second: To be honorable and loyal to my country and my comrades. Third: To maintain and guard all the war secrets of the II Front. Fourth: To never abandon a weapon under any circumstance, which are considered the property of the country and must not be deserted. Fifth: To denounce traitors and deserters.

In an interview with Herbert Matthews on June 5, 1957, Batista denounced the DRE and the 26th of July Movement: "These groups seek, through terrorism and disorder, to damage or destroy their nation's economy, as well as its prestige, and to create political chaos, if necessary, in order to satisfy their own, personal, anti-patriotic ambitions. . . ."

With the contract they signed on November 10, the men in the Escambray formalized their membership among the "criminal element" that Batista, his army, and the police were hunting all over the country.

EDUCATION

The dream for which each Rebel fought was filtered through his personal experience. Around the campfire and during long treks across the countryside, Morgan came to know the stories of the men around him.

Ramirito, the young sentry, had seen Batista's soldiers come to the general store where he worked, order coffee and cigarettes, and swagger away without paying, laughing—no one dared stand up to them. For Ramirito, these daily *abusos* represented both the corruption of the current state of affairs and a personal insult to his authority at the store. Ramirito became involved in the urban resistance in the towns of Camajuani and Regla, running errands and messages for those more directly involved. It wasn't until he scrawled "Viva Fidel" on a wall in Regla that things became too hot for him and he sought the relative safety of the hills and this nascent guerrilla army.

For others, the fight was intensely personal and carried with it elements of ferocious revenge. A tall, broodingly handsome man named Jesús Carreras stalked around camp with a slight limp. The rum he sipped calmed him at times and at other moments stoked his rage. He and his brother, Tomás, had been involved in the resistance against Batista for years. When Fidel and his men disembarked from the yacht *Granma*, Jesús and

Tomás had spread word of their return from Mexico throughout the small towns and cities of the province.

Carreras's father practiced medicine and instilled progressive ideas in his children. Carreras himself had studied to be a laboratory technician, but he'd abandoned this work completely when Batista's police had raped his sister, who was also involved in the urban resistance. He came to the hills angry, with no empathy for supporters of Batista's regime, stoically resigned to his fate, whatever that might be. There was an element of hard danger and pragmatism about the man that frightened some of the younger, more fun-loving and idealistic Cubans. Carreras, for example, volunteered to execute the spies and traitors who threatened the Second Front's position. Though executions of traitors were not uncommon in either the Sierra Maestra or the Escambray, Ramirito, for one, refused the task that Carreras was willing to perform.

Morgan's new companions found him some clothes fit for his new vocation, and he discarded his casino suit. He inspected the weapons the small band possessed and found they were a mixed batch of mostly cheap Italian and Brazilian rifles, a few good American Garand rifles, one Czechoslovakian machine gun, and some hand grenades. Morgan held up an Italian carbine in one hand and announced with authority, "*Mierda!*—Shit!" In the other, he raised a Garand, "*Bueno!*—Good!" Ramirito laughed, enjoying the American's pronouncements, loving the theater he brought to the group.

New recruits filtered into camp. One was another foreigner, a Haitian named Henri Fuerte, who hoped to help the Cubans and then to return to Haiti and overthrow the brutal regime of "Papa Doc" Duvalier there. There were no brigades of internationals organizing to help the Cuban Rebels like the ones that had formed in Spain to fight Fascism and Francisco Franco in the late 1930s. Still, perhaps inevitably, a few people, freelancers like Morgan and Henri Fuerte, hopped planes or boats and found their way to Cuba.

Morgan began to acclimate. He got used to being called "Weeleeam" and to the diet of beans and the starchy, boiled malanga. He wouldn't eat *jutía*, or "rat," as he called it, in one instance preferring, to the revulsion of his Cuban friends, to skewer a piece of spoiled, moldy sausage and burn it over a fire until he deemed it edible.

He felt the soreness in his muscles from climbing the *lomas*, as the men called the slopes. Between the diet and the exercise, he dropped weight quickly. Not so much weight, he hoped, that he would lose the strength that the other Rebels were coming to admire. Already they were turning down his invitations to wrestle. Morgan would approach one of the more athletic guerrillas, "Come on. Come on," circling, baiting. A man would accept the challenge, only to find himself pinned flat on his back within seconds, startled by the big man's quickness and power. It was a good thing for Morgan that new recruits kept joining the force—they were fresh meat for his competitive appetite.

This wrestling prowess lent Morgan an added bit of authority when Menoyo asked him to put the guerrillas through a kind of rough and ready basic training. The American showed them basic skills he'd learned in the army. He'd joined at age 18. Since there weren't enough weapons to go around and the Rebels couldn't spare bullets for target practice anyway, Morgan taught maneuvers. He demonstrated how to approach an enemy force unnoticed, to set up an ambush, to dig a fox hole, to find effective cover when caught under fire, and the basics of hand-to-hand combat. Men carrying sticks instead of guns crawled on their stomachs through the scrub, pulling themselves forward on their elbows, listening to a *yanqui* bark orders at them in English or, occasionally, one-word Spanish. "*Lento!*—Slowly!" "*Rapido!*—Quickly!" "*Ahora!*—Now!" They learned to toss knives, though none achieved the accuracy and command of their instructor. He taught them to pluck a hollow reed and use it as a kind of natural snorkel to disappear and escape the enemy underwater. The play was deadly serious. The men all knew that it might help them win a battle against professional army troops and, moreover, that it might save their lives.

As he worked and played with the men, Morgan began to learn Spanish. Like a two-year-old child, he pointed to things, asking, "*Como se llama?*" in his Midwestern accent. "What's that called?" Then he would repeat the word he was told. Everyone was taken with the affable, energetic gringo and tutored him at every opportunity, pointing and calling out words: tree, chicken, gun, tarpaulin, rice, beans. Run, walk, laugh, yell, shoot. Bird, airplane, army, farmer. Traitor. They quizzed him relentlessly.

Once, returning from a trek, Morgan sidled up to Menoyo as they passed the edge of a tenant farmer's small pasture, looking for a chance to show off his Spanish.

"*Gallego,*" said Morgan, "*mira aquel vaco.*"

The serious Menoyo and all the other men within earshot roared with delight at the American's mistake. "*Vaca,*" said Menoyo between gasps, "not *vaco.*"

Roughly translated, Morgan had said, "Spaniard, look at that male cow." Morgan would keep calling Menoyo "Gallego," in reference to his Spanish heritage, but he would learn that cows were always *vacas*, always female, that bulls were *toros*.

On another hike, Morgan, worn out, flopped onto the ground. The men looked at him, a bit startled by this act of insubordination.

"*No soy mulo*," he announced, pronouncing the word *mulo*, or mule, with a long American "u" rather than the softer "oo" that would be correct in Spanish. "I am not a mule."

After a pause, Menoyo laughed. "*Descansamos*—Let's rest," he said. The men rested.

On their daily treks, the Rebels made regular visits to the campesinos who farmed the land for city-dwelling landowners. They recruited the tenant farmers and their workers as allies, guides, messengers, and informers who could provide information on the army's activities.

In these hills, the primary cash crop was coffee. A tenant farmer would lease a section of land, plant coffee, and when harvest time came around, he'd hire as many as six or seven men—depending on how many children he had of his own—to harvest the beans. In addition to coffee, most families planted a truck garden that included malanga, as well as beans, limes, and bananas. They kept chickens and pigs. The more comfortable ones might own a cow or two. The Rebels would offer cash for vegetables and meat and rice. The cash came in handy because what the campesinos couldn't grow or make for themselves, they bought on credit from company stores run by the landowners; they were always in debt.

Though becoming known as a Rebel sympathizer carried a high degree of risk, the Rebel talk of land reforms enticed the tenant farmers, since they all dreamed of owning their own land someday.

On one farm visit, Morgan had his first look at the inside of a *bohío*. The wary but hospitable peasants invited the Rebels in for coffee cut with black beans and seeds. Even here, at the heart of Cuba's coffee-producing land, the poorest campesinos couldn't afford coffee. After the harvest ended, women would scour the ground beneath the coffee plants for the beans that had slipped from the fingers of the pickers. What Morgan saw was a tidy poverty under a thatched roof: one room; dirt floor; a family of six sleeping side by side. Over and over he'd been struck by the generosity of the Cubans he'd met, the acceptance and friendship of his fellow Rebels, and now by these poor people, sharing the little they had with men who they hoped wouldn't hurt them and who just might help to make their lives a little better. As time passed, Morgan would find that he could relate well to these country Cubans

And the Cubans took to Morgan. When they thought of him, some of these men and women recalled the childhood stories and poems they'd heard about the exploits of another American who had landed on their island and taken up a military cause. As a boy from Brooklyn, Henry Reeve, "El Inglecito," as he was known in Cuba, had been a flag bearer during the Civil War in the United States. When that war ended, he looked for an opportunity to become a real soldier and found it in Cuba in the 1870s. There he led wild, violent attacks on the Spanish that earned him a place among the pantheon of Cuban freedom fighters. His legend was fixed when he was killed, galloping into battle, only one leg remaining, wearing a white lily on his lapel as a tribute to one of his mistresses. In a culture that above all valued a man's strength, courage, and virility, Reeve had not only earned respect, he had mastered the art of the grand gesture, of adding to a deed the drama that would cement it into memory.

All Cubans themselves are immigrants by choice or by

force. No native population survived the Spanish conquest and disease. The people who populate the island came from Spain, Africa, China, England, Ireland, France, and by way of other Caribbean countries. One of Cuba's most lauded generals in the fight for independence from the Spanish was General José Miguel Gómez, a Dominican who is buried in Cementario Colón—Columbus Cemetery—in Havana. Cubans, in other words, were accustomed to including in their national projects the ambitious strangers who arrived on their shores. The country was, after all, an island with valuable ports, which from the earliest colonial period had received boats carrying rich cargoes and international crews.

Morgan was what the other Rebels called a *maranero*, or trickster. He was the kid who would short sheet his sister's bed and he was the boy who, back in junior high, had climbed a tree to peek in a girl's window. And he was the man who loved to tease his fellow Rebels. For Ramirito, Redondo, and the others, Morgan was exploding a stereotype of the arrogant, aloof Anglo. "He is like a Cuban," they would say, referring to his expressiveness, his love of laughter and play.

FIRST BLOOD

Mid-February, 1958

Morgan and his new comrades could only train and scout until they received the arms and munitions that Faure Chomón, the secretary-general of the DRE, was bringing by boat from Miami. Chomón had acquired the weapons with money donated by Cuban exiles, enemies of Batista awaiting his overthrow so that they could return to the island. Among the contributors was the former President of Cuba, Carlos Prío, who hoped to return to the country he'd abandoned when Batista seized power.

If everything went as planned, the smugglers would leave U.S. waters undetected by customs officials or the coast guard and arrive on Cuban shores without drawing the attention of the Cuban navy or police. But Chomón and his cargo were late, and Menoyo and the men worried that they might have been captured or lost at sea.

How and where should the SNFE begin its rural campaign? At the moment, they were a ragtag bunch of young men with some experience in urban resistance, a handful of guns, and the shared dream of a free Cuba.

Finally, on February 13, about two weeks after Morgan had first appeared at the camp, Faure Chomón limped in with the shipment of arms. Chomón's crossing from the Florida Keys had been delayed by storms in the gulf, which had nearly capsized his small boat, the *Escapada*. Instead of the usual two-day crossing, he and his crew had spent nine days at sea and come ashore exhausted, starving, and dehydrated. In spite of the ordeal, they had managed to unload their cargo into a truck on Cuba's north-central coast, slip undetected into the hills, and transport it into the mountains.

Like young baseball players being handed their first uniforms, bats, and gloves, Menoyo's men thrilled at the sight of the shipment of arms. It was an odd assortment of weapons from shady dealers and pawnshops from Miami to New Jersey. There were fifty Italian carbines, a Thompson submachine gun and two English Stens that could fire 550 rounds per minute, two Springfield rifles, a Garand, five Remington semiautomatic rifles, one M1 and two M3s, carbines, and thousands of rounds of munition. Menoyo handed the Sten to Morgan, knowing that he was one of the few men in the group who could handle a submachine gun.

In addition to the weapons, there were tents, uniforms, knapsacks, lanterns, and other essential tools and supplies, including a few old military helmets. One of these was a big, heavy Nazi helmet that a pawnshop proprietor had tossed in with the guns. Only one young man, a country boy named Publio, had a head big enough to wear it—and he did.

Every piece of hand-me-down war refuse would find a home. The weapons that didn't work would be investigated and retooled by a bespectacled Spanish machinist named Regino Camacho. Camacho could turn a rifle into a submachine gun, or fit the clip of an American repeating rifle into the equivalent Italian firearm.

In the time he had spent crossing the ocean from Florida to Cuba, the wiry Chomón, with his sparse Trotsky beard and skittish professorial demeanor, had formulated a new plan. The best thing to do, he announced to Menoyo, would be to return to Havana and use the arms to attempt another coup. Go right for the top. Knock the regime's head off. This plot, he argued, would be more efficient than a drawn-out guerrilla battle. With all these weapons, how could they fail?

Though Chomón and Menoyo ostensibly belonged to the same organization, their loyalties to the DRE did not emanate from the same source. The former was deeply committed to the organization and knew that the Spaniard operated more independently, like his brother Carlos before him. Neither man enjoyed the idea of answering to the command of the other. Chomón believed his tenure with the Directorio had earned him authority, whereas Menoyo looked to his time in the mountains and his sibling relationship for the same. While Chomón gathered arms in the relative safety of Miami, Menoyo had been living off the land in Cuba, dodging army patrols.

How could Chomón change the plans? Eloy thought the new plan was idiotic, that the arms they'd worked so hard to acquire would be discovered and confiscated by the secret police in Havana. Every assassination plot that Menoyo and Chomón had been part of or witnessed had ended in fiasco.

However, to Chomón, the idea of starting a guerrilla war in the mountains seemed risky and made him uncomfortable. Menoyo's intensity regarding the point also indicated a shift in philosophy; it was important, he now believed, to allow the Cuban people more time to come to the side and the aid of the Rebels. Killing Batista too soon would truncate the revolutionary process.

As the two leaders argued, the loyalties of the men in the camp were tested. It was becoming clear that a split would occur: Who would stay with Eloy and who would follow Chomón to Havana?

When Morgan had climbed into the mountains, he had walked right into Cuba's complex and multifaceted history. One could look back more than one hundred years for the antecedents that precipitated the struggle Morgan joined and in them begin to tease out the ideological differences that would emerge between the Rebel factions that, in 1958, were focused on ousting Batista.

In *Shah of Shahs*, his book about the revolution in Iran that toppled the last shah, Ryszard Kapuscinski offers a neat and apt conception of revolutions. There are, he posits, two kinds of revolution: the one by assault and the other by siege. The former is a quick, violent decapitation of a regime. It is, Kapuscinski suggests, the more superficial form of revolution, one that allows the defeated adversary to preserve "a part of his forces." It is a top-down approach that might be seen as a kind of violent reform—change the guy at the top and, after some tinkering, things will be better. Carlos Menoyo's attack on the Presidential Palace represented an attempt at revolution by assault.

The latter, Kapuscinski argues, creates the possibility for more profound structural reform of a society's politics and culture: "The success of a revolution by siege depends on the determination of the rebels, on their will power and endurance. One more day! One more push! In the end, the gates yield, the crowd breaks in and celebrates in triumph."

With this concept of revolution in mind, it's interesting

to consider the role of José Martí in Cuba's political history. Martí is essentially the father of Cuban independence. He is to Cuba all at once what Thomas Jefferson, George Washington, and Walt Whitman are to the United States. Martí created the intellectual framework for Cuba's independence, fought the Spanish for Cuban independence, and wrote literature that helped create an indigenous Cuban identity. "Guantanamera," a Cuban song that went around the world, became popular when verses drawn from the Martí poem, "Yo soy un hombre sincero," were added. It speaks to the simple values of love, friendship, loyalty, of the connection between man and the land, and of the plight of the poor. The following lyrics are from Martí's poem, found in his collection *Versos sencillos*:

> Yo soy un hombre sincero
> De donde crecen las palmas
> Y antes de morirme quiero
> Echar mis versos del alma.

I am an honest man / from where the palm trees grow / and before I die / I want to release the verses of my soul.

> Con los pobres de la tierra
> Quiero yo mi suerte echar.
> El arroyo de la sierra
> Me complace más que el mar.

With the poor of the earth / I will throw in my lot / The mountain stream / gives me more pleasure than the sea.

As he thought about Cuban sovereignty, Martí worried not only about Spain but also about the United States. He was afraid that Cuba, a small country so close to such a powerful one, could never be truly independent. Soon after returning to Cuba in 1895, Martí died in a skirmish. Three years later, the Spanish lost Cuba. Immediately, Martí's worst fears were confirmed. Even as Cuba won its independence from Spain in 1898, the credit for the victory went to Teddy Roosevelt and his Rough Riders, who had galloped in at the last minute to steal the limelight from the Cubans who had fought for decades. Piling insult upon insult, Roosevelt, rather than one of the Cuban generals, accepted the surrender and withdrawal of the Spanish troops. From the first day, therefore, "Cuban independence" had been something less than true independence. The Americans were always meddling, always keeping an eye on the Cubans. In fact, written into the 1902 Cuban constitution was the right of the United States to intervene if it didn't approve of the Cuban government's administration of the island's affairs. Although the Platt Amendment, the clause that legalized U.S. intervention, was struck from the Cuban constitution in 1933, its effects on the Cuban political psyche remain. Sacrifice for the country's sovereignty is of primary value in the Cuban collective conscience.

In the history of twentieth-century Cuba, the figure of José Martí plays something like the rope in a tug-of-war. Every Cuban leader, whether he's from the Right or the Left, allied with or against the United States, attempts to pull Martí's image and philosophy into the service of his political interests. Some, like Fidel Castro, turn a light on Martí's national pride and his insistence on Cuban independence free of the fetters of imperial control. Others emphasize Martí's passion for human rights, individual determination, and the belief that the vote, while imperfect, is the greatest political tool known to man. Though Cuba ratified a strong, liberal constitution in 1940 that engendered three consecutive peaceful elections, one could argue that Martí's popular poems and essays were more important founding documents than the legalistic prose of the constitution was.

The politician Dr. Ramón Grau San Martín had aligned himself with Batista in the 1930s. Early in the following decade, he reorganized the Revolutionary Cuban Party, or PRC, and renamed it Partido Revolucionario Cubano Auténtico, claiming that the "Authentics" would be the *true* representatives of José Martí in Cuba.

The Cuban people elected Grau president in 1944. The Auténticos took power and quickly strayed from Martí's ideals. Hugh Thomas writes that Grau did "more than any single man to kill the hope of democratic practice in Cuba" by turning his presidency into an "orgy of theft." The last American ambassador to Cuba, Philip Bonsal, would note that he knew of "no other country among those committed to the Western ethic where the diversion of public treasure for private profit reached the proportions that it attained in Cuba." As much as 60 percent of Cuba's public funds may have ended up lining the pockets of private individuals during the presidencies of Grau, Carlos Prío Socarrás, and finally Batista (who was not an Auténtico).

There are those who would argue that some leeway might be given with regard to Thomas's assertion. At least Grau and Prío were freely elected. Sooner or later, some felt, if the constitution remained intact and the democratic process were allowed to proceed more or less unhindered, the voters would eliminate corruption. As Martí himself had said, the vote could be a powerful, if imperfect, tool.

When Carlos Prío, another Auténtico, won the presidency in 1948, the handsome, well-intentioned leader presided over a period of healthy economics and steady, constant graft. Prío believed in liberty and social democracy, but he had rich tastes, as well as friends and relatives to whom he owed big favors. Prío lived on a farming estate outside Havana called La Chata, known for the waterfall that tumbled into the swimming pool, a barbershop that could seat twelve, and sit-down dinner parties at which he would entertain more than two hundred guests. The transition between Grau and Prío did little to impede the flow of public funds to private pockets.

In 1948, from Daytona Beach, Florida, Batista won a Cuban senate seat and again fixed his sights on the presidency. As the election of 1952 neared, it became clear that Batista would not win. So he called in his chips with his friends in the military and promised double military pay. On March 10, 1952, Batista claimed power from the Cuban military headquarters at Camp Columbia, in Havana. Instead of facing Batista down—a move that might have forced international diplomatic intervention—Prío slipped out of the country with millions in stolen loot and went to Miami.

Overnight, the Auténticos became an opposition party. They did not think that Cuba's political culture needed to be rebuilt from the bottom up. They believed it could be fixed—or better, reclaimed—from the top. In other words, replace Batista. The democratic process that had brought them the presidencies of Grau and Prío could be rejuvenated and, if necessary, improved upon to make it less corrupt. They continued to view the constitution of 1940 as a pillar on which democracy could rest.

The Revolutionary Student Directorate group to which Menoyo was linked was affiliated with the Auténticos, but the goals of the young insurrectionists and the corrupt politicians were not altogether aligned. Menoyo and others carried the banner of social justice, advocating a more equitable society and a redistribution of land that would benefit Cuba's poor. They wanted the corruption of Grau and Prío eliminated from Cuban politics. However, until Eloy took men into the mountains, the members of the DRE had favored the top-down approach described by Kapuscinski: the revolution—or reform—by assault. The DRE and its followers saw no need to rebuild Cuba's political culture from scratch.

In contrast, the Ortodoxos, a group that splintered from the Auténticos in 1948, identified Cuba's problems as going much deeper than Batista. A charismatic political organizer, philosopher, and writer named Eduardo "Eddie" Chibás led the split and claimed for his group the true revolutionary tra dition of Marti, which he said the Auténticos had abandoned. Chibás put constant pressure on Prío, bringing to light the government corruption and Prío's spending habits, reminding the country of the value of political ethics and its responsibility to the poor. To a degree, the Ortodoxo Party became the party of purists, of those who saw Cuba's problems as not only political but cultural. Fidel Castro had been affiliated with the Ortodoxos, who favored a bottom-up approach to revolution. Indeed, Fidel's efforts in the Sierra Maestra resembled a political campaign in which the candidate is surrounded by body-guards who double as guerrilla soldiers. He was coaxing the Cuban people along, preparing them for significant change, fighting not only with guns but also with ideas for a better, more equitable Cuba.

After witnessing so many failed attempts to assassinate Batista, Menoyo now thought, like Fidel, that a longer process, one that gradually captured the minds and support of the Cuban people, might be preferable to a sudden coup d'etat.

Six days after Chomón's arrival, as his argument with Menoyo simmered, a Rebel sentry spotted an army patrol of six men wending their way toward the Rebel camp. Menoyo gathered his men to give them instructions.

The Cuban Army had barracks appointed at regular intervals along the perimeter of the region where the Rebels were training. Occasionally army patrols made sallies into the mountains.

"I don't want any shots fired," Menoyo said. "The first option is to let them pass. We'll hide and hope they go around us. If they discover our presence, we will let them come toward the camp. When we have them surrounded, we will ambush them and force them to put down their arms."

He scanned his men as he spoke to see if they understood. He looked specifically at Morgan, whose vocabulary was growing but still lacked a solid command of the Spanish language. The American nodded, as if to say, "Right, right, right."

"*Que no tiren!*—Don't shoot!" Menoyo hissed. "Not unless your life is in danger," he continued. "If we must, we will take them as prisoners. Look for my command."

The men fanned out, taking their places. Morgan stayed close beside Menoyo as they picked their way down the slope, choosing a path parallel to that of the climbing enemy patrol. Finding a dip in the ground, they squatted, barely breathing, and waited for the soldiers to go by.

Many people, including one of Batista's generals, who was secretly sympathetic to the Rebel cause, had said it would be impossible to build a successful Rebel front in the Escambray. "There are too many roads," he'd observed. "You can't hide. The army will be able to cut off your supply lines easily. And it's too close to Havana. The government cannot afford to have

Rebels that close to the capital. They will throw all the troops they have at you and wipe you out quickly."

All the drawbacks of the Escambray could also be considered strengths, Menoyo thought. How demoralizing would it be to the government, to the army, if a second guerrilla front were established so close to Havana, in a place where no one thought the Rebels would ever dare try? This could be the beginning of the guerrilla war in the Escambray.

The six soldiers, relaxed, not alert, eased their way up the mountain path, their guns hanging from their hands. Their khaki uniforms flickered in splotches of light that filtered through the trees. Now they were within ten yards. The Rebels sat completely still, waiting for Comandante Menoyo's order. Out of the corner of his eye, Menoyo saw a slight movement.

Crack-crack!

Menoyo saw the first soldier drop and smoke puffing from Morgan's gun.

Hijo 'e puta! Son of a bitch, the idiot opened fire!

A firefight burst through the trees. Within seconds two Cuban soldiers were dead. The other four escaped through the dense forest, down the mountain toward their barracks, where they would alert their unit of the Rebel presence.

Pulling a translator along, Menoyo found Morgan and grabbed him, furious.

"Damn it, why did you fucking shoot? I specifically said no shooting! And if you didn't understand what I was saying when I gave my orders, why did you keep nodding, like an idiot?"

"I thought you said to shoot to kill the first soldier," Morgan answered.

Everyone was shaken. The first blood had been spilled. The fight was real.

It was an inauspicious beginning for a friendship that would become indelible, and for a Rebel soldier who would become formidable.

LIFELINE

There was no time to absorb the event. The Rebel position was compromised; the guerrillas had to leave the camp immediately. Soldiers would be close behind them. It was a tense moment, one that forced action, but it was not entirely undesirable; for these men to have an impact, confrontation was necessary.

The battle brought the disagreement between Chomón and Menoyo to the breaking point. The two would separate, and each volunteer would follow the commander of his choosing. Initially, however, they fled as one unit deeper into the mountains of the Escambray, north of the port city of Cienfuegos.

In the group of thirty-five or so, fifteen stayed with Chomón. The remainder—including Morgan; Ramirito; Artola; Carreras; Henri Fuerte; the young campesino, Publio; and a doctor, Armando Fleites, who had come on the boat with Chomón—followed Menoyo. Roger Redondo and a few others stayed behind to stash in a cave the arms and supplies that could not be carried.

As they began their journey west, the guerrillas were led by a peasant farmer called Bombino, who knew the terrain well and could help them survive in the hills. They hiked at night, avoiding contact with the campesinos, and slept during the day in their hammocks.

Only three days out from Banao, as they skirted an area

not far from a military outpost at La Diana, one of the men descended to a small stream to get a drink of water and fill his canteen. He quickly returned with the news that a large army patrol was making its way directly toward them, surely sent to look for the Rebels who had killed their comrades. Menoyo and the rest decided that there would be no way to avoid this group; the only choice was to fight.

This time they would ensure that the element of surprise was theirs. Based on Morgan's training, they prepared an ambush—they would attack from more than one angle at once, being careful to allow an escape route for the patrol. The goal would be to inflict some casualties, cause the army to retreat, and then to gather whatever useful supplies might be left in the wake of the fleeing soldiers.

The Rebels arranged themselves as the patrol approached. And when the Rebels attacked, a ferocious fight blistered across the small valley. At one point, as the soldiers stormed toward them, some of the Rebels began to retreat. Then they noticed Morgan out in front of everyone, moving ahead, completely focused on the fight. The men, heartened, pushed forward.

In the three hours of fighting, the Rebels suffered no casualties and managed to kill or wound thirty in the patrol before it retreated. The tactics worked. Three men stood out in the fighting, risking exposure to gain better angles on Batista's men, working to take the fight to the army: Menoyo, a man from the city of Trinidad named Edel Montiel, and Morgan. Any questions the Cubans still had about the depth of the *americano*'s commitment were put to rest.

Once again, the group managed to avoid destruction. One could say that little more than dumb luck, a bit of training, and the unwarranted confidence of youth kept them alive. Not once did the men doubt that they would survive or that, from this humble and inauspicious beginning, the ultimate victory would be theirs.

After the skirmish at La Diana, the two Rebel factions finally divided. Faure Chomón and his men headed north toward the town of Fomento. From there they would make their way to Havana. Menoyo and his contingent pressed on west into the mountains.

The difficult treks Menoyo's men had made around Banao could not prepare them for the sustained effort of hiking nights on end with little rest and even less food. They learned to cup cigarettes so that the orange ember would not be seen in the night, to lower their sweaty faces to prevent detection by a plane passing overhead. They learned to walk the "military crest" of a hill, just below the summit of a ridge, so that they wouldn't be silhouetted against the sky and easy to spot from below by soldiers or from above by planes.

They never spoke above a whisper. Bombino taught them which *vehucos* -vines—held water and could be cut for a few precious, refreshing sips. When the men were especially weak with hunger, they shared cans of condensed milk.

Each Rebel carried his precious weapon slung over a shoulder or across his chest. He bore a heavy canvas backpack— *mochila*—that contained a hammock, a green tarpaulin, a couple of cans of the precious condensed milk, a poncho, perhaps a change of shirt, a bit of soap, some string, and matches. If a soldier was lucky, he might have cigarettes, which he always shared. The rest of the *mochila* was filled with general items from the camp: munitions, cookware, an ax, a radio, walkie-talkies. Many of the men carried good luck charms, saint medallions, photographs of their mothers or girlfriends, whatever might remind them of the lives they'd left and to which they hoped to return.

Ramirito wrapped a bullet in a handkerchief and nestled it into his breast pocket, hoping that it might protect him.

Though he talked little about them, Morgan carried a photograph of his two children, who were back in Toledo. He also wore a small patch depicting an American flag that he'd stitched to the shoulder of his Rebel uniform. Though he wore this American symbol with pride, the more he thought about his country's support of Batista, the more troubled he became. The American people, he began to believe, thinking about the stories that Jesús Carreras and Ramirito had told him, would never agree to support a dictator like Batista if they only understood what it meant to the lives of these people.

Shortly after the skirmish at La Diana, Ramirito slipped and fractured his foot. He hobbled along, even dropping behind the laboring Morgan, who had fallen ill with a virus that caused him to shiver with fever and pause for long moments while his stomach convulsed.

One night, as the two thrashed forward to keep up with the others, Morgan collapsed. This time it was not in jest. Morgan gestured with his hands to the gimpy Ramirito, pointing to the ground: "Let's stop here."

Word that they had stopped made its way forward, and Menoyo came back to check on the two stragglers.

"*Gallego*," Morgan said, "*no puedo más*—I can't anymore."

"If you can't go any farther, I will have to shoot you," Menoyo said. There was no laughing this time. No adapting to the weakest among them. The survival of all depended on the entire group's ability to remain hidden from the Cuban Army. If these men were captured, there was no telling what they might say, what information they might divulge, even against their wills. Menoyo was serious. He would shoot them.

Morgan climbed back onto his feet. As sick as he was, he would summon the strength to move, and he would not leave his young friend behind. He gestured to Ramirito to get up, while reaching into his backpack for a length of rope. He tied one end of the rope around his waist and got Ramirito to put the other around his.

"Okay, Gallego," he said.

Morgan walked, pulling the rope taut, offering Ramirito some balance. The two comrades limped forward, the sick man pulling the injured man as they pushed on toward their destination in the Escambray.

As he ploughed along, thinking, whispering his rudimentary Spanish, Morgan grew more and more frustrated by the knowledge that these men were not only fighting Batista and his army, but they were fighting the support the U.S. government gave Cuba's illegitimate leader. Indeed, that was a constant subject of frustration to the Rebels. Furthermore, he expected that the only way to truly challenge that support would be to get the attention of the U.S. public, make them pay attention to the Cuban situation and insist that their leaders not interfere with the Rebels.

A year earlier, when Batista had announced to the world that Fidel Castro was dead, Herbert Matthews of the *New York Times* had been smuggled into the foothills of the Sierra Maestra to find out if this were true and, if possible, to get an interview with the Rebel leader. Matthews's wife, who had accompanied her husband to Cuba, tucked the notes from the interview into her girdle to sneak them out of the country. Not only was Fidel Castro alive in the mountains, declared Matthews in the articles that followed, but Castro, his democratic values, and his loyal followers seemed unbeatable. Batista called the story a fake, saying that Matthews had not been to Cuba, but the *Times* published a photograph of Matthews and Castro sitting and talking together on the forest floor. The world, inside and outside of Cuba, took notice.

It occurred to Morgan that he might be in a unique position to influence the American people. If only they knew what he had come to understand about Cuba and the Rebels in less than a month. No one in the United States or in Cuba was even aware that a second guerrilla band existed in the fight against Batista. He could write a letter and send it to newspapers in the United States, or to Herbert Matthews himself.

And so, barely a month after he arrived in the mountains, Morgan tried to put into words exactly what the Cuban struggle was coming to mean to him.

The letter he sent to Herbert Matthews began with a title that rests ambiguously between an assertion and a question: "Why Am I Here." In the paragraphs that followed, Morgan attempted to lay out his reasons for joining the Rebels.

The two pages Matthews received, typed on flimsy stock, were full of misspellings and grammatical errors, some of which are corrected with the quick slashes of a black pen. At times, the misspellings are so bad that they make one think that Morgan must have written the letter by hand and that someone else, perhaps with an imperfect command of the English language or unable to decipher his penmanship, had typed the letter.

Why am I Here

Why do I fight here in this land so foreign to my own? Why did I come here far from my home and family? Why do I worry about these men here in the mountains with me? Is it because they were all close friends of mine? No! When I came here they were strangers to me I could not speak their language or understand their problems. Is it because I seek adventure? No here there is no adventure only the ever existent problems of survive. So why am I here? I am here because I belive that the most important thing for free men to do is to protect the freedom of others. I am here so that my son when he is grown will not have to fight or die in a land not his own, because one man or group of men try to take his liberty from him I am here because I believe that free men should take up arms and stand together and fight and destroy the groups and forces that want to take the rights of people away. To once and for all time be sure that men will never again have to fight and die to be free. This is a wonderful world in which we live. But it will be at its best when every man is free and no where in the world are men oppressed because one man wants to rule others. I am here, because here are men who believe as I do here are men fighting for liberty and justice in their land and I am here to fight with them. HIGH IN THE ESCAMBRAY SIERRA.

High in the lomas of the Sierra Escambray live and fight a group of men who without a doubt are one of the toughest opponents to dictatorship and communism in Latin America these are men who are not professional soldiers but doctors, lawyers, farmers, chemist boys, students, and old men banded together in the cause of Cuban liberty.

Here the impossible happens every day. Where a boy of nineteen can march 12 hours with a broken foot over country comparable to the American Rockies without complaint. Where a cigarette is smoked by ten men. Where men do without water so that others may drink here men march 20 miles on a cup of powdered milk carrying rifles, ammunition, and 50 lb packs, men untrained in the ways of war who meet and defeat the Cuban army at every turn. Here men talk in low voices in small groups of the family that they have left behind and what they will do when the revolution is over. Here men fight and die for the simple freedom that we as Americans take for granted. I know these men well as I live and fight with them and am proud to be a part of them. Inborn in all men is a sense of justice an freedom but here it is developed to a degree that puts Americans to shame; we take for granted the right to elect a president of our choice, to speak our minds freely, to know that our press and radio is not censored that we will not be imprisoned unjustly or without trial, these are freedoms no man can take from us in America but only 100 miles from Miami, men must fight and die for these same freedoms in a country ruled by a dictator supported and supplied with arms by the United States, to as an American it does not make sense.

I cannot say I have always been a good citizen but being here I can appreciate the way of life that is ours from birth. And here I can realize the dedication to justice and liberty it takes for men to live and fight as these men do whose only possible pay of reward is a free country. In the press of the US I read an article written by an expert on Latin America who stated that the opposition to Batista was confused but here we have men from all political parties and men like myself who care not for politics, fighting together as the Directorio Revolucionario all with an undying hatred for the man who calls himself president of Cuba.

Over the years we as Americans have found that dictators, and communist are bad people with whom to do
business yet here is a dictator who has been supported by
the communist and he would fall from power tomorrow
if it were not for the American aid. And I ask myself why
do we support those who would destroy in other lands the
ideals which we hold so dearly?

William A. Morgan
Sierra de Escambray
Febrero 24 de 1958

Until this moment, the most electrifying intrusion of the
Cuban struggle into the International arena had been Herbert
Matthews's own reports a year earlier. Morgan's missive added
a more personal note. Here was an American willing to risk his
life by taking up arms to overthrow Cuba's dictator.

In an article about the Second National Front of the Escambray, published on April 3, 1958, roughly a month after he
received the letter, Matthews wrote, "One of the least-known
features of Cuba's dramatic history these days is that of the
so-called second front in the Sierra de Escambray of Las Villas
Province in the center of the island. Yet it is playing a role that
will earn it a position of some prominence when the full story
of contemporary events is chronicled." He also mentioned a
"33-year-old" American fighting with the Second Front and
quoted from Morgan's letter. Though Matthews got some of
his facts wrong, such as Morgan's age, the missive was successful in that it expanded the world's sense of the opposition to
Batista and brought the Rebels' story a little closer to home for
the American people.

One thing that Matthews wouldn't mention in his article
was an odd paragraph attached to Morgan's letter. It seemed to

be an imaginative reflection that the American Rebel had written, and, for some reason, had sent along with his statement. The paragraph described the Nazi helmet—which had made its way to Cuba amid Faure Chomón's smuggled shipment of arms—worn by young Publio. The helmet was an anomaly on these Cuban slopes, not unlike Morgan himself. In the paragraph, he took the voice of the helmet.

An explanatory note in Spanish introduces "The Helmet of Publio" and identifies Publio as a nineteen-year-old Cuban peasant. Publio's helmet, it says "made the North American, William A. Morgan pensive and so at the end of February he sat down and wrote the following:

'I was made in germany for the use of the mighty wermacht. Here I saw the rise to power of Adolf Hitler and the glory of the third reich. I saw the conquest of France, the Netherlands, Austria, Checkslovaca, and findaly all of Europe. I saw the mighty german panzers on the sands of Africa. I was there when the allied armys invaded Italy and France and I saw the destruction of Hitler's power and all it stood for in Europe. I came to U.S. a souvenier of a G.I. and then to a pawn shop and finely to an arms dealer who sold me with other arms to a man who took me to the Lomas [hills] of Cuba. Now I rest on the head of a farmer boy of nineteen and here I will see the death of another dictator and the liberation of Cuba.'"

≡ Nineteen days after they fled Banao, Menoyo and his group arrived at their destination outside Guanayara. A rural family greeted them and set out food and gathered supplies for the haggard guerrillas. Morgan and Ramirito came into camp behind the rest. Men were eating already, seated at a table and on the ground around an outdoor kitchen. They ate meat with rice and beans, filling and stretching their shrunken stomachs until they could barely move. Someone handed Ramirito a pair of boots and he squeezed his swollen, broken, bare foot into the shoe with a shout. But it offered him support, something of a cast to help the healing.

When Morgan and Ramirito finished eating, they made their way behind their hosts' simple country house and across a clearing to the edge of the woods, where they strung hammocks for the night. For the first time in three weeks, they could relax. As the adrenaline drained from their bodies, it was replaced by exhaustion. That night they would sleep the sleep of the dead, and in the morning they would awake to the task of setting up a new guerrilla base in the mountains. Ramirito, limping along in his new boots, thanked God for his life, his full stomach, the chance for his foot to heal, and the strength and courage of the American beside him.

Over the course of the exhausting trek, Eloy Gutiérrez Menoyo had developed increasing respect for the American, who demonstrated a force of will that impressed both the young leader and his men. The heavy man who had wheezed into camp was now trim, smaller than when he first arrived. But each day, his stature among the Rebels increased.

Morgan's Spanish was improving, and Menoyo soon entrusted him with the command of a Rebel column. Though they couldn't communicate easily, and certainly not about more abstract topics, each recognized aspects of himself in the other man. Morgan saw how the men responded when Menoyo announced a plan and then marched ahead without looking to see if anyone followed. El Gallego always led by example. Menoyo admired the same qualities in Morgan. He saw that Morgan, in a short time, had come to love the men with whom he fought. He led with his heart.

FREE TERRITORY

By the end of March, the split between the DRE and Menoyo's group was official. As Menoyo had predicted, Chomón's plan to assassinate Batista came to nothing, and the carefully smuggled arms were lost in a police raid on March 30 in Havana.

Menoyo proposed that all efforts be focused on the Escambray and consolidated under his command. The DRE refused, stating that their strategy was one of decentralization, and concentrating all their resources on one front would weaken the insurrectionist efforts. When the leaders of the SNFE protested, the DRE voted to expel them from their organization. And so, the Second National Front of the Escambray became a stand-alone band of Rebels, still philosophically nonsectarian, still accepting anyone who wanted to fight for the liberation of Cuba, but independent of the political group from which it had sprung.

With his beard coming in thick and reddish brown, Morgan was looking more and more like a guerrilla. He continued to train recruits as they joined the force; Menoyo organized them into columns, each numbering between fifteen and thirty men. These columns would set off for separate sections of the Escambray with the express purpose of intercepting army patrols, engaging them, and either taking hostages or inflicting casualties. This offered a great opportunity for a hunter-gatherer approach to increasing their supply of arms: Dead or captured soldiers would give up their weapons.

The immediate goal of the Second Front was to create as large a *territorio libre*—free territory—in the mountains as they could. By definition, this free territory would be beyond the control of the Batista government; it would be a place that the Cuban Army would not dare enter—a country within a country.

Each of the army barracks that dotted the region housed anywhere from fifteen to thirty men who patrolled the area, usually in groups of five to ten, walking defined routes, looking for signs of Rebel activity, interviewing local residents, and, when possible, arresting or killing Batista's enemies. To ensure that they completed their route each day, the patrols were required to get the signatures of certain community members in the towns and hamlets they passed through.

The Rebels made these patrols their first targets. They ambushed the soldiers, terrorizing them as they made their rural rounds. Every time they destroyed or frightened off a patrol, Rebel territory in the Escambray increased.

The soldiers and commanders of each barracks were then faced with a choice: They could constrict the patrol route, thereby ceding territory to the Rebels; they could increase the size of the patrols, in which case each barracks would require a greater number of troops; or they could call in a larger force and attempt to wipe out the Rebels quickly. The problem with the last option was the logistics. Even if the army were to commit a large number of troops to the area, they still might not find the fleet-footed Rebels, who rarely rested in the same place for more than a day or two.

The Rebels spent entire days trudging through the mountains. On one such trek, Menoyo and a group of his men came upon the estate of a large landowner. They entered the house, a scraggly group of rebels in an opulent, rural mansion. The owner was not home, but the house was fully staffed with maids, butlers, and even a bartender. Menoyo, having tended bar at his club in Havana, thought it would be amusing to test the bartender's experience. Standing there in his dusty Rebel uniform, a machine gun slung across his back, he ordered a Sazerac. Without hesitation the bartender filled a glass with the comandante's cocktail of choice. Even to a Cuban, the degree to which cosmopolitan sophistication had penetrated the country's culture—from the coastal cities to the heart of the island—was surprising. The rich in Cuba had everything they wanted whenever and wherever they desired it.

In late March, a farmer alerted the Rebels to the presence of a Batista spy in a cabin not far from the Rebel camp. As the Second Front increased its territory, it attracted more attention from the army. Whenever possible, Batista's troops recruited spies to help them track the movements of the hard-to-catch Rebels.

Morgan told Menoyo, in his imperfect Spanish, that he would take care of it. "*Gallego, voy abajo coger el chivato*—Galician, I'll go down to catch the snitch." Menoyo agreed, and in the middle of the night, Morgan sneaked to the house where the informant was staying. He crept to the door and then burst in, catching the man without a struggle. The spy was a local boy named Rolando Ocaña Carter, and it wasn't long before the young man's mother caught wind of her son's capture. Terrified that the Rebels would execute Rolando, she sought out Menoyo to plead for her son's life. "The American took my son prisoner," she said. "Please don't kill him."

"Don't worry," responded Menoyo. "He's more useful to us alive. He knows the terrain better than any of us. He can act as a guide."

To keep their captive from escaping, the Rebels dressed him in one of their own uniforms and strapped an empty pistol to his side. He looked just like one of them. If an army patrol were to see Rolando, they would think that he had switched sides and betrayed them—and they would kill him. Indeed, the one time he did try to escape, soldiers shot at him and he was forced to return to the uncomfortable safety of the Rebel camp.

When news spread that Menoyo and his men were establishing themselves in the mountains, disparate groups of Rebels began to make their way to the Second Front. A man named Wilfredo Peña brought a group of more than thirty from around Trinidad. Genaro Arroyo delivered another collection of men to Guanayara, all affiliated with the 26th of July Movement.

Back in Banao, Roger Redondo, who had been protecting the guns left behind by Chomón and Menoyo, had rounded up enough recruits—more than forty—to carry all the weaponry to Menoyo. They arrived in early April, increasing the total number of guerrillas in the band to more than one hundred.

When Redondo rendezvoused with the SNFE in the small village of Naranjo, the William Morgan he saw barely resembled the man he had known six weeks earlier. Morgan could communicate in rough Spanish on nearly any topic, and he was earning a reputation for daring feats.

Redondo was amazed at the transformation. Morgan was becoming *aplatanado*. Literally, this meant "bananaed." Figuratively, it signified that he was becoming Cuban.

In addition to the groups, individual volunteers trickled into the mountains, one or two at a time. They came, for the most part, as a matter of personal conviction or because their activity against the regime had rendered their existence in the cities perilous.

In Cienfuegos, a tall, long-faced twenty-year-old named Felix Rafael Vázquez Robles sat on a bench at the corner of Avenida San Fernando, where students congregated, and the wide boulevard of Paseo del Prado. Everything from revolution to baseball was discussed along this shady boulevard. It was April 2. Robles leaned forward, looked down the bench, and announced to his friends, "I'm going to the Escambray tomorrow. If anyone would like to come with me . . ."

Robles, known as Bibe or as Caunao, after his small hometown just outside the city, was an Auténtico and a member of the DRE. He was also the son of a Cuban revolutionary who had been involved with a student-military alliance that managed to topple another Cuban dictator, General Gerardo Machado, in 1933. Machado's fall coincidentally led to the rise of a young, charismatic military officer named Fulgencio Batista. Now, twenty-five years later, Bibe was going into the hills to oppose the same man his father had supported.

The young men to whom Bibe announced his decision that morning were also involved in student politics. They marched, argued, advocated, and protested. However, it was no small step from condoned tinkering at the edges of a system to armed rebellion. These middle-class boys just looked at their friend and shook their heads.

The next day, Bibe took a bus to Cumanayagua, a dusty agricultural community. There he caught a collective jeep taxi to El Nicho, a tiny town of coffee growers. The last patch of road into town had been built by the Spaniards (or, more accurately, by their slaves) with ship ballast that they had brought from the Old World. The hamlet consisted of only a small cluster of houses and one large building, where workers brought the harvested coffee to be cleaned and roasted before the beans were transported to the capital.

From El Nicho, Bibe began the long trek into the hills toward Charco Azul, where he was supposed to wait for the Rebels at the house of a man named Tomás Perez. The road tapered to a path. He skirted a clear, blue pool fed by a curtain of water cascading down a thirty-foot cliff and continued climbing.

He found the house and waited; it was after nightfall when the Rebels arrived. Menoyo, Carreras, and Morgan walked in, leaving about forty or fifty others outside. Bibe was surprised by how young Menoyo was; barely older than himself, he thought. The young comandante didn't speak much, but he smiled at the newcomer. Bibe noticed the men teasing Morgan about his Spanish. Though joking, they were talking about a daring mission accomplished by the American when he captured one of Batista's spies. Bibe listened, wide-eyed.

After dinner, Menoyo and Carreras interviewed Bibe and accepted him into the group. He was the first recruit from Cienfuegos to join Menoyo's force, but he would not be the last. Within weeks, the trickle of volunteers would turn into a stream and include some of Bibe's middle-class friends, the same young men who were incredulous when he had first announced his mission.

Bibe had arrived just in time to take part in what would be the greatest test yet of the Second National Front of the Escambray.

In early April 1958 the SNFE blew up a hydroelectric plant that provided power to a small village and one of the army barracks beside the Hanabanilla River. When the lights went out, both the soldiers at their posts and the residents realized that the Rebels truly intended to disrupt their day-to-day lives.

Then on April 9 a national strike, poorly organized by a faction within the 26th of July Movement, led to an intense and brutal period of repression by Batista's police. Though some suggest he was only tangentially involved, Fidel Castro's image suffered as hundreds of Rebel supporters, young men and women in the cities, became targets. In the eastern city of Santiago de Cuba, just south of the Sierra Maestra, police assassinated thirty people. Men and women who'd never considered joining a guerrilla force soon found themselves hanging hammocks and tarpaulins between trees or running supplies into the mountains. Many who might have tried to make it into the Sierra Maestra with Fidel trekked instead into the Escambray to join the SNFE. Their reasons had to do with logistics—the Sierra Maestra range was isolated and a difficult trip—and with the 26th of July Movement's loss of standing following the strike debacle.

In response to the incident at Hanabanilla and the growing presence of the Second Front, Batista sent a force of a thousand men to clean the Rebels out of the Escambray. In response, the Second Front consolidated its columns for a trek from Guanayara to Topes de Collante.

The Rebels broke camp before dawn and made their way along the edge of a wide valley where a slow-moving river meandered. It was prime coffee-growing land, and plantations covered the valley floor and crept up the slopes. The area was called Charco Azul—Blue Pool—after a place where the river widened and reflected the mountain sky. The prisoner Morgan had captured, Rolando Ocaña, knew the terrain best and guided the Rebels through the valley.

At seven o'clock shots rang out, whizzing over the snaking Rebel column. Some of the Rebels ducked and dropped to the ground, others scattered behind trees and thick stands of coffee plants. A few, including Menoyo and Morgan, peered in the direction of the shots, attempting to determine the enemy's numbers. From the movement they detected in the distance—clumps of khaki uniforms scurrying closer to them for another salvo—the army force appeared significant, at least as large as their own column of nearly one hundred.

More shots came at them from across the river, then more from the slope on their other flank. Menoyo and his men were surrounded by Batista's soldiers.

Menoyo managed to get word to his men to hold their positions and fight back. If they scattered and ran, chaos would ensue and there would be no telling how ugly it could get. The last thing Menoyo wanted was to lose his entire force just as they were getting started.

Dropping and scrambling on their bellies as Morgan had taught them, the men took up positions behind rocks and trees, carefully moving to find angles that afforded them both protection and clear shots at their enemies. The two sides hammered away at each other, shifting slightly here and there, looking for an advantage. For hours there was little movement; neither side could gain the advantage. By now the sun had climbed in the sky and found its way into the valley. The men sweated, fired, loaded, shifted position, sipped from their canteens, fired again. Three Rebels had been shot dead. Two were injured. A bullet nicked Redondo's knee, but he continued fighting.

As afternoon set in, a flurry of shooting erupted behind one army unit. Luckily for the Rebels, Lázaro Artola had started out later with a second column and was traveling behind and parallel to Menoyo, higher up on the ridge on the other side of the river. Although Menoyo had been unable to send word back, Artola quickly assessed the situation and moved in. Some soldiers panicked, while others attempted to hold the position.

Morgan found Menoyo and told him their best chance was to force their way across the river and through the army unit on the other side. If they made it across successfully, they could then join forces with Artola and split the unit into fragments. After nearly seven hours of fighting, Morgan thought there couldn't be much fight left in the soldiers and the chaos of splitting the battalion would finish them for the day. It was a risky move. Menoyo was unsure, but Morgan was adamant.

"I'll do it," said Morgan. "Follow me down to the river. When I've cleared it, wade across behind me." The Rebels crawled behind the American, moving closer and closer to the bank. Suddenly Morgan leaped to his feet and ran into the river, his Sten spraying bullets at the soldiers who'd remained in the bushes. They shouted, caught by surprise. Three or four were cut down immediately. The rest scattered. Seeing this, Morgan turned and gestured to the other Rebels. They hurled themselves over the bank, splashed to the other side, and quickly they made their way to Artola's position. A few scattered shots could still be heard, but the fight was over.

The Rebels had escaped the ambush thanks to Menoyo's initial leadership, Artola's assistance from behind the enemy lines, and Morgan's nerve.

In total, the Rebels lost five men in the fight. Wilfredo

Peña was seriously wounded, and the men carried him to a small farm, where Armando Fleites removed the bullet lodged in Peña's gut. In a civil war of skirmishes, this would be one of the biggest single-day casualty tolls for the Rebels of the Escambray.

Despite their having been ambushed, from what the Rebels could determine, they'd managed to kill about thirty soldiers, several of whom were killed by Morgan as he led the men out of the trap. They were exhausted by the physical and emotional effort. Fleites said that they "were so tired after nine hours of fighting that they wanted to die."

True to form, the government-censored *La Correspondencia*, the daily newspaper of Cienfuegos, reported the incident in this way: "In the island's interior various incidents have been reported with small groups of revolutionaries that are being pursued and attacked by the public forces. In Las Villas province, where complete order reigns, the guardians of the peace suffered five casualties, but inflicted on the saboteurs a much greater quantity."

The confidence of the young Rebels was greatly buoyed by their success at Charco Azul. They now believed they could beat anything the Cuban Army sent at them. After Charco Azul, the SNFE announced in a memo to Herbert Matthews that its presence in the mountains was "no longer a dream" and that it was "crushing the forces of the Dictator Batista."

Letters to Matthews aside, the SNFE had problems getting its message out. When it broke from the DRE, the Escambray contingent lost the support of the organization's infrastructure, which included media and propaganda departments. As well as having covert outlets in Cuba, the DRE had connections to radio stations and newspapers in Miami. The SNFE, a purely military organization, was at a distinct disadvantage when it came to publicity—particularly in spreading word of their success.

Morgan and Menoyo described the problem in a memo to Herbert Matthews: "As intense, heavy fighting was going on daily and due to the fact that there were no adequate facilities to keep the people of Cuba well informed, it was utterly impossible for the Front to alert the nation and the world as to what was going on. . . ." The DRE, they complained, was claiming credit for SNFE military victories: "Other rebel units [referring particularly to the DRE] capitalized heavily on the heroic record of the [SNFE] by usurping to themselves the victorious results of the Front in several areas. In short, here was a group of men [the DRE], light-years away from the fighting lines, claiming in a loud voice that they had been combating in the battlefields of Cuba. The claim was nothing more than a big, big, big lie."

When the DRE stopped helping the SNFE, the Auténtico organization stepped in, placing articles in the *Miami Herald* and the Spanish-language Miami newspaper *Diario Las Américas*.

But the SNFE needed to build an urban infrastructure of its own. Enter Max Lesnik. In Havana, Max founded the SNFE's urban underground—a network of supporters who would perform some sabotage but focused primarily on gathering resources for Menoyo and his men. He also worked to get the word out about SNFE victories and designed the group's insignia, a fist holding the torch of freedom superimposed on the Cuban flag, and sold bonds to raise money for the guerrillas. As the head of propaganda, Max scattered leaflets around the city, informed people who were in a position to tell others sympathetic to the anti-Batista cause, and created spots for the illegal radio transmitters dedicated to pro-Rebel news. He also collected money and supplies for the SNFE and carefully organized deliveries into the mountains. His was a dangerous job. He constantly moved from safe house to safe house, since capture by Batista's secret police would have meant torture, prison, and possibly, death.

Max was a son of revolutionaries: His father, a Russian Bolshevik, fled to Cuba, where he met Max's mother, who descended from a long line of Cuban independence fighters. Max's politics bent left, not toward Communism, but rather toward democratic socialism. Under his mother's influence, his fervor burned closer to the teachings of José Martí, who focused on the Cubans' right to determine their own path without excessive influence from either Spain or the United States. Max was an energetic and smart nationalist who loved to give fiery talks, to debate, and to wrestle.

Max attended university and studied law where one of his fellow students was a passionate and brilliant young tough named Fidel Castro. Max, like Castro, was deeply involved in student government. In Cuba at this time, student leadership positions carried real political power. The students knew how to confront, challenge, and embarrass the government with their idealistic messages. There were constant clashes between students and the police. Still, they were viewed as the vanguard, not as the national leaders. They were future leaders in training, building their reputations and credibility for later. The insurrection in Cuba would turn tradition on its head. Out with the old and in with the new. Within a year, Cuba's youth would be running the government, not harassing it.

Shortly after the success at Charco Azul, Max Lesnik visited the guerrillas in the mountains. He wanted to assess the strength of Menoyo's troops and discuss what to do about the surge in volunteers wanting to join the Rebels.

Max had heard of "El Americano" and was curious to meet him. In addition to the information that made its way down from the mountains, he'd read Herbert Matthews's *New York Times* article of April 3, and was interested in verifying its contents. It seemed curious to him that a man with Morgan's credentials — a World War II hero, a Korean War veteran — would be up in the hills of Cuba looking for more military action.

Also, it did not escape Max's attention that Morgan's biography was not dissimilar to that of Carlos Menoyo, Eloy's brother. Carlos was ten years older than Eloy and was born in Spain in 1924. If Morgan was 33, as Matthews stated, he was the same age as Carlos. When Eloy's eldest brother, José Antonio, was killed in the Spanish Civil War, the Menoyos sent Carlos to France. There, at the age of sixteen or so, he joined the French resistance fighters, the Maquis. He fought the Germans in Libya and in 1944 participated in D Day in Normandy. By the end of that year, the young Spaniard was under the command of General George Patton. To his family, Carlos was a World War II hero.

Max waited for the Rebel columns in the tiny town of Naranjo. The few guerrillas there regaled him with stories about the hardships and exploits of the last months. They couldn't stop talking about the feats of El Americano. Max heard about the trek from Banao and how Morgan had saved Ramirito, the capture of the Batista spy, the heroics on the river at Charco Azul, and the good humor of the *maranero* who brought levity to the tense and exhausting missions.

That evening, when Menoyo, Fleites, and the rest returned from the day's patrol, Max found himself at a small table with Morgan, playing dominoes. Cubans love to play dominoes, preferably outdoors, whistling and exclaiming to the cha-cha beat of the tiles hitting the table. Morgan, like many a cocky Cuban, played the game with a flourish, predicting his victory, slapping his pieces down on the table for emphasis. And he talked.

Max learned some things about Morgan that contradicted the Matthews article. For example, he was younger than Matthews had said, only days away from his thirtieth birthday. He had not fought in World War II, though getting more information out of Morgan about his military service was no easy feat, since Morgan didn't like to talk about it. However, it was clear that he'd been trained. The men confirmed that he was an expert with a knife and excelled at hand-to-hand combat.

As he and Max discussed the insurrection, Morgan confided in the young lawyer his thoughts about Che Guevara. "I think he's a Communist," he told Max. Lesnik was surprised. No one was saying this except Batista. He wasn't sure what to make of the proclamation's coming from the American Rebel. America, he knew, had a peculiar, hysterical relationship with the idea of Communism. In Cuba, for the most part, people were much more relaxed with the Communists. Communists ran a couple of unions and had made pacts with Cuban presidents, including Batista, until the American government insisted that Batista crack down on them. As far as Max knew, J. Edgar Hoover's FBI was behind the persecution of the Cuban Communist Party. Perhaps, thought Max, Morgan didn't distinguish between democratic socialism and communism. He wondered if Morgan might have trouble seeing nuance, that his tendency—often a useful characteristic in battle—was to see the world in black and white.

Morgan's comment about Guevara worried Max. Either it was particularly astute or it was a crude notion that could cause trouble for everybody if it got around and took on a reality of its own. Max wasn't sure what to think of this American. He could see that the men of the Second Front were looking to Morgan as a leader. Morgan's swagger, his humor, and the stories passed around about his courage were infectious and inspired the other Rebels. Like a Cuban, he talked with his hands.

What concerned Max was not Morgan's magnetism per se, but that it was the charisma of an American. What impact might this have on the psychology of other Rebels? The fight in which the Rebels were engaged was a fight against a Cuban dictator propped up by the Americans. Max hoped Morgan's leadership would not diminish, however subtly, the confidence of the Cuban people. He didn't want the Rebels' success to be attributed to the feats of this curious, vaguely mysterious American. Cuba did not need another Teddy Roosevelt.

For the most part, Max was alone with his worries. He saw that Menoyo was growing particularly close to the American, entrusting him with more and more responsibility. While Max would not forget his concerns, they would recede into the background. More pressing issues were at hand, namely, how to maintain momentum in the fight against Batista and how to arm the surge of recruits who were making their way into the mountains. With any luck, thought Max, there would be only a few more years of struggle before they wore down the resolve of the dictator and forced him to hold fair elections or, better still, leave the country.

Even as its numbers increased to nearly one thousand men and women, the Second Front could not risk a direct face-off with the Cuban Army. However, using the guerrilla tactics of constant movement, surprise, and ambush, it could keep the Cuban Army off balance and nervous about entering the ever-expanding free zone, which came to be known as the Territorio Libre. The perimeter of the Free Territory was continuously patrolled by SNFE columns, who took names such as Black Berets and Tigers of the Jungle, which was Morgan's column. As Rebels secured the Free Territory, they set up headquarters in a section of the mountains called Nuevo Mundo. There, the eighty-year-old Spanish proprietress of a coffee plantation, by the name of Doña Rosa, invited Floy to make his general headquarters in her large stone house.

As its position in the Escambray stabilized, a three-part strategy emerged for the SNFE: It would dominate the zone militarily; it would plan larger offensives designed to break the will of the regime; and it would work to improve the quality of life of the residents.

The SNFE acquired its own radio plant and began broadcasting reports. Their channel was called Seis Barbudos Feroces – Six Ferocious Bearded Men. They installed the transmitter in Doña Rosa's house, and a news team, Roger Rodríguez and Rafael Garriga, broadcast accounts of the combat victories. When they spoke of the Tigers, they referred to El Americano, and for the first time, people beyond the front began to learn about the American who was making a difference in the struggle against Batista.

The Rebels ran phone lines around their territory so the various camps could communicate with one another. They operated a factory in which they made uniforms and shoes. A dentist cared for the Rebels as well as local residents. Through an underground network, a postal service moved mail around Cuba and to the United States. The Rebels even began opening schools for the children of the mountain farmers.

The SNFE command rigorously enforced its basic policies for interacting with the local people. All food, goods, and services received from farmers and laborers had to be paid for. And if a Rebel took up with a woman from one of the hamlets, he had to marry her. The Rebels tolerated supporters of Batista, provided they did nothing to aid the dictator or the Cuban Army. Ramirito's mother, a Batista supporter, even made her way into the Free Territory to visit her son, to bring him food and make sure he was all right. In a photograph taken during her visit, she's wearing a simple white dress and a big smile as she stands next to her boy. She seems not only glad that he's alive but proud of her son, in spite of their differing political sympathies.

These policies brought stability, which improved the lives of both the Rebels and the locals. In addition to working their coffee plantations, many farmers grew enough food to sell some commercially. Some grew small plots of rice, a staple for any Cuban meal, along the rivers and streams in the valleys. The Rebels bought rice, beans, bananas, tomatoes, and vegetables from the farmers. They could buy a pig for five dollars. Even from the Rebel-controlled areas, the farmers continued to ship coffee and vegetables to markets in the cities. Processed food, however, came into the mountains infrequently. Salt and sugar were hard to come by. The Rebels had to adjust to unsalted rice and beans, and to coffee sweetened with honey from local hives instead of the Cuban sugar to which they were accustomed.

Still, some stores operated in the region. A Syrian who maintained his allegiance to Batista ran one not far from SNFE headquarters. In response to the reduced supply of canned and dry goods coming in, the proprietor raised his prices exorbitantly, charging as much as a dollar for a can of milk that would normally cost twenty cents, thereby gouging some extra cash from the Rebels and their collaborators. When the Rebels asked him to lower his prices, the man refused.

Morgan decided to deal with the situation his way. With a small escort he rode to the store and "liberated" all its goods. He filled up knapsacks and bags with everything the little shop held, loaded it onto the back of a mule, and spent the rest of the day riding around the area, delivering free food to appreciative locals.

Incensed, the storeowner sent his son after Morgan to demand that he return the food or pay for it. Thinking they would have a bit of fun with the young man, Morgan and his men tied the boy to his mule facing backward, and, with a firm slap to the mule's hindquarters, sent the pair back down the hill to the boy's father. Delighted with themselves, they assumed that would be the last they'd hear of the shopkeeper.

Now enraged and insulted, the Syrian alerted the army and put it on the trail of the Rebels who were playing Robin Hood. An army patrol gave chase and surprised Morgan's group as they set up camp in the late afternoon. The Rebels won the skirmish, killing the soldiers, but one of Morgan's men, Edmundo Amado, was shot five times in the chest. Remarkably, he hung on to life. Morgan dispatched a messenger to find and bring back the Second Front's nurse, Julio Martínes.

Well after dark, Martínes, accompanied by a friend of Ramirito's named Miguelito, approached what they believed to be the site where Morgan and his men were huddled with the wounded man. Under the pitch black of the new moon, Martínes and Miguelito could barely see each other, though less than ten feet separated them. They flashed a signal light. A torch sparked in response and they moved forward to call out the Rebel password.

Unbeknownst to Morgan's group, Eloy had changed the passwords earlier that day. The Second Front's password system functioned as a call-and-response. The approaching party would say one word and listen for the answer. When Martínes and Miguelito approached in the dark, they said, "*Rana*—Frog," expecting to hear "*Toro*—Bull" from the shadows across a small stream.

Instead they heard someone say nervously, "What did they say? What's the word?"

They heard a man respond to the question in heavily accented Spanish, "I don't know. Did they change the password?" They recognized Morgan's American pronunciation.

Then, "Come out with your hands up!"

The two men were scared, hoping that no one on the other side had an itchy trigger finger.

"Weeleeam!" Martínes called as the two raised their hands in the air, "it's me, Martínes, with Miguelito."

The men were allowed to approach. They splashed across the stream toward a gory scene. The nurse spent much of the night operating on the wounded man. Somehow Amado lived, though he never returned to combat.

The Syrian shopkeeper packed up and left the area. The Rebels, however, could never be too careful, even in the Territorio Libre.

By late summer, the Second National Front of the Escambray controlled as much as one third of Cuba's largest province, Las Villas. They'd repelled what would be the last significant Cuban Army offensive in the war against Batista. Through it all, Morgan's Tigers of the Jungle had never lost a single confrontation with the dictator's forces.

DIPLOMACY

As the Rebels strengthened their opposition to Batista, the United States government struggled to define its own position on Cuba. While it's true that the United States had supported Batista, sold him arms, and pushed him to take a harder line with the Communists in Cuba, the government's view on the Cuban situation was by no means homogeneous.

Arthur Gardner, the U.S. ambassador to Cuba until July 15, 1957, thought that Batista was doing a magnificent job. When he was interviewed by the Senate Internal Security Subcommittee after he'd relinquished his ambassadorship, Gardner said, "I don't think we ever had a better friend [than Batista.] . . . It was regrettable, like all South Americans, that he was known—although I had no absolute knowledge of it—to be getting a cut . . . in almost all the things that were done. But . . . he was doing an amazing job."

Others, however, were less favorable in regard to the Cuban leader because of his heavy-handed approach to those who opposed him and because the elections he repeatedly promised never materialized. The CIA's number two inspector general, Lyman Kirkpatrick, wanted Batista gone. Some of Batista's friends accused U.S. agencies, namely the CIA and the State Department, though, of assisting Castro to power. Many people believe, although it has not been documented, that the CIA even made a contribution of at least fifty thousand dollars to the 26th of July Movement.

While many did want to see an end to Batista's reign, they did not necessarily want to see Castro at the helm of the island's government. He was an unknown, a revolutionary with possible links to Communists even though he wasn't considered by most people to be one himself. In the interest of stability, American officials hoped to anoint a more seasoned bureaucrat—someone they'd done business with in the past, for instance. One popular pick was the head of the Havana Bar Association, José Miró Cardona. But at that point it wasn't clear to anyone who would hold power if the Rebels were victorious.

At the State Department, William Wieland, by no means a supporter of Batista, said, "I know Batista is considered by many to be a son of a bitch . . . but American interests come first. . . . At least he is our son of a bitch." Batista protected American business and harassed Communists. What more, in other words, should the U.S. government demand? Which should be favored, democratic values or political and commercial interests?

When the new ambassador, Earl Smith, arrived in Havana in July of 1957, one of the first things he did, on the recommendation of Herbert Matthews, was to travel beyond the capital city, where Batista took great care to mask the success of the insurgents. Smith's visit to Santiago coincided with the funeral of a young 26th of July hero named Frank País, who'd been assassinated. City residents staged a huge demonstration, and, as Smith looked on, police turned fire hoses on the crowd and treated a large contingent of angry women roughly, knocking them down and shoving them into paddy wagons. The new ambassador, though no friend of the Rebels, was horrified.

Less than three months into Smith's tenure, a faction within the Cuban Navy staged a coup in Cienfuegos. As the mariners took over control of the navy barracks, about four hundred Rebels joined them. For a few hours, Cienfuegos was under the control of the insurrectionists. But the Cuban military responded with overwhelming force, taking the city back with tanks and armored cars, quickly capturing many Rebels and hunting down the rest. In a brutal action, Capitán Alejandro García Olayón and his men went from house to house apprehending and executing anyone they even suspected of participating in the uprising. They looked for cuts, bruises, ripped clothing. They did not seek justice; they went to instill terror. About three quarters of the Rebels were killed. Some, it was said, were buried alive.

Not only did the government act in a particularly brutal way, it was using the resources the United States had given it for fighting Communism to put down a popular revolt. The violence and the misappropriation of funds gave people in both the State Department and the CIA cause for concern. But still they remained on the fence. A former State Department employee who was on the Cuba desk during the time said, "We weren't sure what to do. We were flying by the seat of our pants."

≡ Despite Batista's insistence that the Rebels were Communists, the U.S. government couldn't establish any real evidence that the Rebels were influenced by Communist ideology or the Soviet Union. In fact, a U.S. Army Intelligence report in 1958, which described Morgan as one of the primary combat trainers in the Rebel army, references a political officer from the U.S. Embassy who believed that the

> movement was reformist rather than revolutionary. [The Rebels] had never indicated they were for fundamental change of government policies. [He] remarked there had been only four consistent planks in the Rebel programs:
> 1. Some form of land reform.
> 2. Government control (eventual Cuban control) of public utilities.
> 3. Reform of armed forces (clean out graft and corruption).
> 4. Some type of career civil service (to eliminate graft in government jobs).
>
> The few statements made concerning economic changes all boil down to more jobs for Cubans.

Finally, in early 1958, as the Rebels continued their push, the churches in Cuba unified in their opposition to Batista, providing institutional support to the idea that the Rebels' aims were not Communist.

Then, on March 14, 1958, the U.S. State Department acted, freezing a shipment of weapons on the docks of New York, initiating an arms embargo against the Cuban government. The U.S. government knew it had to begin to appear neutral if it hoped for any kind of diplomatic relationship with those who might assume power if Batista were forced to leave.

Around the middle of the year, due to their success in battle and Max Lesnik's propaganda efforts, the Rebels of the Second National Front of the Escambray began to receive more attention from the American intelligence community. Now that Batista's departure seemed possible, if not likely, the United

States needed to better understand the balance of power among the opposition groups.

Reports of an American tearing up the Cuban Army in Las Villas caught their attention.

Miami's Spanish-language newspaper, *Diario Las Américas*, published two articles that repackaged and updated some of the information from Herbert Matthews's April 3 *New York Times* article. These articles gave American intelligence agencies their first real sense of what was happening in central Cuba. A third article in *Diario Las Américas* then reported that "the command of William Alexander Morgan has been fighting for a long time against army forces in the zone between the Soledad Central [a sugar-processing plant north of Cienfuegos] and the South Circuit. Morgan's men, excellently trained by him, a World War II veteran, attacked the soldiers, causing many casualties among them and seizing a large number of weapons from them." Around the middle of June, the CIA began to file reports about Morgan.

In addition to newspaper reports, American intelligence officials were picking up the crackle of illegal radio broadcasts coming from the Escambray, which identified someone as "*El Americano*." Perhaps, the CIA speculated, Morgan was "The American."

A month later, the CIA gathered more information from the Escambray. In a report dated July 22, 1958, the agency noted that

> Rebel activity has increased considerably in Las Villas
> Province since April 1958. There are several rebel bands
> from five to twenty men each. Another group of twenty or
> thirty rebels is led by an American who is believed to be
> a veteran of the Korean War and experienced in guerrilla

warfare. . . . About 20 June 1958 some 80 members of the Guardia Rural (Rural Guard) made their headquarters for a few days in the houses of the LORA family plantation in the Nuevo Mundo area, near Cumanayagua, which is about twenty miles northeast of Cienfuegos. The American rebel and his group ambushed the Rural Guard and practically wiped it out. In general, the Rural guards are alienating the natives of the region by their actions. In one incident . . . at a small coffee plantation . . . the Guards showed poor discipline and behavior, and they took everything they could lay their hands on without payment of any kind."

The FBI picked up the following UPI wire report of August 1958:

"Cuba's Rebel Radio reported today that a rebel force 'led by an American' in Las Villas Province of Central Cuba, has killed 40 Army troops in a clash at Curva de Marcial.

"The Radio identified the American Rebel troop's commander only as 'Morton.' He had been mentioned previously by Rebel Radio as a 'Yankee fighting for the liberty of Cuba.'"

"Morton" was, undoubtedly, Morgan.

What, if any, conclusions, the U.S. government agencies were drawing about Morgan remains unclear at this point. The government seemed more interested in the big picture, and in figuring out how to direct its own influence, than in categorizing the particular efforts of individual Rebels — even this curious American. It would be another few months before it would begin assembling every scrap of information on Morgan its agents could get their hands on in order to try to understand his motives.

TOLEDO

*People can't, unhappily, invent their mooring posts, their
lovers and friends, any more than they can invent their
parents. Life gives these and also takes them away and the
great difficulty is to say Yes to life.*
                              James Baldwin, Giovanni's Room

On a map of the United States, Toledo appears remote and
isolated, tucked into the corner of northern Ohio just south
of Canada and Michigan's eastern edge. However, during the
second half of the nineteenth century, it was a place of growing importance in the nation's burgeoning web of industry and
transportation. In 1868 local entrepreneur Jesup W. Scott expected Toledo to become a "Future Great City of the World."
The railroads would run through it; it boasted a port on Lake
Erie and lay within a day's travel of Chicago, Detroit, Cleveland, Buffalo, and New York City. "All the rough work was
done," wrote one commentator in 1871, "to make Toledo one
of the great and beautiful cities of America."

When Alexander W. Morgan took a job in the finance department of Toledo Edison and moved his family the 120 miles
from Cleveland to Toledo in 1929, the city was an up-and-
coming industrial center, still striving to distance itself from

its outpost past. Between 1910 and 1930, Toledo's population nearly doubled. The arrival of the four Morgans—Alexander, his wife, Loretta, and their two children, Anne Marie "Carroll," and the baby, William—helped to edge the number of Toledans close to 300,000.

Alexander Morgan bought a large, boxy house at 2909 Collingwood Boulevard in the city's most fashionable neighborhood. Collingwood runs like a spoke toward downtown. If you drive slowly along that route, you realize that here Toledo's snug, Midwestern values are on display. Large houses squat on sloping lawns. Vast churches do not strain up so much as out, reaching to draw worshippers in. There is an ornate high school that looks like a frosted gingerbread castle, named after Jesup W. Scott, Toledo's biggest nineteenth-century booster. On Collingwood, it seems, the optimistic convergence of industry, piety, education, and success is everywhere.

The résumé of Alexander Morgan suggests an archetypal American of the 1930s and 1940s. He was a husband, father, business leader, and active member of the community. In addition to his work at Toledo Edison, Alexander dedicated a great deal of time to church and to hobbies. Several societies and clubs at Rosary Cathedral counted him among their members. He collected stamps and owned a moving-picture camera. The film he made of Rosary Cathedral's dedication ceremony in 1931 won first prize in a national competition, and following this success, the Boy Scouts of America contracted him to shoot "exemplary Scout activities" for a documentary film.

One might think of him as the kind of American-next-door who inspired Norman Rockwell's paintings in praise of the everyday struggles and successes of the modern middle-class family. While America might have been founded by exiles and rebels, and expanded by adventurous speculators, its day-to-day existence depended on the calm and dutiful lives of men like Alexander Morgan.

Alexander worked a lot and moved quietly through his community, attracting little attention. His wife raised a higher profile. While her husband worked and practiced his hobbies, Loretta made church life her vocation. "She's one of those people," people would say, with just a hint of sarcasm in their voices, "who thinks she will go straight to heaven."

Loretta was a slim woman who cut an immaculate, stylish figure and wore the latest hats, cocked tastefully to one side. Her friends and neighbors thought of her as a "classy lady," if a bit cool and "holier than thou." Loretta became the highest-ranking laywoman in the church, a position colloquially known as Miss Cathedral.

Though some might have thought her a bit stuck up, Loretta Morgan was motivated by a desire to help the needy. As Miss Cathedral, she recruited the women in her largely Catholic, silk-stocking neighborhood to come to the aid of the ill and the poor. The women followed her, though most did not feel close to her.

Together, Loretta and Alexander Morgan strove to make a world for their children that resembled the values of Collingwood Boulevard. The Morgans were undoubtedly preparing their son for a life like theirs: He was to receive a good, Catholic education before working his way into Toledo's manager class, raising a family, and doing what he could to help the less fortunate. But it was apparent from early on that conformity wasn't for Billy Morgan.

"He was getting into trouble a lot," said Geri Brandon, a classmate at Rosary Cathedral School. "The nuns would send him to the coatroom. . . . In those days the nuns really took the kids in there and whacked them. But," she continued, "he was a nice kid. Always tried to get along with everybody. He was just mischievous."

Jack O'Connell, who had attended high school with Billy, said, "The classes I had with Morgan were taught by priests, so he wasn't going to get too far out of line with them or he'd *really* get whacked. You would look at him and say, 'Who the hell is winding him up?' He was restless. I don't think anyone was that friendly with Bill."

Geri tried to soften the memory. "He wanted to be accepted badly. He was so tickled if someone stopped him, talked to him, gave him a little bit of time, you know. Or if he was ever included in school, if there was a project and he was included, he just beamed. He was nice." She paused. "He didn't have a mean bone in his body.

"He just wasn't one of the . . ." It seemed as though she was going to finish the sentence with "popular kids" or "in crowd" but thought better of it. Her voice trailed off and she concluded, "He was sort of a lost soul."

Billy's struggles left his parents feeling helpless and re-moved. Loretta enlisted the help of the church to get him onto a more acceptable track. She repeatedly implored Monsignor Bernard Smith to "put some discipline to" Billy.

In 2001, at age 96, Monsignor Smith's health was failing, but he claimed to remember Billy Morgan and his antics clearly. He recalled the young boy as a loner with few friends. What trouble the boy made exactly, he wouldn't tell, continuing to respect, all these years later, the religious contract. "Billy had a very mixed-up life" was all he'd say.

≡ The social landscape of Toledo offered a set of alternatives for an alienated, rebellious youth in the 1930s and 1940s. If Billy Morgan was easily distracted, there was a great deal happening in Toledo to woo him away from his parents' design. In addition to imagining a career as a manager, factory worker, cop, fireman, soldier, or priest, kids in Toledo might fantasize about becoming a labor organizer or chasing bootleggers and gamblers for the FBI or even of becoming one of those racketeers with shiny suits and their own codes of loyalty.

Toledo had a split personality. On the one hand, it was considered the perfect place to raise a family. On the other hand, it offered services that would earn it a reputation among soldiers during World War II as the "greatest R&R town in the country," a characterization bolstered by the city's boisterous gambling houses and brothels.

The Mob ran these temples of vice. People tend—or prefer—to think of the underworld as distinct from the world that "regular," law-abiding people inhabit, but in Toledo the movement of illegal goods mingled the spheres of the underworld and the overworld financially, physically, and, especially, imaginatively. Slightly smaller and quieter than Cleveland or Detroit and close to Canadian waters, Toledo became famous not only for making bottles in the Owens Bottle plant, but for filling those bottles with bootleg booze. The market for liquor—along with the markets for gambling and sex—stitched together a complex social fabric. Toledo parents drank bootleg whiskey and secretly regretted the death of racketeer Jack Kennedy. At the same time, Toledo society promoted civil and church law and feared the violence associated with the suppliers of their cocktails.

For children like Billy Morgan, this meant that some of the exciting young adults he heard about were involved in illegal activities. It also meant that violence was often near. The bootleggers and racketeers added bursts of color to Toledo's news. These real-life characters were known by names that sounded as if they'd been lifted from comic books: "Firetop" Skulkin, "Chalky Red," and "The Muzzler," as well as the Licavoli clan and the Purple Gang from Detroit. When Billy was five years old, in the summer of 1933, the Licavoli gang murdered Jack Kennedy, and Toledo lost the most glamorous character of its Mob mythology. Kennedy had been known as a kind of Robin Hood, generous and fair, a homegrown gangster who cared for his community and helped the needy.

According to Mary Harpen Wright, a local children's-book author, a Toledo version of the traditional children's games of cops and robbers cropped up during this time along the sylvan stretches of Collingwood. It was called "FBI and bootleggers." As any kid knows, once you start playing, who the winner *should* be is no longer clear.

It was in this setting that Billy Morgan—unpopular and a failure at school—came of age, and his attention was drawn to the busy fringes of Toledo society.

In the fall of 1943, during the first semester of his sophomore year, Morgan dropped out of high school, finally taking leave of the classmates who'd never understood him. He headed to the piers. It was the middle of World War II, and nearly all the young men in Toledo joined up to serve the minute they turned eighteen. The U.S. Merchant Marine, desperate for ship hands, dropped its age limit to fourteen. With his mother's permission, fifteen-year-old Billy signed on as a deckhand. Perhaps his parents hoped that the hard, physical work could do what they and the church had failed to do—teach their son some discipline.

Down on the docks, Billy got mixed up in what the Toledo police, in their reports, would call the "hoodlum element." This was a rough crowd, maybe even some sort of gang, that brawled with rival tough guys and held up a convenience store or two. It's likely that these young toughs intermingled with Toledo's mob, though how and to what degree remains unclear. Some of the scars the Cubans saw on Morgan's body when he removed his shirt that first day in the mountains were the result of his days as a teenage thug.

≡ One finds signs of Billy's disaffection with the hoodlum life in his attempts to join the U.S. Army. Toledo was proud of its sons who served overseas and took every opportunity to honor them in the newspapers and with parties when they came home to rest. The Thirty-seventh Infantry Division was dubbed the Buckeye Division because it consisted largely of men from Ohio, many of whom hailed from Toledo.

The war also provided Toledo a significant economic boost. The city was quick to see the opportunity the war might afford its industries, and offered mechanical training programs in vocational schools and high schools. Toledo's Willys-Overland Company, inventors of the jeep that would be dubbed the "little hero of the Pacific," trained women to drive in emergency conditions. Between 1941 and 1945 Willys manufactured more than three hundred thousand jeeps. Because so many of Toledo's factories were receiving defense contracts, the federal government counted the city among thirty-three strategic inland-defense areas. That only heightened the war anxiety, making Toledans think they might be bombed by enemy sorties that would come skimming west along the St. Lawrence Seaway.

On V-J Day, more than one hundred thousand Toledans jammed the streets to celebrate all night long. Traffic stopped and people danced and frolicked about the town, knowing their boys would come home, enjoying the moment before the war boom slowed and postwar economic struggles settled in.

Before V-J Day, Billy Morgan had tried three times to enlist in the army, hoping to extract himself from marginal life and to find purpose in the nation's struggle overseas. Joining the army would have been a way back toward respectability, a way to put his hoodlum reputation behind him as something to be written off as a restless period during difficult teenage years. Billy turned eighteen on April 19, 1946, and by August, when he was allowed into the army, the war was over and he was shipped off to Japan as part of the occupying force there.

The army wanted to get fresh troops to Japan quickly so it could send the combat veteran home. To do this, it truncated the basic training program. Morgan spent only three weeks at a base in Arizona before he was sent to the Pacific with the Thirty-fifth Infantry.

The details of Morgan's time in Japan are murky. His military records were lost in a fire in the 1970s that destroyed a building that housed army archives in St. Louis. Tens of thousands of records burned, including the files of several controversial figures whose military careers prepared them for later work as covert contractors for the CIA or the FBI. Conspiracy theorists wonder at the convenience of the fire that obliterated the records of people whose names had surfaced during the House Select Committee on Assassinations's investigation of the death of John F. Kennedy.

The experience of Jim Rynn, also from Toledo, casts some light on what Morgan's experience may have been like. Rynn joined the Thirty-fifth Infantry, known as the Cacti Regiment, the same year as Morgan; however, he never knew Morgan.

"Once they got us over there, it was like a year's worth of basic training. We stayed in an old Japanese barracks with no heat. We trained in the snow and in cold mud. It was kind of desperate living that first year. I got scarlet fever that winter and was sent to the hospital in Osaka.

"We ate leftover turkeys. There were three thousand guys with the shits. We each had two blankets, no sheets. It was so cold we'd pile all our clothes on top of the blankets. We'd line up in the mess hall for breakfast, and there was never enough to go around. We'd eat toasted bread and put jelly diluted with warm water on it. We got a cuppa coffee.

"At some point they do IQ tests. They'd look at these and decide what you were qualified for. They picked me to run a jail in downtown Kyoto. Guys would get pretty drunk. Some of them were pushing drugs or something. Lots of us would get shacked up with Jap girls. Our little jail was for guys who went AWOL.

"The truth is, we didn't know shit from Shinola."

The life was, in other words, miserable. Many men who'd joined the army with enthusiasm and pride became bitter and disillusioned. They had a difficult time justifying their time away from home, much of it spent, as in Rynn's case, policing one another. The eighteen-year-old Morgan, apparently, did not take well to it. He met a Japanese girl and disappeared with her. After a brief time, the MPs caught him and threw him in a jail like the one Jim Rynn ran. According to the FBI records that still exist, Morgan overpowered a guard in the jail and escaped to spend more time AWOL with his Japanese girlfriend.

When the MPs caught him a month later, he was court-martialed and sentenced to five years' hard labor before being shipped back to the United States. He served three years in federal prisons in Chillicothe, Ohio, and Milan, Michigan. He was released with a dishonorable discharge. Morgan's attempt to reenter the mainstream through the army had failed miserably.

≣ Upon his release from prison in 1950, Morgan returned to Toledo an angry and broken young man. He was twenty-two years old and faced the difficult task of remaking himself with little experience on which to build. His mother used her influence at the cathedral and with Monsignor Smith to get Bill a job as a janitor.

According to Alexander, his son was furious at the U.S. Army for the way he'd been treated. Assuming that the story about going AWOL and beating up an army prison guard is accurate, it's difficult to see why Morgan was so mad. An Army psychologist who interviewed Morgan while he was in prison described him as "smart," "angry," and "self-destructive." Perhaps Morgan had created a heroic image of what his army experience would be and couldn't reconcile that with the reality. Or maybe there was more to the story.

Gerry Hemming, an American friend of Morgan's in Cuba, says that by early 1947 covert operations were being run out of Japan into Korea. He says that Morgan told him he'd been involved in such operations and had gotten into a disagreement with his case officer. Something went seriously wrong. According to Hemming, the whole AWOL episode was a cover story.

Morgan's résumé from 1950 until he arrived in Cuba is that of an itinerant tough guy willing to do just about anything that struck his fancy. His upper-middle-class parents were incredulous, unable to believe the situations their son got involved in. Once, while on vacation in Florida, Alexander and Loretta came across him hitchhiking beside the highway. They'd had no word from him in months.

After Morgan left his job at the Rosary Cathedral in the early 1950s, he briefly held a variety of jobs. The details and chronology of this period are sketchy at best. It appears that in 1954 and 1955, he spent time in Miami. There he made his first contacts with Cuban exiles organizing against Batista. Morgan's father would later say that Morgan met Fidel Castro in Miami, which is possible, as Castro was there in 1955 raising money for the Revolution—until the U.S. government asked him to leave. Castro left Florida for Mexico, where he staged his return to Cuba.

Morgan claimed that he did some work for the infamous Mafia kingpin Meyer Lansky. One report suggests he was a bodyguard for Lansky, whereas another says Morgan worked for him as a fruit vendor.

His story grows even more eclectic. He is said to have picked up work in a carnival, apparently as a fire swallower, where he met a snake handler, Ellen May Bethel. "Theresa," as he nicknamed her, became his wife.

The couple moved to Toledo and, over the course of their four years together, had two children, Anne and William Jr.

In an effort to settle down and provide for his family, Morgan studied electronics at a local technical school. He then went to work as a sound engineer for a company in Dayton, called Mus-Ad, Inc., which produced and packaged background music for department stores and restaurants. Two associates in this business were a man named Joseph "Yap" Yoppolo and Irving "Slick" Shapiro, minor figures in the Toledo and Dayton area underworld who occasionally got involved in nefarious activities, mostly, it seems, in the interest of making a quick buck. An acquaintance described Morgan at this time as "aggressive and adventurous, on the goofy side, with a strong sense of loyalty to his friends."

Perhaps he was bored—with the work, with Ohio, or even with family life. In any case, in 1957 Morgan got involved with running guns to the Rebels in Cuba. Though it was illegal, a substantial arms-delivery industry had sprung up in the United States involving a rather odd assortment of mobsters, teamsters, and ex-GIs, who worked their connections and raided old weapons stores to fill the needs of the Rebels.

The Mafia was trying to protect its interests by catering to both Batista and the Rebels. It is estimated that during the late fifties the Mob cleared approximately $100 million a year from its Cuban businesses, which included gambling, prostitution, drugs, and even abortion. By keeping cozy with Batista and aiding Fidel, it hoped to ensure the status quo regardless of the outcome of the civil war.

A number of freelancers were motivated by profit or status, and maybe also—at least in Morgan's case—by idealism and adventure. Before he went to Cuba, Morgan left Toledo a number of times to travel between Florida, Texas, and Arizona, fixing deals that would land guns in the hands of Cuban Rebels.

≡ "You know," said Bob Brandon, a high-school classmate of William Morgan's, "I was talking with a friend of mine who said, 'Bill Morgan was an adventurer.' I think that's right. He was just adventurous." At a kitchen table in Toledo forty-four years after Morgan traveled into the Escambray Mountains, another of his classmates said, "He was always getting into trouble. He was different."

An adventurer. Different. The words were offered not as compliments but as polite descriptions of a young man whom many in Toledo felt had lost his way. Identifying Morgan as an adventurer relieved friends and acquaintances of the more complex task of trying to understand the personal and political motivations behind his journey to Cuba.

An *adventurer* seeks the thrill of experience. The term implies that there's no significance to the search beyond the adventure itself. In other words, an adventurer does not act for the greater good, but rather in his own interests.

Morgan said he went to Cuba to find out what had happened to his friend. Later he claimed to be "protect[ing] the freedom of others." Either way, he was taking justice into his own hands.

This kind of vigilante action has deep roots in American popular culture: in America's own revolution and the rough-and-tumble days of the American frontier, where a gunslinger might keep good people safe, where John Brown could choose violence as the means to end slavery.

A little common sense allows most of us to figure out which vigilantes deserve to be called freedom fighters and which ones are little more than criminals attempting to find justification for their crimes. In some cases, however, one man's freedom fighter is another man's terrorist, one country's hero another's traitor.

William Morgan was not the only American to lend his services to the cause of freedom in Cuba. According to some estimates, as many as twenty-five Americans fought with the Rebels against Batista, drawn by idealism, opportunity, or merely the intoxicating energy of the young, charismatic Cuban rebels.

Apart from Morgan, perhaps the brightest media light shone on three military brats in their teens—Mike Garvey, fifteen; Vic Buehlman, seventeen; and Charles "Chuck" Ryan, nineteen—who began by passing guns to the Rebels through the fence at the American navy base at Guantanamo Bay. In early 1957 the three sneaked away from their parents on the base and joined a group of Cuban volunteers who were setting out to join Fidel Castro in the mountains.

An article published in the *Miami Herald* in 1999 chronicles the boys' story.

"I didn't like Batista's police standing on the street corners with guns," Garvey remembers. "I didn't like what his cops did to young people. People were disappearing."

"Me and Ryan would go to the whorehouses at Canamara (a GI hangout near Guantanamo). We were there for fun. But they were all talking politics.

"Batista said on the radio that Fidel was dead," Garvey remembers.

"Then, Cubans started asking us, 'By the way. Can you get us any guns?'" They gave us the money. It didn't seem like Fidel was dead.

"At Windmill Beach the sailors had beer parties. We'd go out there and get drunk. The sailors thought we had access to teenage girls, and they'd say, 'She's a

fox. Hey buddy, what's her name? Can we buy you a
six-pack?'

"We'd say sure. And guns too."

When the boys went into the mountains, the ever savvy
Fidel milked the event for its propaganda value. Journalists
appeared from *Life* magazine, and a film crew from CBS made
it into the camp to capture the boys in Rebel uniforms sporting the 26th of July insignia. The outspoken Chuck Ryan told
the film crew, "They should be proud of their sons," referring
to the boys' parents. "I only hope that they can try to realize
what their boys are doing. . . . Their boys are fighting for an
ideal . . . for their country and the world."

They wrote letters to their parents, to President Dwight
Eisenhower, and to the ambassador Arthur Gardner. They
sent this letter to Gardner on March 11, 1957:

Dear Mr. Arthur Gardner,

I am not in the habit of writing letters to Presidents,
Ambassadors, and Newspapers. We would like to thank
the Government and the Base [Guantanamo] authorities
for the effort in trying to find us. My two friends and I
have brought our thoughts together and I will attempt to
tell you some reasons why you should stop trying to get us
to return to our home.

We are determined to stay here, where we are carrying
on with the Cuban people in their fight for freedom. Our
government sends airplanes, tanks and guns to Batista.
I know that these guns are given to him to fight communists. The Cuban people feel that the guns are given
to him to fight them in their move for freedom from his
dictatorship.

The people of Cuba who are fighting in [the] Army of the 26th de Julio will be the future leaders in Cuba and if they feel that the government of the United States is against them [they] will not favor the U.S. in world affairs. We need Cuba as much if not more than they need us. We are trying to bring them some friendship from our country. We feel that young men in the United States would help if they had a chance to. We trust that our government will make every effort to help us not hinder us. We are fighting side by side with the Cuban people. I personally will fight Batista until Cuba is free or I have not any life in my body.

> *Respectfully yours,*
> *Charles Edward Ryan*
> *Mike Garvey*
> *Vic Buehlman*

None of them stayed long. Fidel sent the youngest two back home once they had served the purpose of attracting press. Ryan stayed a bit longer, but by October 1957 he, too, left for the United States, having become disaffected by what he perceived as infighting among various Cuban political and opposition groups.

Another American participant was a Korean War veteran named Howard K. Davis. Davis, like Morgan, went to Cuba with a broad set of experiences. He had set off proudly for Asia with all the patriotism and faith in his government that a young man could have. When he came back he still loved his country, but he didn't trust its government. To his mind, friends of his had died because of bureaucratic incompetence, because politics muddied the mission.

"They would tell us to take a hill. We would take the hill. Then they would tell us to withdraw from the hill. Then they would tell us to take the hill again. Each time we took the hill, men would die. Each time we took the hill we weren't advancing our line," Davis says of his experience in the Korean War.

After the war Davis found himself in Miami, working odd jobs and contemplating how to make the world a better place. If governments wouldn't do it, why shouldn't individuals act on their own, find a worthy cause, and go fight to advance it? Left to *us* and *our* guns, Davis and his Korean War buddies thought, American foreign interests could be brought into line with American values. To their minds, the only choice was to work outside the system.

It was easy in the mid to late 1950s to encounter the Cuban Rebels in Miami. Fund-raisers for the cause were advertised in the local papers. People would show up and pile crumpled bills on a table. The money would buy arms and supplies for the men and women intent on toppling Batista from power.

Davis became connected with a group within the 26th of July Movement that was attempting to open a Rebel front on the far western tip of Cuba, in the rolling, tobacco-growing province of Pinar del Río. He made it to Cuba and into the hills, where he met a ragtag bunch in need of training and supplies. They were spotted by the Cuban Army almost immediately. Davis scrambled out of the area, fled to Havana, and got back to Miami without being picked up by Batista's police.

But that was just the beginning for Davis. He continued to support the Revolution until it began to smell like Communism to him. At that point he switched sides and for years operated against the Castro government. For some of this work he got paid. Often, though indirectly, his employer was the CIA.

In the 1943 Central Catholic High School "Fighting Irish" freshman picture, Billy Morgan's classmates frown at the camera. They seem altogether worldly. Like the other boys, Billy wears a sweater over a shirt and tie. But unlike them, the hint of a private smile plays across his lips. He's not posing, but rather seems caught in a daydream, fixed on the middle distance. Fifteen years later the same ears, bright eyes, and sharp nose would be apparent in photos taken of him in Cuba. His hair was parted in the same place. His face was lined around eyes and mouth, but the boyish features and expression remained.

If "being adventurous" means to do what Billy Morgan did, what did it mean to stay home in Toledo, keep your head down, work hard, and raise your kids? In most of our society, it means you're a good citizen. From his youth, the "right" dream in Toledo never seemed to be one that Billy Morgan took to. "Right" in Toledo made him restless. "Right" in Cuba imposed a very different set of responsibilities. There, he was an equal in the company of doctors and lawyers. He'd found a place where he could flourish.

OLGA

Olga María Rodríguez Fariñas was living a double life in Santa Clara. During the day she was a favorite among the professors at the Normal School, where she was studying to be a teacher. At night, when she wasn't preparing homework until two or three in the morning, she was planning or executing plots to disrupt Batista's government.

The twenty-two-year-old was not particularly talkative, but her intelligence—she was at the top of her class—and quiet strength made her a leader among her peers. She was attractive, with light brown hair and hazel eyes lightened by a splash of green, and her coloring was fair enough for other Cubans to call her blond.

Olga was the second of six children, born to a poor family in Santa Clara. Her reserve hid a ferocious ambition to make things better for her family. One way she could do that was to enter a profession that offered regular work. Another was to fight to make life in Cuba more equitable.

In 1957 Olga, along with her friend Blanquita, distributed campaign literature when Olga ran for and won the position of student-body president at the teachers' school. By the late spring of 1958, Olga needed only two courses to finish the four-year program and become certified as a teacher. However, in the small city of Santa Clara, her name had been linked to the insurgency, and so life at home was no longer safe.

Olga packed a few clothes and stopped by Blanquita's house. The two young women, born exactly a week apart in September of 1936, had been friends since they were fourteen. Though she was only days older, there was something of the protective big sister in Olga when it came to Blanquita. She didn't want her friend mixed up in the Revolution. Occasionally she would ask Blanquita to deliver a letter or a message. Blanquita never asked questions about the contents of a letter or the subject of discussion at Olga's secret rendezvous.

Upon her departure Olga said nothing to her "little sister," but to Blanquita's mother she said, "I'm going to the hills to fight. Don't tell anyone for two weeks. I need time to get there." Blanquita wouldn't see Olga until the Revolution was over, several months later.

After she left, people in town would receive little notes from Olga requesting that they send cotton pads for the Rebels' medical kit or pens and paper for the children attending the schools in the Free Territory. In general, although they didn't participate in the battles against the Cuban Army, women were involved at many levels of the insurrection. They carried messages and supplies, planted bombs in the cities, spied on the army and on officials, stitched together olive-green shirts and pants in a textile plant that produced Rebel uniforms, cared for the injured in Rebel clinics, and taught in the Free Schools that the Rebels opened in the mountains for the children of the campesinos. In the Sierra Maestra, a celebrated Cuban actress by the name of Violeta Casals became the voice of Radio Rebelde—Rebel Radio. She reported Rebel victories and pronouncements, letting people know that the insurgents were making progress.

Olga found a place with the Rebels of the Second Front, working as a nurse and later as a teacher in the Free Schools. After a time Blanquita heard a rumor that Olga had become involved with one of the Second Front's most important leaders.

▤ Meanwhile, Menoyo had promoted Morgan to the rank of *comandante*—major, the most senior title in the Cuban Rebel army—and named him Chief of General Organization, his second in command. Nearly all official communication of the SNFE came out of Morgan's office, stamped with the seal of the Second Front's general headquarters and signed William Alexander Morgan in this son-of-Toledo's tight, schoolboy scrawl.

In July of 1958 Morgan wrote letters to his family in Toledo to explain to his parents and his American wife what he was doing in Cuba. The themes echoed the letter he'd sent to Herbert Matthews in February: "I am here with men and boys—who fight for freedom for their country that we as Americans take for granted—they neither fight for money or fame—only to return to their homes—in peace. . . . And if it should happen that I am killed here—you will know that it was not for foolish fancy—or as Dad would say a 'pipe dream.'" In a letter to Bill Jr., he struck a fatherly tone: "Always be a man. Defend your rights; respect the rights of others. Love your God and your Country and stand up for both. Listen to what your mother tells you. You may not like [it] but believe she is right. Study and work hard son and I know your country and your mother will always be proud of you."

In the letter to his wife, he acknowledged that Theresa would probably want to file for divorce.

In fact, she already had filed on grounds of desertion. The divorce was granted in August. A short time later, Theresa married an American diplomat, who took his new family to live in Turkey.

By the time he met Olga María Rodríguez Fariñas, Morgan had achieved a degree of respect and status he had only ever dreamed of. He would later say that in the United States he "never would have amounted to anything," but that in Cuba he could be a "big man." In the Escambray, he was the chief of general organization for the second most prominent Rebel fighting outfit in the nation.

In the summer of 1958, Olga met a kind, funny, dashing American and fell in love. In an interview in the *Toledo Blade* in 2002, she said, "He joked with me from the start. I had short hair, and I was wearing fatigues, and he'd pull the cap over my head, and say, 'Hey *muchacho*—Hey boy.'

"I could see that he knew about our problems, and felt for my people. I know that he had many troubles in his life, but he had a big heart."

A romance in the mountains would not be a simple thing. In fact, it was strictly forbidden under the rules of the Second National Front of the Escambray. Menoyo had instituted a policy to deter the young men from pursuing and fighting over the limited number of women. The rule was simple: If you had relations with a woman, you married her. For the most part, this rule was meant to discourage unseemly situations between the Rebels and the local residents. Getting accurate information about the movements of the Cuban Army was even more important to the Rebels than having good-quality weapons, and their most valuable source of intelligence was the eyes and ears of sympathetic farmers and laborers. Trust between the Rebels and the local population was essential. Hope for a post-Batista Cuba would quickly dissipate if the residents of the Escambray thought these bands of young men were preying on their women.

Olga and Morgan's romance developed slowly. Meanwhile the most critical period in the fight to depose the dictator was fast approaching.

CHE

In late spring the various opposition groups began talking about unity, arguing that only by working together, by centralizing the command and direction for all the groups, would it be possible to win the war. Shifting from his early position that a decentralized campaign offered the best chance for success, Faure Chomón now proclaimed "boastful sectarianism" to be "Batista's best ally." Only Fidel Castro resisted the call for unity, knowing that beneath the talk of strength in cohesion, the other Rebel organizations were jockeying for power and influence in a post-Batista Cuba, power that Fidel hoped to consolidate for himself.

In June 1958 the SNFE sent Victor Bordón to the Sierra Maestra to meet with Fidel. Bordón, a longshoreman from Las Villas and a member of 26th of July, was carrying letters in which the SNFE recognized "Dr. Fidel Castro as the body and soul of the Rebel cause, as the leader of the armies of liberation and as its guiding star." It was an interesting move on their part, an attempt to put rivalries and differences aside to come together under the umbrella of Fidel's leadership.

Bordón returned from the trip saying that it was a success. It was soon discovered, however, that he was lying and, probably due to the degree of personal risk, hadn't gone into the

Sierra Maestra at all. He never spoke with Fidel. Incensed, the SNFE leaders threw Bordón in the jail where they kept prisoners of war and traitors.

The men under Bordón's command protested and separated from the SNFE, withdrawing to the small mountain town of San Blas. Ramirito and Redondo went there to work things out with Bordón's men. Eventually, the holdouts returned. Bordón was released from prison but was discharged from the SNFE for "violation of the military code, the discipline of the army and directives." He was also accused of conduct that was "a blemish to the Front and to the office entrusted to him."

The actions and reactions of Bordón and his men were, perhaps, representative of the general feelings of fatigue and anxiety among the Rebels at that time. They were reaching a breaking point and could no longer sustain the effort or the difficult lifestyle. And some, it seems, were beginning to worry about what benefit they might reap from a Rebel victory.

During the summer in the Sierra Maestra, Fidel and his men repulsed an all-out effort by the Cuban Army to finish them off. They defeated the Army at every turn and significantly increased their armory with the weapons and munitions they captured. By August 18, when the government troops began to withdraw, Fidel knew that the government's military power and resolve were cracking. Unable to defeat the crafty and persistent Rebels, the morale among the soldiers had collapsed.

Now that the eastern section of Cuba was secure, Fidel sent Ernesto "Che" Guevara and Camilo Cienfuegos to the Escambray to unify the groups for a final push against Batista. When he sent his commanders on their errand, none of them knew that the SNFE had tried to reach out to them two months earlier.

It took Che and Camilo and their troops about six weeks to reach the Escambray. They arrived in mid-October. The ill-fated encounters there between Che and the command of the SNFE, particularly Morgan, Menoyo, and Carrerras, would alter the destiny of everyone involved.

Che and Morgan had things in common. Morgan was born on April 19, 1928, in Cleveland, just two months before Che's birth in Rosario, Argentina. Both came from upper-middle-class families. Both had, in essence, been itinerant for years before finding focus and personal meaning in the Cuban Revolution. Now they were the only two non-Cubans in the Rebel forces who held the rank of comandante. (Menoyo, though Spanish by birth, was a Cuban citizen.)

Their personalities and political ideas, however, could not have been more different. Morgan believed in the individual's right to self-determination. He advocated for a government with a light touch, one that would allow a man to improve himself on his own terms. He was, in other words, against Communism and hoped that the fight in Cuba would help the peasants become new men. Che had been interested in Communism for some time. He believed in the utopian idea of the "New Man," a selfless person who sacrificed his own interests for the greater good. Che's serious and determined image would become a symbol of revolutionary valor around the world, whereas the story of the courageous trickster Morgan would fade from the record of the Revolution.

Fidel had charged Che with the task of unifying all the opposition groups in the Escambray under his, Che's, command. These included the area's largest group, the Second Front; the DRE, Bordón's group, which was operating apart from the Second Front; and the tiny Communist organization called the Partido Socialista Popular—People's Socialist Party (PSP). This was no easy thing to do. Among other tensions, the SNFE, still smarting from its earlier dispute with Faure Chomón and the subsequent attempts by the DRE to take credit for some its successes, felt disregarded by the other organizations. When he arrived, Che made tactical decisions that tapped into the concerns and insecurities of the Second Front and increased the difficulty of his task.

On his way to Las Villas, Che met first with the PSP, and it became the first organization to accept his command. To the Second National Front of the Escambray, which had maintained a policy of not admitting Communists, this was troublesome at best. To many SNFE members, it confirmed Morgan's assessment seven months earlier when he had told Max Lesnik that Che was a Communist.

Che sent a letter to the Second Front announcing his mandate as given by Fidel. He did not ask to meet with the leaders of the group to discuss the situation. On the evening of October 16, as he and his column walked toward the Free Territory, they were met by Jesús Carreras. Carreras demanded the password. Che didn't know the password, since he'd not been in communication with the Second Front. In a tense encounter, Carreras then refused Che and his men entry to the Free Territory. Che was furious. He responded by ordering that the men of the Second Front report to him and abandon their leadership. At this point, the Second Front of the Escambray counted nearly fifteen hundred armed Rebels, 90 percent of whom were from the area around Cienfuegos.

Two hundred two men, including Bordón and his followers, decided to report to Che. They packed their belongings and grabbed their guns, but as they went to meet their new commander they were stopped by Morgan, Carreras, Redondo, and six other men loyal to the Second Front. Morgan told them that it was fine that they were going, but they couldn't take the guns with them. Those, he said, were the property of the Second Front.

The nine men confronted the two hundred. Some of the departing soldiers shouted back, but Morgan calmly restated his position. It grew so quiet that the men could hear every sound emanating from the surrounding forest. For Redondo, it was the most frightening moment of the whole conflict. Finally one of the departing men stepped forward and laid his gun on the ground. The rest followed suit, then departed—unarmed—to join Che.

Later, Guevara would demote Bordón from comandante to captain and purge many of his men from the force. Like Menoyo and Morgan, he found them unfit as guerrilla soldiers.

After these incidents, Morgan issued a military order threatening that any person or group that entered the Second Front's territory without previous agreement would "first be notified, then expelled or exterminated by the army of the Second National Front."

It wasn't until more than two weeks later that Menoyo and Che would meet and reach an "operational pact," which described how the two groups would coexist in Las Villas. Menoyo explained to Che that Carreras had been following orders. "When anybody enters our zone there must be an agreement on passwords, in order to avoid confrontation. This is territory liberated by us, where our guerrillas operate. In consequence, if in the evening or in the night you ask troops for the password and they can't give it, they are enemy troops. This is an elementary thing, which [Guevara] later understood perfectly."

Even this meeting with Menoyo, however, did not go smoothly. When they were to sign the agreement they'd developed, Guevara signed it "Che." Menoyo was insulted. "This is a formal document!" he said. "Do you expect me to sign it 'Gallego'?"

Guevara had provoked altercations with three of the most important people in the Second Front's command. None, except possibly Menoyo, would ever get over the slights. Later, Guevara would participate in eliminating these men from the Revolution and from its history.

ENDGAME

On September 17, 1958, the Havana daily newspaper *Tiempo* reported that William Morgan had been killed the preceding night in a fight with the Cuban Army. That same day, the head of the Department of Investigation for the Cuban police said that he believed it was true and produced two photographs of a dead man.

The FBI received the report from the Cuban police and filed the information with the U.S. Embassy, the CIA, and the army, navy, and air force. The FBI also sent copies of the photographs to the Miami and Cleveland field offices to see if anyone could verify the identity of the corpse. They then sent copies of Morgan's fingerprints to the U.S. Embassy in Havana to see if they matched those of the dead man.

Curiously, on October 24, more than a month later, the FBI's investigation was still open. It wasn't until the middle of November that the American embassy and intelligence services were sure that Morgan was, indeed, still alive. Their lack of knowledge about what was transpiring in the Escambray is striking.

What the story really demonstrates, however, is that Morgan had become a significant symbol of the Revolution in the minds of Cubans. The erroneous story was most likely planted by the

Batista government as part of its last-ditch propaganda campaign to demoralize the Cuban people. It had reported Fidel Castro's death numerous times. Only weeks before the story about Morgan was printed, the government had announced that Che Guevara had been killed.

Morgan, for his part, was alive and well in the Escambray, working with Menoyo to maintain an ever growing force in the face of the political drama Che's presence had brought to the region. To manage such a significant Rebel army, the Second Front was organized into fifteen departments, all managed by Morgan, who, in turn, reported to Menoyo. Among these were a department of sanitation, a press bureau, an investigation and information corps, a chief of personnel, a department of armaments, a messenger corp, a department of engineering, a chief of general instruction, a treasurer, an agriculture department, and a person charged with managing Rebel–peasant relations.

As Morgan tended to his responsibilities, his relationship with Olga continued to develop. When Menoyo found out about the affair, he was upset that his chief of general organization was breaking the rules. Morgan was setting a bad example, and Menoyo felt he had no choice but to punish his second in command. He suspended Morgan for two weeks during a critical juncture in the campaign. During his suspension, Morgan and Olga were married and spent their honeymoon in the cabin of a local man named Ventura. The couple's first child would be born nine months later.

By the end of November, Morgan was reinstated and was itching to get back into the fray. Early the following month, the Rebels saw soldiers beginning to leave their barracks. Unsure of just what this meant but confident in its own abilities, the Second Front began to confront the army more directly.

It attacked and took control of the city of Trinidad. At Topes de Collante, during a lull in a vicious firefight, Menoyo's men watched in awe as their commander walked right up to the massive hotel sanatorium, which had been converted to an army barracks, and demanded the surrender of more than a hundred Cuban soldiers. The soldiers gave up the fight, stacked their weapons, and turned themselves over to Menoyo's command.

On the 24th of December 1958, Morgan and his men won a hard fight in Cumanayagua. As the townspeople celebrated the guerrillas' efforts, an airplane buzzed toward them. It was one of Batista's army planes, approaching as if to bomb the Rebels back out of the city. The thirty-year-old American climbed to the roof of a building with a machine gun slung across his chest. He beckoned the plane forward with his free hand and then took aim. People on the streets below ducked into shops and squinted up at the improbable scene: a lone gunman standing against an airborne bomber.

The plane banked away from the town.

People cheered, *"El Americano!"* as Comandante William Morgan came back down to the street smiling. In a culture that valued a man's strength and courage above all, William Morgan's past mattered little. He had reinvented himself as a Cuban hero.

On that day in Cumanayagua, the war was not yet over. The people of Cuba were tired of the death and the torture. They were tired of young men and women disappearing, and they were tired of never knowing the truth about what was happening in the mountains. Were the Rebels really winning? Were they losing? Leaflets scattered like trash along the sidewalks offered accounts that differed from the official line. Rebel radio channels reported Rebel victories. Stories filtered out from caves and safe houses suggesting that the morale of the army was slipping away, that the troops were running scared. Many Cubans had only just begun to hear about the heroic acts of Fidel, El Che, Raúl, Camilo, Eloy, El Americano. Most people had seen Rebels only in the newspapers: dead, skinny, bearded men lying twisted on the ground. For the majority of the population, the war had been a time of confusion and misinformation. Roadblocks slowed traffic. Soldiers patrolled the streets. Occasionally, gunshots would crack across town and in the paper the next day there would be more photographs of dead Rebels, accompanied by an official message that the insurrection was coming to an end. Soon, Batista claimed, life would return to normal.

≡ A week after Morgan's performance in Cumanayagua, Che Guevara, along with supporting columns from both the SNFE and the DRE, won control of Santa Clara, the capital of Las Villas.

In Caunao early the next morning, "Bibe" Vazquez, who had spent New Years Eve with his girlfriend in his hometown, was awakened by gunshots. He raced outside and saw men by a small bridge, shooting into the air. When he asked what they were doing, they told him that, just a few hours earlier, Batista had left the country by plane with his family and closest advisers. Bibe could barely believe what he heard, but he knew exactly what to do. He ran to his jeep and raced the twenty kilometers to Cumanayagua. He arrived breathless. When he found the comandante, he told him the news.

"We've won! Batista's left."

Morgan turned to his men and shouted, "*Todos para Cienfuegos!* — Everyone to Cienfuegos!"

The Rebels who Batista had said were dead now emerged. Men and women came down from hills and up from basement rooms and reentered Cuba's conscious life. It was as if a tide had suddenly gone out and in its absence the seabed was revealed for the first time. *Los Barbudos*—The Bearded Ones—became visible. They were thin, longhaired, dirty, and exhausted, but they had the energy that comes from victory: They were ready to take control, to set things right, to make the island a better place. They were students, teachers, farmers, laborers, lawyers, doctors, nightclub owners, peasants, and idealistic adventurers. Most of them were young; many were very young. In the mountains these men had forged new relationships with each other and with the Cuban people. Their youth, their beards, and their olive-green uniforms all came to represent the hope for a more just and egalitarian society. Batista was gone. His corrupt cronies in khaki uniforms and silk suits were gone, too.

Morgan's recruits whooped and shouted when they heard the good news. They had won! Some cried, relieved and joyful that after the months of fear and privations of war, they might soon return to the lives they'd left behind.

Everyone, including Olga, crammed into jeeps and hurtled down the dusty roads toward Cienfuegos. As they went, they fired victory salutes into the air.

Looking down the slopes ahead of them, they saw the tops of swaying sugarcane and, beyond, the ocean glinting in the sun. There, beside the water, lay one of Cuba's loveliest towns, Cienfuegos, the city of One Hundred Fires. It would be the first time in months that any of them had entered a city without a fight. Morgan's beard touched his chest. He had been fighting in Cuba for nearly a year.

When the guerrillas rolled onto the broad, central boulevard that entered Cienfuegos, the crowds swarmed to welcome them: "*El Americano!*" Already, the citizens of Cienfuegos knew who Morgan was. "*Bienvenidos!*—Welcome!"

Morgan called back, "*Hola! Victoria! Libertad!*—Hello! Victory! Liberty!" He draped the flag of the SNFE—bars of blue, white, and gold with the flame of freedom emblazoned at the center—over his shoulders. He flashed a broad, relaxed smile. That smile had been about all he had to give when he first hiked into the mountains to join the Rebels.

If one can imagine an instant in which winter swings suddenly to summer, it would resemble Cienfuegos as its citizens realized they were free of Batista. The victory party was kicking up all over the countryside, with loud blasts from cow horns and car horns and a steady drumbeat that pulsed through the streets. People going about private business in their apartments or houses heard the noise and knew what the news must be. On all the radio stations, with the martial chords of "El Himno del Libertador"—"The Hymn of the Liberator"—playing in the background, the gravelly voice of Victor Hugo Alemán, who until now had recounted Rebel victories only over the illegal airwaves, crackled with authority: "The Forces of Comandante Gutiérrez Menoyo have taken charge of the city!"

Girls put on dresses. Women donned the forbidden red and black of the 26th of July Movement.

From the balconies, doors, and windows, people unfurled symbols of Cuba and the Revolution. Caravans of cars carrying ecstatic citizens joined the Rebel convoy. Rebels hopped out of their jeeps to mingle with the crowd and to accept kisses and hugs. Twenty-sixth of July appeared and Rebel armbands, which only a day earlier had been reason enough to land someone in jail, adorned the revelers.

People hugged and laughed and sang, with friends and strangers alike. Political prisoners were already being released into the world they had dreamed of and fought for. Shouts of "*Cuba Libre!*—Free Cuba!" rose above the din.

La Correspondencia proclaimed that "there is no more marvelous spectacle in the world than that of a people who feel new liberty; the feeling of the citizen who has remained year after year enslaved and living in shade to newly see, in all its splendor, the radiant sun of liberty. [This] first day of the year that will make history. . . ."

As they approached the center of Cienfuegos, Morgan and his men turned right, off the Paseo del Prado, and headed for Parque José Martí, a broad plaza bigger than a football field, which is surrounded by the city's administrative buildings. The bright, clear sunshine reflected off the park's pavement and the stone and plaster of the colonial buildings. The Jeeps, jammed with well-armed Rebels, pulled up to the municipal offices. A Cuban flag flew from a third-story balcony. Morgan's men fanned out to secure the area as he and Olga stepped inside.

Up to this point, Morgan had been only a shadowy guerrilla in the mountains, a foreigner fighting for Cuba, his name a signature on Rebel documents, his nickname attached to accounts of Rebel victories. Now he would begin to play a role in the governance of post-Batista Cuba. The stage would shift, and he would be thrust into the glare of television lights and camera flashes as reporters pressed this American adventurer, this drifter-turned-freedom-fighter for tales of his experience in the mountains and his predictions for what would follow.

It is one thing to be a guerrilla soldier in the mountains. There's a simplicity to that life. There are good guys and bad guys, traitors and heroes. There's a hierarchy and a mission.

One lives closer to the animal edge: Stay warm. Stay dry. Find food. Kill and don't be killed.

Fidel Castro has referred to his days in the mountains with nostalgia as a time when he could focus on a clear and straightforward goal. There's a rarefied air about the Rebels who fought in Cuba; they've been somewhere most of us have never gone and will never go. The time they spent in the mountains lingers about them, and perhaps it makes the mundane compromises of daily life more difficult. Fidel's olive-green Rebel uniform and scraggly guerrilla beard are tokens that connect him to the time when he must have felt most alive. When Ramirito speaks of the months in the mountains, his face flushes and his eyes sparkle. It isn't only the fighting and the camaraderie he misses; it is also the security of knowing without any doubt that he was doing the right thing.

Morgan would later say that he didn't go into the mountains with ideals, but when he came back down he carried ideals with him. He was a changed man, propelled by love for the people he'd come to know and by faith in the idea that he'd helped to make their lives better.

The struggle against Batista was now in the past. The one for Cuba's future was just beginning.

1. William Morgan arrived in Cuba in early 1958 and joined the Second National Front of the Escambray. By the middle of the year, he'd become one of the most important Rebel fighters.

2. Roger Redondo, the epitome of Rebel cool, poses for a photo in 1958.

3. Eloy Gutiérrez Menoyo left his nightclub in Havana to lead a group of Cuba. This group became the Second National Front of the Escambray.

4. In the Escambray Mountains, the Rebels slept in hammocks strung between trees. When it rained they made roofs out of tarpaulins.

6. Ramiro Lorenzo was the first to see William Morgan arrive at the SNFE camp in Banao.

5. Ramiro Lorenzo, one of the youngest members of the SNFE, is visited in the mountains by his mother.

7. Eloy Gutiérrez Menoyo was a Cuban hero once the Rebels achieved victory. Today, most Cubans still consider him a hero.

8. Max Lesnik (left), Ramiro Lorenzo (center with sunglasses), and Eloy Gutiérrez Menoyo pose for a photo after beating Batista's army.

9. Comandante Jesús Carreras's fate would be tied to that of his friend, William Morgan.

10. Members of the SNFE gather in the living room of Eloy Gutiérrez Menoyo's parents' house. Eloy Gutiérrez Menoyo, William Morgan, Roger Redondo, and Ramiro Lorenzo are among those present. Menoyo's mother stands between her son and "El Americano."

GUERRILLA DE LOS TIGRE I FUENTE

11. The SNFE Rebels take a moment to mourn the death of one of the Rebels who fought in Morgan's column, the Tigers of the Jungle.

12. On January 1, 1959, Fulgencio Batista left Cuba. The same day, the mayor of Cienfuegos smiled for the cameras as he passed control of the city to William Morgan and his men.

13. William Morgan was one of only two foreigners to hold the rank of comandante in the Cuban Rebel Army. He became the subject of much speculation on the part of U.S. intelligence agencies.

14. Fidel Castro passed over Eloy Gutiérrez Menoyo and William Morgan for important posts in his new government.

15. In Havana, Olga Morgan, wearing boots and a Rebel uniform, enjoys the Rebel victory with her friends.

16. William Morgan and his pregnant wife, Olga, pose for a photo. They were married in the Escambray Mountains.

17. Shortly after the Rebel victory, Morgan went to a barbershop and shaved off his guerrilla beard.

18. In his role as double agent, William Morgan kept the Dominican authorities abreast of his—false—plans to overthrow Castro.

19. Cubans nicknamed the Dominican dictator, General-issimo Rafael Leónidas Trujillo, "Bottle Cap" for all the medals he wore on his chest.

20. Morgan and Menoyo confer during the television program that revealed the details of the "Trujillo Conspiracy."

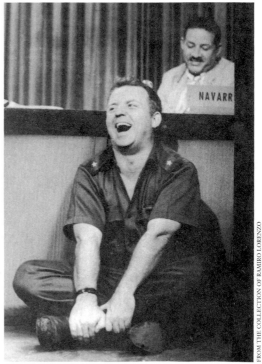

21. Morgan, always the jokester, enjoys a funny moment.

22. Morgan interrogates one of the Trujillo Conspiracy participants. Fidel Castro looks on and applauds.

23. Fidel Castro, Menoyo, and Morgan enjoy the "biggest leg pull in the history of the Americas" when they trick Trujillo.

24. Fidel Castro, President Osvaldo Dorticós Torrado, Che Guevara, William Morgan, and Eloy Gutiérrez Menoyo, among others, make a show of solidarity after the *La Coubre* explosion in Havana Harbor.

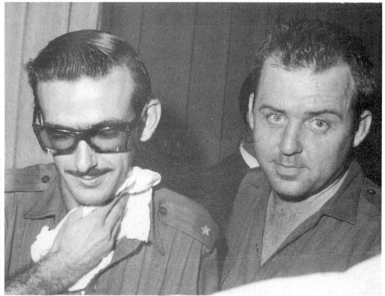

25. Eloy Gutiérrez Menoyo and William Morgan shared a profound friendship and a distrust of Communism.

Freshmen — 1943

26. William Morgan left school not long after this class photo was taken; he never fit in with his peers.

27. After twenty-two years in a Cuban prison, Eloy Gutiérrez Menoyo advocates peaceful dissension and negotiation with Castro as the best means of creating political change on the island.

Part II

REVOLUTION

VICTORY

While Menoyo secured Trinidad, Morgan met with the mayor of Cienfuegos, and they agreed that the Second National Front of the Escambray would take control of the city. Morgan was named the military chief of Cienfuegos and, as such, assumed the responsibility of preserving order and securing all city property until a Revolutionary government could be established.

Then the mayor invited the press into the room. Smiling, the Cuban politician and the guerrilla from Ohio shook hands as the mayor ceded control of the city to Morgan.

Morgan announced three decrees for the sake of order and safety: No civilians would be allowed to carry weapons; no bars or restaurants were to serve alcohol; there would be a 10:00 P.M. curfew. Anyone found in the streets after that time would be detained. Additionally, in the interest of health and safety, the Red Cross would not be subject to the rationing quotas controlling the limited supplies of gasoline.

With that, Morgan left the meeting, and he and his men moved purposefully around the city, taking control of the navy base, the armory, the banks, and the treasury. All the military sectors turned themselves in without resistance, laying down their arms for the invaders and for the civilians charged with collecting weapons.

The Rebels established their command center in a Jesuit high school and set up control posts in the naval district and other strategic points around the city. They sealed off municipal buildings to prevent sabotage. Once this was done, delegates were appointed and assigned the task of maintaining the city offices. Olga Morgan was named a municipal delegate of Cienfuegos.

Later that afternoon, Eloy Gutiérrez Menoyo arrived from Trinidad in time to endorse and ratify the act that granted temporary governing authority to the Rebels.

A reporter for *La Correspondencia* marveled at the way Morgan and his men comported themselves, describing the scene as a celebration, a "party of hearts": "Not one note of discord do we have to lament. Not one excess. Not one violent intent. Natural happiness . . . What stood out, above all things, was the good example given by Comandante Gutiérrez Menoyo's subordinates, imposing [the] authority and moral force . . . of the citizen who believes in the truth of his rectifying mission."

The Cuban people believed that, together with the Rebels, they would make their country better. They hungered for a virtuous political culture that would root out the corruption, the prostitution, the violence, and the gambling, which had dogged their country for so long. They felt that they were getting a fresh start.

All afternoon and into the night, SNFE troops kept arriving, roaring and honking down the wide Calzada del Dolores—Sorrows Road. They came to celebrate and to bask in the adulation being heaped on them. *La Correspondencia* referred to them as the "priests of the new Republic." They would always be *los barbudos*, even after some of them began to shave.

It was like an introduction and a curtain call at the same

time. People in Cienfuegos got to see the faces and hear the voices of men they had only heard about. One native son returning triumphant was the SNFE's chief surgeon, Antonio Díaz Viciedo. Though he was "of advanced age" and unwell, Dr. Díaz Viciedo had not hesitated to offer his services to the Rebels, suffering inclement weather and rough living conditions to help patch up wounded fighters.

Rafael Garriga, the Rebels' chief of propaganda and information, met with reporters at *La Correspondencia* and organized interviews with principal or newsworthy members of the SNFE. Primary among these were William and Olga Morgan. People would want to know everything. What was it like in the mountains? What had brought Morgan to Cuba? What had Olga done in the mountains? How did they fall in love? Had Morgan's men really won every conflict they fought against the Cuban Army? Was the couple planning to stay in Cuba? Had Morgan spoken yet with Fidel?

When the reporters interviewed the busy Comandante Morgan at last, he was tired and did not have that much to say. "Speak to me in Spanish," he said. "Because after thinking so long in this language, I'm forgetting my English."

≡ In Toledo, newspaper reports began to appear about the local man who was "one of Castro's Rebels." Toledans read the stories, fascinated, incredulous. Some remembered Loretta Morgan's son and the years they'd spent with him in school. It had never occurred to them that they would read about him in the news, except, perhaps, for a mention in the police report. Now the *Toledo Blade* was reporting his sensational exploits, and they were hard to believe:

"An adventure-minded Toledo man, who joined the Cuban

rebels a little more than a year ago, has been named chief of the Fidel Castro forces in Cienfuegos, Las Villas Province." The reporter interviewed Morgan's mother, who said, "I'm just so happy to know that he's alive."

The *Blade* reporter spoke with Morgan by phone from Cienfuegos. "All I'm interested in is settling down to a nice peaceful existence," said Morgan. Describing the exploits of the troops under his command, he declared, "My men fought in 15 or 16 battles—more than any other rebel force—and had heavier losses than the others. . . . These people have been fighting for things we take for granted in the United States. They want their freedom. . . . We have no Communists here in Cuba." Wrapping up the interview, he told the reporter how tired he was, saying he'd only had six hours of sleep in the past week. "I'm going to shave, get cleaned up and take a nice long sleep."

≡ On January 1, 1959, Fidel Castro began making his way slowly toward Havana from Santiago. Rather than fly, he chose to ride in a caravan of Jeeps, trucks, and cars, stopping to give speeches in towns and cities along the way, fixing his image in the minds of the people from one end of the island to the other. He was, without a doubt, Cuba's most prominent Rebel. By the eighth, when he and his ever growing convoy of uniformed Rebels with their beards, Catholic medallions, and colorful, African Santería beads rolled into Havana, Castro was the man Cubans expected to make their country independent and great. The trip was a brilliant political move, a first step toward consolidating the power he has yet to relinquish almost fifty years later.

In every town on the way, Fidel squeezed his way to the podium through joyous mobs who pushed and shouted and reached to touch him. The young Revolutionary then stirred this passion to a patriotic frenzy. After listening to Fidel, every Cuban became a Rebel, ready to defend the fatherland and the Revolution (the two were becoming one and the same) against any threat, internal or external.

When Fidel learned that Morgan, Menoyo, and the SNFE were occupying Cienfuegos, he diverted his caravan southward to make an unscheduled appearance there. He did so in the interest of unity and to ensure that one primary face be associated with the Revolution. He knew about the strain between Che and the SNFE comandantes. He also knew that the majority of Rebels in Cienfuegos had fought under Morgan and Menoyo and would, presumably, continue to be loyal to their commanders. It would be best to make a gesture of both authority and inclusion early on.

Fidel arrived on January 6 at one in the morning, to find the vast central plaza full of expectant Cubans. Morgan and Fidel met as Fidel charged toward the balcony of the municipal building to speak. The Cuban and the American exchanged a hearty handshake, hellos, and congratulations on the victory. With Morgan at his side, Fidel spent the next two hours telling the Cienfuegueros about his hopes for post-Batista Cuba.

The caravan rolled away in the wee hours of the morning. If there'd been any doubt about Fidel Castro's preeminence before his visit, there was none afterward. No one in Cuba could rival his oratory power. No one could stir the crowds the way he could, or make Cubans feel as proud. People might feel warmth and affection for other Rebel heroes, but Fidel's performances left little doubt that he was the *Jefe Máximo*—the Maximum Leader—the man with the vision to carry Cuba forward into the future.

By the time Fidel arrived in Havana two days later, the new president, Manuel Urrutia Lleó, and the cabinet—both hand-picked by Fidel—were recognized by the United States as Cuba's new government. U.S. Ambassador Earl Smith had been recalled—his support of Batista would render it impossible for him to work with the Rebels. And Fidel, although technically only the head of the military, was clearly the man in charge.

In Havana, the *Jefe* met with Menoyo before any of the other Rebel comandantes, a gesture that acknowledged the importance and power of the SNFE. The big, brash Cuban towered over the slight, soft-spoken Spanish-born leader of the SNFE. Eloy, with his thick glasses and crooked smile, shook hands with the embodiment of Cuba's freedom. Castro thanked him for all he had done in the Escambray.

At the end of their conversation, he asked Menoyo about Morgan: "How much do we have to pay this American adventurer to go home?"

"He's not an adventurer. He's a revolutionary. He's like us," said Menoyo.

Fidel rubbed his chin, looked askance, and said, "*Peor todavía*—Even worse."

CHAOS

The joy most Cubans felt could not mask the chaos and violence of change. The shift from past to future in Cuba danced along to calls for unity, the roar of airplanes taking off and landing, and the sharp report of rifle shots. Havana's firemen raced to extinguish blazes set by revenge-minded revelers. Citizens beat the tops off parking meters with hammers and baseball bats and ravaged some of Havana's fancy nightclubs, symbols of corruption and decadence. It was all happening very fast.

The tectonic shift of political realignment was beginning. Planes flew from Havana to Miami filled to capacity with fleeing passengers while others returned with Cubans who hoped to reclaim what had been theirs.

A few hours after Batista left, an army leader named José Pedraza departed for Ciudad Trujillo (now Santo Domingo) in the Dominican Republic, arriving the morning of January 1. Batista, whom Pedraza called "yellow bellied" for ceding Cuba to the Rebels, was already there. Pedraza immediately began plotting Castro's demise and his own return.

At approximately the time Pedraza landed in the Dominican Republic, Carlos Prío, the former president who had made his own unceremonious exit when Batista took over the government, arrived in Havana from Miami. He expected to work his way back into a cozy position in the government and renew the graft that had made him and his family rich. Friends and followers greeted him warmly on his arrival.

The 26th of July Comandantes Che Guevara and Camilo Cienfuegos, under explicit orders from Castro to seize two strategic military sites, left Las Villas for Havana shortly after the Rebel victory. Che took over the military barracks at La Cabaña, and Camilo took control of the military headquarters at Camp Columbia. The transition of military authority went relatively smoothly.

By January 2 the atmosphere in the capital was calmer as the guerrillas-turned-peacekeepers ensured that citizens spent more time celebrating than destroying the property deserted by the toppled regime. Patrols of SNFE Rebels arriving from Cienfuegos spread around the city to help the 26th of July Movement maintain order. Even the pro-Batista U.S. ambassador, Earl Smith, had to admit as he departed that the Rebels did a remarkable job, under the circumstances.

An American teenager, Jim Hickey, sat on the porch of his house and watched a mob strip the abandoned house of a Batista loyalist next door. They took everything, right down to the doorknobs and the bathroom fixtures. However, from his vantage point he felt no threat. The Rebel soldiers, many no older than he was, kept a close eye on the situation, allowing only specific outlets for the mob energy.

Although it had publicly recognized the Revolutionary government, the United States maintained its schizophrenic mindset. Prior to the victory, within the U.S. government there was disagreement about whether or not to support Batista. Now the debate was over whether or not to back the Revolutionary government. The central question—Is Castro a Communist?—was a vestige of the name-calling tactics Batista and his allies had used to curry U.S. support. Regardless of its origin, the question would not go away.

The island was already crawling with hundreds of CIA and FBI agents and informers. Only a few years before, Cuba had been shifted from the jurisdiction of the FBI to the CIA. J. Edgar Hoover, however, maintained a keen interest in the country, having decided that the 26th of July Movement was Communist. Castro, therefore, entered power already having been labeled an enemy by the FBI director.

The CIA was internally divided on the Communist question and took a more liberal wait-and-see attitude toward Castro. Under Batista, the CIA had established the Bureau for the Repression of Communist Activities (BRAC) to harass and discourage Communists. To the agency's discredit, Batista used these CIA-trained men against the insurrectionists, regardless of their ideology. Though the new regime dismantled BRAC, many of its members remained in Cuba.

If the United States was divided on Castro, Castro was equally undecided on how to position Cuba with respect to the United States.

Fidel was furious at the United States for supporting Batista. After an American-made bomb blew up the home of a campesino family in the Sierra Maestra, Fidel had written to his confidante, Celia Sánchez: "I swore to myself that the Americans were going to pay dearly for what they were doing. When the war is over, a much wider and bigger war will begin for me: the war that I am going to launch against them. I am saying to myself that is my true destiny."

Most important to Fidel was his image as a Latin American

revolutionary, incorruptible by U.S. power and money. Facing down the United States would send a clear signal to the Cuban people and to the world that Cuba would be a truly sovereign nation. "Imperialism" was his favorite, oft repeated accusation, and resistance to "imperial forces" was, for Castro, the ultimate national goal. In a speech in early January, he said, "I am not a Communist. My political ideology is very clear. Before anything else, we believe in the interests of our nation."

Herbert Matthews viewed post-Revolution Cuban–American relations with considered optimism in a *New York Times Magazine* article on January 11, 1959:

The most difficult diplomatic problem that now faces the [U.S.] Department of State in Cuba [is that] . . . for many years the United States favored Batista. Until March of 1958, they sold him arms that killed other Cubans, arms supervised by three military missions that remain in Cuba. The United States has had in Cuba a pro-Batista business community . . . and Ambassador Smith has sent clearly hostile signals to Fidel Castro, a man who is a hero to the majority of his compatriots. . . .

The Cubans are convinced that the Department of State is poorly informed [about the nature of the revolution]. As a consequence, although they exaggerate the friendship between Batista and the United States, the anti-Americanism is today perhaps stronger than it ever has been in the history of Cuba. . . . [T]his could be dangerous, but for two factors: one, that Cuba needs the United States, and another that the Cuban hostility . . . is directed against the policies, not against the people of the United States. With a new government, new policy, new representatives and the marvelous resourcefulness of the Cuban people, the situation can be rectified rapidly.

≡When he came to power, however, Castro had to contend with far more than the problem of intergovernmental relations with the United States. A vast array of institutions, organizations, and individuals, national and international, local and foreign, would resist the changes he hoped to make. Aware that this would be the case, Castro stated early on that the "hard part [of the revolution] was just beginning."

The challenges would include the integration of the other Cuban Revolutionary groups such as the SNFE and the DRE, the U.S. intelligence apparatus, the bulk of Batista's professional army, which remained in the country, American and Cuban corporate interests, and the syndicates that owned and ran Havana's nightclubs and casinos. Associated with each of these were people who had their own agendas and opinions about the best course for Cuba, and for themselves.

Whereas the leadership of the SNFE immediately accepted Fidel as the leader of the Revolution, it took nearly two weeks for Faure Chomón and the DRE to reach an agreement with the Jefe Máximo. Both groups would be monitoring Fidel very closely to protect the revolutionary spirit for which they had fought.

Members of the Cuban Army were invited to form part of the new Fuerzas Armadas Revolucionarios—Revolutionary Armed Forces (FAR). Many joined, though it was unclear exactly where their loyalties would lie.

For the time being, Cuban businesses celebrated with the populace, expressing their optimism in advertisements that juxtaposed their products with congratulatory messages. An advertisement for Banco Pedroso read, "Congratulations to the Cuban people on the arrival of the Peace." A tractor business, Aspuru and Company, was more directly political: "In these moments in which Cuba inaugurates its new liberty, won with the efforts of the heroic rebels, Aspuru and Company joins the gathering of all Cubans and toasts the Republic and those men who made the return to Democracy possible." Polar Beer proclaimed simply that "The people are never wrong!" while Glostora burnished its hair product with the glow of revolutionary victory more subtly: "Triumphant youths always comb with Glostora . . . [which] dominates hair whether it be soft or rebellious. . . ."

There were also the interests of organized crime, which operated Havana's lucrative and louche party scene. Primary among the underworld stakeholders was Meyer Lansky, who, through powerful connections and blackmail, had remained immune from U.S. law enforcement. No one quietly gives up the kind of money these people were making so, to protect the Revolution from Mob-related violence, a number of the casino managers were picked up and held in a comfortable but highly secure prison. Once the casinos were closed, they were allowed to leave the country.

Perhaps the most controversial and shocking example of postvictory realignment, however, was the execution of Batista's "war criminals."

Shortly after Morgan arrived in Cienfuegos, news spread that Capitán Garcia Olayón, the man who had perpetrated the atrocities against the insurrectionists in Cienfuegos in September of 1957, had been apprehended and executed somewhere between Cienfuegos and Santa Clara. Though there had been no trial, no one in Cienfuegos doubted that justice had been served. The brutality of men like Olayón had united Cubans of all socioeconomic classes against Batista. Olayón was one of the first to be executed, but hundreds would face the firing squad.

In the days that followed, Cuban newspapers published scores of photographs documenting the scars of torture victims and the exhumed corpses of Rebels who'd disappeared at the hands of Batista's regime. These were vivid reminders of the Revolution's justification. Next to them were equally gory photographs of the freshly executed perpetrators, accompanied by descriptions of their crimes and corresponding sentences. One series of photographs captured the death by firing squad of a corpulent policeman who'd been responsible for terrorizing Santa Clara during the insurrection: He walks toward a wall, stands at the wall, and buckles as the bullets strike his body. The final photo shows his vacant, wide eyes staring into the camera. It takes a moment to notice that the top of his head is half gone.

For the most part, Cubans took solace in the knowledge that justice was being served; they accepted the executions as an important, if bloody, house cleaning that would prepare the country for a fresh start.

Though people around the world rejoiced at the Rebel victory, some, particularly in the United States, worried publicly that the executions marked the beginning of an ugly purge that would be used to destroy any democratic opposition to Fidel Castro's power.

Others, however, understood the executions differently. The *Chicago Tribune* journalist Jules Dubois defended them to the

American people: "The executions of 'war criminals' after they have been tried and convicted by the revolutionary military tribunals seem to have created the erroneous impression that a blood bath of vengeance has broken out in Cuba.

"Nothing could be further from the truth and the reality of the situation. . . ." Dubois went on to categorize the tribunals as rapid, but just, considering the cold-blooded murders Batista's policemen and soldiers had committed.

"The opposition and the protests against the executions," continued Dubois, "seems [sic] to arise everywhere but Cuba. The public opinion in this country, from the poorest laborer to the richest sugar magnate, from the atheist to the hierarchy of the Roman Catholic Church, supports the intransigence of Castro on this topic."

The Revolutionary government miscalculated, however, when it held the trial of Army Major Jesús Sosa Blanco in a sports arena before seventeen thousand spectators and scores of reporters from all over the world. In hopes that the trial would demonstrate justice, the Cuban government allowed the event to be aired live on the radio in the United States. There is no doubt that Sosa Blanco had committed atrocities, burning people inside their homes, murdering sons in front of their mothers, and shooting workers who protested their employers' support of Batista.

The accused arrived in the arena smiling and proceeded to defend himself intelligently and with what *Bohemia* would call "unconscionable aplomb." At one point, as the sound of his voice was washed away by the roar of the crowd calling for his death, he said, "Gentlemen, if I am in a Roman Coliseum, then I have nothing to say. . . ." That, of course, was the quote that played in the international press. Sosa Blanco, even at the moment of his death, managed to deal a public-relations blow to the young government.

■ In his book *La revolución Cubana: Una versión rebelde* — *The Cuban Revolution: A Rebel Version* — Lucas Morán Arce argues for a distinction between a rebellion and a revolution. A rebellion, he says, is an individual act of rejection. Many people can join together in this act of rejection, but it does not mean that they share the same expectations for what will come next. A revolution, he argues, is the act of creating a new order after the rebellion. This new order must, of necessity, reject the ideas and visions of many who participated in the rebellion.

Though he made a show of thanking Menoyo, Fidel did not tap the SNFE's leader for a significant military or civil post. Like the leadership of the other Rebel organizations and even prominent members of the 26th of July Movement who weren't in Fidel's inner circle, the SNFE comandantes were given little more than honorary posts.

Menoyo made it clear that he and his men were not seeking government positions, but he was also clear about what he expected from the Revolution. "I only hope for one thing," the young comandante told a *Bohemia* reporter, "that the Revolution that has cost so much blood is not frustrated. . . . We fought for the fall of Batista and for the reestablishment of democratic institutions. We understand that it is necessary to make profound political, economic, and social changes in our country and I'm sure that the triumphant Revolution will make them. My brother Carlos died for the cause of liberty in the attack on the Presidential Palace. My brother José Antonio died for the same cause in the Spanish Civil War. I'm proud of them and their example will always inspire me. The cause of liberty deserves all sacrifices, as hard as they may be."

Castro played up the voices opposing the Revolutionary government, such as Sosa Blanco's, and used them to justify keeping important posts in the hands of a tight circle of loyal and trusted advisers, mostly men he'd fought with in the Sierra Maestra.

Still, what one sees in the Cuban newspapers and magazines of early 1959 is a pluralism of thought, an active debate about what Cuba would or should become in the post-Batista era. Everything—good and bad—seemed possible.

Despite Fidel's concerns, Morgan stayed in Cuba and was made an honorary comandante with a $125-a-month salary. For the first two months, he remained the military chief of Cienfuegos. He and Olga traveled back and forth between the southern port city and the capital. When they drove back to Las Villas, they would visit Olga's friends and relatives in Santa Clara. On one of the first of those trips, they came across Blanquita visiting friends on the outskirts of the city. Olga called to her friend to come with them in the Jeep. "Get in. It's still dangerous here. There is still some shooting. *Vamanos!*— Let's go!"

For the first time in several months, Blanquita laid eyes on her adventurous friend and, in that same moment, got her first look at Comandante Morgan. Blanquita liked what she saw in her friend's husband. He was loving and attentive to his young wife, and he showed concern for Blanquita's comfort, as well: Did you sleep well? Are you hungry? Is there anything you need? These seemed like oddly sensitive questions coming from a man who was a walking armory. Morgan carried an automatic weapon with him at all times. In addition, he kept a handgun on his belt, another on his ankle, and a miniature pistol holstered at the base of his neck, just under the collar of his shirt. Even if he were captured and frisked, he might be left with the gun under his collar.

They went to a café and as they were eating, a loud *bang* exploded from the boulevard.

"Get on the floor!" Morgan shouted to the women as he leaped to his feet and ran out the door to the street. Olga screamed and Blanquita, terrified, scrambled under the table.

A minute later Morgan returned. It had only been a car back-firing. Although Cienfuegos remained calm under the control of the SNFE, at times it was hard to believe that the victory wasn't some big trick—that Batista and his army weren't re-grouping to overwhelm the Rebels.

BAGMAN

. . . Not so far from here
There's a very lively atmosphere
Ev'rybody's going there this year
And there's a reason.
. . . .
Cuba, there's where I'm going . . .
　　　　　Irving Berlin, *"(I'll See You in) C-U-B-A"*

When the *americano* returned to Havana, the management of the Capri Hotel offered him a suite. Many of the Rebels, particularly those who weren't from Havana, settled into the capital's better hotels. Morgan and Olga made the swank hotel their first Havana home. They were greeted upon their arrival by George Raft, the former boxer, "B-movie" actor, and gambling impresario, who played host to the Capri's lavish casino, the burlesque shows in the famous Red Room, and wild rooftop parties around the swimming pool in the sky. The SNFE Rebels met there and threw several victory parties themselves. Ramirito remembered those days with a sly smile. "It was a big party. And there were always women. We had everything we could want."

A photograph of Morgan taken at the Capri captures him

posing with a "Cuban Winchester" (a regular bolt-and-lever Winchester rifle that the weapons doctor, Regino Camacho, had turned into a semiautomatic). Morgan's Rebel beard is trimmed, a cigarette dangles from his lips, and he squints toward the photographer. He's wearing his guerrilla uniform, and the single stars of a comandante shine from his epaulets. His eyebrows are raised just a nudge. The expression on his face seems to say "Can you believe where I am!"

In January a Cleveland man named Dominick Bartone swept into the Capri with big plans for the men of the SNFE. Morgan met a well-groomed man in his late fifties, thick chested, slick haired, wearing a shiny, well-tailored suit. The man reeked of underworld money, and indeed, he's referred to in FBI reports as a member of the Mafia.

Bartone worked for the Teamsters in Miami and was involved in various entrepreneurial and covert activities. He was a fixer, a person who set up deals, got you what you needed. He'd been involved in smuggling guns to the Rebels, and, through Morgan, he hoped to expand his business with the new government. He could provide planes, arms, whatever might be wanted, through his association with a Cleveland shell company called Akros Dynamic Corporation, which has been linked to both organized crime and U.S. intelligence. He was looking for deals and dollars.

Bartone also had Communism on his mind. He thought the Second Front should establish itself as the "anti-Communist" option within the country. He recommended that the leaders of the Second Front tour cities in the United States to tell their story of the fight against Batista. They needed, he argued, better PR and more support from the American people, particularly from politicians and business leaders who could help them along a course toward democracy. He told them people were worried that the Revolution would go Communist, and that would be bad for business.

After their experience in the Escambray, the leaders of the Second Front were most concerned about Che Guevara's influence on the direction of the new government. Beyond their dislike, they were convinced that he would try to manipulate Castro toward Communism. The SNFE leaders weren't worried about the business interests so much as the restoration of individual freedoms that had motivated their fight against Batista.

Morgan wanted the United States to give the Revolution a chance. After risking his life for democracy, he would do anything he could to prevent Cuba from slipping back to totalitarianism, whether on the right or the Communist left. So Morgan and Menoyo decided to explore Bartone's idea of public-relations trips to the United States.

For advice they turned to the press attaché in the U.S. Embassy. The position was a cover job for Paul Bethel, who reported directly to the CIA's station chief in Havana. In his role of assisting Americans with the press in Cuba and Cubans with the media in the United States, Bethel was well placed to gather useful information.

As Bethel's assistant briefed Menoyo on the ins and outs of dealing with the American media, Morgan talked with Bethel, someone to whom he believed he could express his concerns about the revolutionary process. But the two men had little in common beyond the fact that they were both American. Bethel looked at the Revolutionaries with disdain, referring to them as "hairy," and thought of Morgan as little more than a thug. And to Morgan, Bethel was probably just another well-pressed

American bureaucrat who didn't or wouldn't understand the Cuban people or the Revolution. In spite of this, the American comandante told Bethel exactly what he thought, hoping that his insider perspective might influence American policy and persuade the United States to cut Fidel some slack.

In a letter to his CIA boss, Jim Noel, Bethel summarized his talk with Morgan as follows: "The purpose . . . was to say that he was in control of the Second Front Military Organization comprised of '5,000 well armed and well disciplined troops' who were determined not to see Fidel destroyed by the Communists. He believes that whatever is done [by the U.S. in] Cuba must be done with Fidel as the leader since he is the one unifying symbol. Were Fidel to be removed or killed, Morgan believes that certain chaos will result and Communism would take over. Therefore, he is developing a publicity campaign 'to sell' Menoyo, who is described as—you should excuse me—the titular head of the Second Front. He sees Menoyo as a clean, honest person who with the proper publicity buildup might become a principal adviser to Fidel. The purpose, of course, is to undercut the influence of Ché Guevara . . . and other Communists who are exercising influence within the movement today."

Following the meeting with Bethel, Morgan began preparing for a tour of the United States with a group of men and women from the Second Front.

J. Edgar Hoover's man in Havana was the legal attaché in the U.S. Embassy, James Haverty, who reported by telex on February 18 that a "group of approximately 25 members Cuban Revolutionary Army contemplate taking good will trip to United States in immediate future. Group . . . includes . . . William Morgan. Intended itinerary is Miami, New York,

New Jersey, Chicago, Washington, D.C., Philadelphia, and possibly Los Angeles and San Francisco."

Although Haverty didn't include Toledo in his list, Morgan was planning a grand homecoming. On February 27 the *Toledo Blade* published the announcement that "William A. Morgan, former Toledoan who attained the rank of major in the rebel army of Fidel Castro in Cuba, will speak at the Sports Arena March 8 at 8:00 P.M.

"He is now serving as an adviser to Mr. Castro and will tour the U.S. under a diplomatic passport. . . . Toledo will be the first stop for Mr. Morgan and about 30, including several women who took part in the Castro revolution. . . . The group seeks to raise funds for farmers residing in war-damaged Las Villas province, in which Major Morgan led a band of 5,000 guerrillas . . . and to tell Mr. Castro's side of the story to the American people."

Morgan never made it to Toledo. Sometime during late February or early March, Frank Nelson, a man with the servile yet superior air of someone accustomed to running secret errands for powerful men, appeared at the Capri Hotel with an offer for Morgan. After Nelson's visit, Morgan's homecoming was postponed indefinitely.

As Morgan later retold the event to reporters, Nelson got right to the point.

"Morgan, I have a friend in Miami who is interested in your services," Nelson said.

"In *my* services? In what services?" Morgan responded.

Nelson shook his head. "Well, you are an important man in Cuba today and my friend is ready to pay you well if you help him. He's ready to pay you a million dollars."

Morgan startled, but only for a second, realizing immediately Nelson's intent. There was only one man in Cuba whose scalp would fetch a bounty like that.

"I understand that you and your people," Nelson continued, referring to the men of the Second Front, "have been treated badly and I suppose you don't feel particularly obliged. Besides, a million dollars is always a million dollars."

"And what do they want from me?" said Morgan.

"It's an interesting business, but my friend in Miami will give you all the details. The Consul of the Dominican Republic."

"Ah! The Dominican consul. . . . Interesting. I mean, I'm not doing anything here. Besides, they haven't treated me too well. You don't know what it's all about?" said Morgan, encouraging Nelson to continue.

Looking around nervously as though he might be overheard, Nelson lowered his voice. "They want you to lead a movement against Fidel Castro."

As soon as Nelson left, Morgan hunted down Menoyo to tell him about the encounter. Menoyo made an urgent appointment with Fidel, and the two comandantes hurried off to meet the Revolution's leader at the house of his confidant, Celia Sánchez.

Fidel listened attentively to Morgan's account of his meeting with Nelson. Who was Nelson? Why was the Dominican Consul involved? Let's see who's really behind this whole thing, he suggested.

Castro, Morgan, and Menoyo decided that Morgan should tell Frank Nelson he wanted the million-dollar job. By acting interested, Morgan would be in a position to learn whatever subversive plans were being hatched. A plot to overthrow Castro, if Nelson's offer were real, would probably involve a number of people, the removal of whom would strengthen the Revolution.

The three men sketched out a counterplot in which Morgan would play the dangerous role of double agent: He was to pull the counterrevolutionary plot together, meanwhile working behind the scenes with Fidel; and he would have to convince the men conspiring against Castro that he was sincere in his desire to join them. It might just work, since the plotters had identified Morgan as a soldier of fortune who would work for whichever boss dangled the sweetest deal.

Fidel had wished Morgan gone. The American had stayed, and now he was becoming useful.

≣ Francis John Nelson was born in New York City in 1907 and made his permanent home in an apartment on Central Park South until his death in the 1990s. At various times in his life, Nelson claimed to be a freelance writer, a CIA operative, and an FBI informant. More accurately, it seems, he spent his life working for a wide range of power players that included business moguls, the CIA, the Mafia, and foreign intelligence services, people and institutions that wished to cover their tracks or, as infamous CIA agent and Watergate operative Howard Hunt phrased it, maintain "plausible deniability." Nelson often worked as a messenger or bagman, a shadowy figure who would make the payoff or deliver a plan for covert action.

Years later, in 1967, he contacted the FBI to request William Morgan's file, claiming that he was writing a book about Morgan. That he was writing a book seems to have been true, though the manuscript was lost before he died. The FBI report that documents Nelson's request revisits Nelson's own file, noting that in 1949 he was caught as the "middleman in the sale of $25,000 in stolen American Express money orders." He pleaded guilty to the crime and served three years in federal prison in Lewisburg, Pennsylvania. A 1960 FBI report went on to describe him as "untrustworthy, psychotic, unreliable, with the propensity for exaggeration." Adding a shot below the belt to an already dismal portrayal, his apparent neurosis was attributed, speculatively, to a "history of venereal disease." The report recommended that none of Morgan's file be shared with Nelson.

Physical and psychological health aside, Nelson had spent time cultivating contacts in Miami, and in 1959 they included the Dominican consul and newly exiled Batistiano, Augusto Ferrando; the former head of the Cuban National Police, Manuel Benitez; and a character who had already been buzzing around Morgan and the SNFE, Jimmy Hoffa's man in Miami, Dominick Bartone.

To give the appearance that he was actually pulling together a counterrevolutionary force that could topple Castro, Morgan needed cover and resources. Fidel appointed him to an agricultural post on a ranch outside Trinidad. Morgan would return to the area and the people he knew best from his months of fighting as a guerrilla. It was a risky move on the Maximum Leader's part. What if Morgan, operating so independently and so far from Havana, *did* turn against the Revolution? Castro's future—and Morgan's—might well hang in the balance. Morgan staffed the ranch with armed Rebels, primarily men from the Second Front, masquerading as laborers. With this operation, it would appear to the outside observer that Morgan was secretly mobilizing his men against Castro. Logistics for the operation were run out of Morgan's house in Havana.

By March, Morgan and Olga had moved from the Hotel Capri into an enormous house in the well-to-do suburb of Miramar, west of central Havana. The house on Avenue Seven-A and Sixty-sixth Street had been owned by one of Havana's most prominent and successful developers, Alberto Vadia, who had enjoyed the rewards of fat building contracts from the Batista government. He'd left quickly after the Rebel triumph.

Not only did many of the regime's diehard supporters, such as Vadia, leave suddenly, but they left with the expectation that within some short period, perhaps only months, they would return to their comfortable lives. It was a combination of wishful thinking and arrogance that led many of those exiles to believe that Fidel's new government would never have time to mature. Many had U.S. bank accounts where they kept the money they'd earned and looted in Cuba. They took little with them when they departed; they left their houses furnished.

As far as the new Cuban government was concerned, abandonment of the country was a tacit surrender of property rights.

When the Morgans moved into the Vadia home, there were paintings on the walls, linens in the closets, and full bottles of liquor in the bars. A mirror spanned an entire wall of the dining room. The long dining table, which seated more than twenty, was made of glass. In the living room, green velvet drapes hung from high ceilings. A flying staircase swept down from the second floor, expanding with a sensual curve as it descended. In the middle of the house was a courtyard with a swimming pool and a bar. It was like living in a movie set.

The victory, at least at first, was like a fairy tale for so many Cubans, and particularly for the Rebel soldiers. Just over a year earlier, William Morgan had been living with his parents in Toledo. Now he was a popular figure in a foreign country living in one of the capital's finer homes. Many of the young Rebels to one degree or another experienced sudden privilege.

Menoyo loaned Morgan four thousand dollars to live on. From this money and the one hundred twenty-five dollars a month he earned as an honorary comandante, Morgan paid the Cuban government $250 a month for use of the house. The same woman who had cooked for Vadia now prepared meals for William and Olga: Alex cooked Cuban food, rice and beans and pork and chicken. Olga, who was now four months pregnant with the couple's first child, liked squash mixed in with her meat and rice. William preferred *chucherria*—snack food. He would eat bits of cheese and asked Alex to cook him hamburgers. Blanquita came now and then from Santa Clara to stay with the Morgans and help around the house. She remembers that Morgan rarely sat down to a meal; he was always fidgeting and couldn't stay seated for long.

Menoyo, Carreras, and other Rebels trooped in and out of the house. Says Blanquita, "It was impressive. In came *los Verdes*—the Rebels [literally, the Greens]. These big, strong, good-looking men would come to the house. I didn't want to stare, but I couldn't help it. They looked beautiful in their uniforms."

What only the comandantes knew was that Morgan was now "our man in Havana" for counterrevolutionaries hoping to return to the houses like the one he was living in—*and* against them on behalf of the fledgling Revolutionary government.

He and Menoyo met weekly with Fidel to orchestrate the plot to capture their opponents. Though it's not likely that Fidel suspended his wariness of the high-profile American, over the course of the months that followed, the two men developed a rapport, which other Cubans who were close to both of them considered unusual. According to both Roger Redondo and Ramiro Lorenzo, Fidel treated the other comandantes, even those he'd fought with in the Sierra Maestra, with a degree of reserve. He kept them at arm's length. Outwardly, at least, Fidel's relationship with Morgan appeared different. More than once, they saw Fidel drape his arm around El Americano as though embracing an intimate friend. The two men laughed and joked together.

Perhaps Fidel only wanted Morgan to think he trusted him. Since Frank Nelson had come to Havana, Fidel needed Morgan in a way he previously had not. But it is also true that Morgan's popularity couldn't threaten Fidel's preeminence in the same way that, say, Menoyo's or Camilo Cienfuegos's might. Cubans would never expect Morgan to lead their country.

Maybe each of them recognized a bit of himself in the other. One can draw psychological parallels between Morgan and Fidel. Both men took risks that were considered reckless and self-destructive, and both, from a very young age, had found it impossible to do anything in response to authority but rebel against it.

Fidel Castro's father, Angel Castro, had emigrated from Spain to Cuba, worked as a laborer, and over time climbed his way into Cuba's upper economic echelons, becoming a wealthy sugar baron. He married a Cuban schoolteacher who was not Fidel's mother. Fidel was one of five children Angel fathered by the family's cook, Lina Ruz. Angel provided for all his children—those by his wife and those by Lina—and made sure they received the very best Catholic education. Like Morgan, Fidel chafed against his family from an early age. He rejected his father's life and even challenged the way Angel treated the men who worked his plantations. Fidel was a talker and a loner, charismatic and suspicious of everyone.

Morgan was not as well educated as Fidel, but he was tough, rebellious, and charismatic. Filmed interviews of Morgan reveal an intelligent glint in his eyes and an acute sense of timing when he tells a story or makes a point. He is described by his Cuban friends as astute, though not particularly cultured. He had what might be called savvy, and, like Fidel, he read people well, allowing himself to be guided by intuition and a relentless internal drive. Both these characteristics, along with his compassion, had made him a beloved and trusted leader in the Escambray.

One could also argue that both men were driven by the anger that comes from rejection and isolation. Fidel was, and would always be, an illegitimate child. Morgan had suffered exclusion by his peers in Toledo. Neither could change his past; both focused their passions on the future.

TRUJILLO

[William Morgan is] a sweet guy, but very tough.
Adam Clayton Powell,
U.S. Congressman from New York, March 12, 1959,
upon his return from a visit to Cuba

To become a double agent is to enter a world where deception is the norm, a smile here, a joke there, a lie to prove your allegiance to what you don't believe. To do it well, to survive it, you must know where home is, where your own personal truth lies. Otherwise, the role-playing can carry you away.

As he moved into the liminal space where the dirty work of the powerful gets done, what guided Morgan were the relationships he'd formed in Cuba: with his wife and their unborn child; with the men he fought with and the peasants in the Escambray; and with Menoyo's father, who was lending the young American language and concepts for his newfound ideals.

Men of the SNFE gathered frequently at the Gutiérrez Menoyo family home in the Havana neighborhood of Vedado. Señor Carlos Gutiérrez was a fierce, passionate man whom, says Roger Redondo, you wouldn't want as your enemy. Carlos's commitment to social democracy burned as hot as it ever did when he was a Republican medic in the Spanish Civil War. Perhaps it flamed even more brightly once he had lost two sons, José in Spain and Carlos in Cuba, to battles against tyranny.

When Eloy took Morgan home with him from the mountains, Carlos claimed the young American as a surrogate son and as a political project. He admired the young American's ferocity and humor, his willingness to throw himself in harm's way, and the uncanny way he had of emerging intact from dangerous situations.

Referring to his own father's politics, Morgan liked to say, flashing a wry smile, "*Mi padre es un sólido Republicano*—My father is a solid Republican." Alexander was a much quieter, more distant presence in William's life than the fiery Spaniard who preached the possibility of a "third way," a system of government that could skirt the boundary between capitalism on the one hand and Communism on the other.

Señor Gutiérrez was unbending in his political views, and he encouraged Eloy, William, and the other men of the SNFE to be the same when it came to the form of government that should take root in Cuba: not Communism, he said, but the best balance between personal freedom and equality—social democracy. That was a system of government, he argued, that would take care of the less fortunate members of society, such as the peasants in the Escambray, but wouldn't destroy individual initiative. All this appealed to Morgan, who viewed the Revolution as a chance to, as he liked to say, "give the little guy a break." He included himself in this model and would tell anyone who listened that at home in Toledo he couldn't borrow a dime, but that in Cuba he had become a "big man."

≡ Before traveling to Miami, Morgan received a visit from a Spanish priest working for the Dominican Republic's dictator, Generalissimo Rafael Leónidas Trujillo. Padre Ricardo Velazco Ordóñez was a heavyset alcoholic who'd left Spain in 1935 for a mission in the New World, where he spent time in

Panama, Cuba, and the Dominican Republic. He was forced to leave Panama for unnamed abuses, and he wore his robe and collar, seeking access to luxury and power, to the Dominican Republic to tender his services to Trujillo. The Generalissimo enlisted him to infiltrate the Dominican clergy, who, as they agitated for more freedom for the Church, were becoming a problem. Acting as an informant and provocateur, Velazco helped Trujillo harass the Catholic clergy into submission.

Then the dictator sent his lackey priest to Cuba to determine how serious and capable Morgan was for the task of overthrowing Castro. Trujillo wanted Fidel gone, largely because he didn't like the precedent the young leader had set for oppressed peoples in the Caribbean and around the world. Once Velazco had met Morgan in Havana, he reported to Trujillo that he had complete confidence in El Americano.

In April, Morgan traveled to Miami to meet with Dominican Consul Augusto Ferrando. When he arrived at the meeting, Morgan discovered that Ferrando had invited two other men. One was the former head of the Cuban National Police, Manuel Benitez. The other was Dominick Bartone, the man who'd come to Havana in January to sell weapons and airplanes and to assess the political inclinations of the Second Front.

Several months later, Morgan described the meeting to the Cuban press, saying that Ferrando had begun the meeting with, "We understand that you are interested in doing business."

"Of course! I'm a man who works to earn money," Morgan had answered.

Ferrando continued, "We need you to collaborate with General José Eleuterio Pedraza, who will disembark in Cuba shortly. Your mission will be to facilitate his arrival and to take

Las Villas." Pedraza, a Cuban military officer who'd fled to the Dominican Republic on January 1, was preparing a force of Cuban exiles to mount an attack against Castro.

"None of this is easy," Morgan told them.

"We know that," said Benitez, taking over the conversation from Ferrando, "but we will give you everything you ask for. We will pay you one million dollars. Pedraza will bring you half a million that he will deliver when he arrives in Cuba, and we will place the other half in the bank that you choose. You should know that Generalissimo Trujillo is very interested in the plan and will not skimp on anything."

"To begin with, I need some money to get started. I can't do this alone," Morgan said. "I need the help of my boys, but with these guys you have to 'stimulate' them."

"Well," said Ferrando, "ask for what you need."

"To start, I'll need at least one hundred thousand dollars," said Morgan.

Ferrando assured the comandante that money was not an obstacle. "You will have them. We will deliver them to you ten thousand at a time. You just have to send us trustworthy people to collect the money and avoid appearing suspicious by making frequent visits. You won't want for anything. You will have to return to continue this conversation at a later date."

Morgan had set the hook.

Bartone had been enlisted to provide weapons for the counterrevolution. Much of the money that Ferrando and Benitez guaranteed Morgan would go toward the purchase of the armaments necessary to topple Castro.

Manuel Benitez desperately hoped to return to Cuba and his life of easy graft. Once Batista or one of his cronies was restored to power, Benitez expected to become mayor of Havana, a post that he quite openly described as one that would enable him to skim tens of millions of dollars from various city contracts. That spring Benitez had become a primary source for the FBI in the Bureau's attempt to understand and interpret the counterrevolutionary activity developing among the newly exiled supporters of Batista. Benitez was as anxious as anyone to provide information on the "Communist" Fidel Castro and his men, information that would encourage the FBI to subvert and, ideally, topple the Revolutionary government.

Around the time of Morgan's meeting, J. Edgar Hoover made the surprising announcement that he favored an invasion of Cuba as the best means of removing Castro from power, despite the fact that official U.S. policy demanded diplomacy. From the beginning, the FBI was aware (probably because Benitez was informing it) of the developing plot and of Morgan's role as the leader of the counterrevolution. Since the United States was continuing official relations with Cuba, Hoover had to work in subtle ways to support the anti-Castro forces, disseminating information and misinformation to advance his cause, turning a blind eye to legal infractions that might harm Castro. For example, it was a violation of the 1939 Neutrality Act for a U.S.-based arms dealer, such as Bartone, to sell weapons to counterrevolutionaries in Cuba. However, once Ferrando and Benitez raised the money, smuggled weapons poured into Cuba from Miami and the Dominican Republic.

FBI reports disclose the degree to which Hoover and the Bureau were monitoring the gathering coup. They show that by the middle of April, more than six million dollars had been raised for the anti-Castro cause. On May 1 the FBI reported that the coming action had the sanction, if not the material support, of other Latin countries, indicating that there'd been behind-the-scenes activity. "If Castro is defeated," the report concluded, "a revolutionary junta will rule pending free elections within six months. Dr. Emilio Nuñez Portuondo, former Cuban Ambassador to the United States and United Nations delegate, will undoubtedly be president of the junta." A footnote justified the report's classification as secret because "disclosure could jeopardize international relations."

Morgan was now in a position to trick not only the Cuban exiles and the Dominican leader, but also the most powerful law-enforcement agency of his native country.

While the participation of Bartone and Benitez appears fairly straightforward—each, in his own way, was looking to make money and keep corrupt economic patterns alive in Cuba—the involvement of the Dominicans in the plot was a more complicated matter.

Batista had never been a close friend of Trujillo's. The Cuban fancied himself a popular leader, a dictator "of the people," who was tough when he had to be for the sake of the country. In the past he'd distanced himself from Trujillo, whose hunger for absolute power and adulation would be comical if he weren't so ruthlessly brutal.

With U.S. support, Trujillo had staged a coup in 1930 and installed himself as president of the Dominican Republic. By 1959 Trujillo, who did not think twice about murdering anyone who stood in his way, was known particularly for two atrocious events. The Dominican Republic and Haiti share the island of Hispaniola. Haitian laborers moved back and forth between the two countries, working in agriculture on the Dominican side and returning to their families in Haiti. In the mid-1930s a population of Haitians lived in the mountains along the national boundary, many of them in Dominican territory. Trujillo sent his army to the frontier in 1937, where the troops massacred as many as twenty thousand of these poor, itinerant workers. He eventually paid the Haitian government $750,000 in damages.

Another event that sent shivers down many spines was the strange case of Jesús Galindez Suárez. In his book, *Trujillo: The Death of the Dictator*, Bernard Diederich details the life and death of Galindez, a Spaniard who fled his native land at the end of the Spanish Civil War and ended up in the Dominican Republic working for Trujillo. After seven years there, he left to study for a doctorate at Columbia University in New York. His dissertation, a detailed account of the inner workings of the Trujillo regime, caught the attention of the Dominican leader, who ordered Galindez's kidnapping. An American pilot named Gerald Murphy flew the Spanish academic to Santo Domingo where, after he was confronted by Trujillo, Galindez was lowered inch by inch into a cauldron of boiling water. The pilot was murdered a short time later.

Cubans were frustrated by the violence and corruption in their own political history, but they were horrified by Trujillo. The editor of *Bohemia*, Miguel Ángel Quevedo, routinely mocked the Dominican thug's taste for plumed bicorne hats and nicknamed him "Chapita" — "Bottle Cap" — for the chestful of shiny medals that he wore on his military uniform. No one in Cuba respected the Dominican leader.

If, as he had said in his letter to Herbert Matthews a year earlier, it was difficult for Morgan to understand how the United States could support a man like Batista, who suppressed his people's freedoms, the idea that the U.S. might favor Trujillo over the Cuban Revolution must have been the nadir of disillusionment.

With the flush of revolutionary confidence still on their cheeks, many of the Cuban Rebels, including Castro, talked openly about going after Trujillo. Following the tradition of "El Libertador"—"The Liberator"—Simón Bolívar, who had pushed the Spanish out of South America in the nineteenth century, these Rebels thought in terms of "the Americas" and considered their achievement in Cuba a first step toward liberating the entire continent of tyranny and dictatorships. A U.S. Department of State memo from January 20, 1959, notes a "Democratic Affirmation" meeting called by revolutionaries in Havana to discuss strategies for overthrowing Trujillo. Morgan was listed among those in attendance.

By April, Castro was already lending logistical support to two hundred Dominican exiles who planned to reproduce the tactics and success of the Cuban Rebels in an invasion of the Dominican Republic. But even before the Revolution in Cuba, Trujillo viewed the upstart Cuban Rebel as a threat. In 1947, after Trujillo had held power for seventeen years, a group of Dominican exiles and Cuban volunteers attempted to launch an attack against him from a small island called Cayo Confites, off the Cuban coast. Although the invasion never happened, Fidel Castro was known to have been involved. Since that episode, Cuban–Dominican relations had been tense.

The day Castro took power in Cuba, Batista's interests became aligned with Trujillo's. Castro was an enemy of both men.

Trujillo began putting together a foreign legion, a ragtag army of several hundred mercenaries from Europe and the Caribbean, for the express purpose of "liberating" Cuba from

Fidel Castro. General Pedraza worked in parallel, collecting a group of Cuban exiles and preparing them to fight to retake their country.

Between them, Nelson, Bartone, Benitez, Ferrando, and Velazco brought together a seemingly bizarre conglomeration of interests that included, at least by association, Batista and his supporters, the Dominican government, the FBI, the Mafia, the Teamsters, and possibly the CIA. A betting man would not like his odds if he had to go against these forces. As they developed their plans and accumulated arms and money, the exiled Batista supporters, not surprisingly, were confident that Castro would not last through the summer. They had resources and the support of the Dominican government, and the U.S. government was, at the very least, not interfering with the plans. In addition, they had a man inside Cuba—Morgan, with a ready fighting force of five thousand Cubans.

Cuba and the Dominican Republic and all the insidious characters working between them appeared headed for a showdown. And Morgan was the catalyst.

EXPANSION

After meeting with Ferrando, Benitez, and Bartone, Morgan returned to Havana a success, having loosened the purse strings of the conspirators. Fidel monitored the situation personally, demanding full reports of Morgan's activities and a complete inventory of every gun and bullet that would make its way into the country.

As they discussed the situation, Morgan, Fidel, and Menoyo decided that the best way to coax other conspirators into the open would be to draw the plot out, to make it bigger. In a moment of inspiration that Roger Redondo has called brilliant, Morgan proposed springing one of Batista's high-ranking army officers from a Cuban prison. The man selected, a naval comandante named Reynaldo Blanco, was due to be executed. Helping Blanco escape, the American argued, would increase Morgan's legitimacy in the eyes of the conspirators and, more important, would free Blanco to recruit other Batistianos and anti-Revolutionaries into the plot.

Blanco had spent his whole adulthood in Batista's military and had nowhere to turn but against Castro. During the insurrection, it was said that he'd developed a taste and a talent for torturing dissident prisoners. He was a big man with a pencil-thin moustache edging his upper lip and small, deep-set eyes that shone out from beneath a low-slung brow. He looked every bit the part of the cruel and decadent officer he was.

The escape came off according to plan, and Blanco went into hiding, sometimes staying at Morgan's house in Miramar while he recruited soldiers and politicians into the counterrevolution. Under Blanco's influence, the plans for the coup became more elaborate, requiring simultaneous actions in multiple regions of the country. The uprising was to commence with the assassinations of Fidel and Raúl Castro in Havana. Morgan's men in Las Villas would divide the country in two as anti-Castro pilots were freed from prison on Isla de Pinos—Isle of Pines—and hurried into Cuban fighter jets. Conspiring army personnel were to snatch a tank unit and seize the military headquarters. Sympathetic air force personnel would sabotage the planes that the FAR—Revolutionary Armed Forces—needed to defend itself. A counterrevolutionary force that would now include air support, tanks, and foot soldiers was to take over the country.

Despite Pedraza's already having selected Emilio Portuondo to succeed Castro, another group began to form in the living room of Morgan's home in Miramar. A former minister of labor, Arturo Hernández Telleheche, became the president of the latter Cuban government-in-waiting. Morgan's companions from the Second Front, loyal to the Revolution and to Fidel, mingled with the conspirators, playing their own parts in the drama. Roger Redondo and Ramirito were guards. Armando Fleites was named prime minister of the shadow government, and Max Lesnik was voted out for being too close to Fidel to hold an important post.

The upbeat American inspired confidence, and the spirits

of the plotters ran high. The conspirators were not all about work; they managed to throw some parties. At one such gathering, Comandante Blanco handed a young Revolutionary a fistful of money and said, "After this is over, we will all live very well."

The conspirators could barely contain their glee at the thought of wresting control of the government away from the *barbudos* and cashing in. One of the men jokingly said that William Morgan must be related to privateer Henry Morgan, who had terrorized Caribbean waters in the seventeenth century. Generally referred to as a pirate, Henry Morgan, a Welshman born circa 1635, was actually commissioned by the English Crown to protect Jamaica from the Spanish (and eventually awarded governorship of the island) and to invade Cuba and capture Spanish weapons and gold. In a famous episode of seafaring trickery, Morgan floated a ship manned by dummies made of straw and pumpkins toward a fleet of Spanish gunships. The Spanish sailors laughed as the small ship approached, thinking it an easy conquest. But when the little boat drew close, it exploded into flames, destroying the Spanish ships and marking another conquest for England.

William Morgan enjoyed the comparison in ways the conspirators could not know and adopted "Henry" as his swashbuckling code name.

"3JK . . . 3JK . . . Henry speaking . . . come in . . ." Late at night, Morgan would raise his contacts in the Dominican Republic on radio equipment he'd purchased with the money flowing in from Miami. The radio crackled and Morgan, in his rough Spanish, ordered more money and arms and kept José Pedraza and the head of the Dominican military intelligence service (the Servicio de Inteligencia Militar, or SIM),

Johnny Abbes García, up do date on the unstoppable force he was building inside Cuba.

As the conspiracy grew, so did the ambitions of the counter-plotters. Morgan and Fidel now believed it possible to capture the shadow government, dissenters in the Revolutionary Army, the Cuban militia training in Santo Domingo, and, quite possibly, Trujillo's entire foreign legion.

Between May and June, two events, one inside Cuba and one on the shores of the Dominican Republic, expanded the significance of the counterrevolution.

In May the Cuban government passed a controversial agrarian reform law under the slogan "Not a Single Peasant Without Land." Immediately following, the government began dividing the property of large landowners into smaller parcels for former tenant farmers and laborers. Fidel had been advocating land reform since Batista took power, and most people who'd participated in the Revolution, including Morgan and other members of the SNFE, believed that dispensing land to Cuba's rural poor was the best first step toward making the island's society more equitable.

Cuban periodicals struggled to determine what the programs meant. A *Bohemia* headline from July cut right to the chase: "The Law of Agrarian Reform: Communism or Social Justice?" The author, a devout Catholic named Andrés Valdespino, remarked that with these laws the Cuban Revolution entered its "most creative and positive stage. . . . But also the most polemical [stage]." Valdespino, an opponent of Communism, sided with the reformers, saying that they were completing the hard work they'd set out to do when they fought the bloody insurrection against Batista. He understood that not everyone would like it, but he considered the measure to be a necessary discomfort along the route to greater equality among Cubans. Valdespino grounded the land redistribution laws in social Christian thought—what might be described today as liberation theology—not Communist ideology.

Once again the anti-Castro plot expanded, as cattle ranchers, disgruntled by their reduced land holdings, complained vociferously and began to find their way into the counterrevolution. The head of the national Asociación de Ganaderos—Cattlemen's Association—Armando Caiñas Milanés, was slated to be Tellechea's minister of agriculture.

Then, on June 14, two hundred exiled Dominicans, led by a Cuban Rebel comandante named Delio Gómez Ochoa, floated up to the Dominican coast and landed with the intention of slipping into the hills and replicating the success of the Rebels. Whether Trujillo had been tipped off about the invasion or was simply well prepared, his army greeted the guerrillas as they disembarked. The troops quickly overwhelmed the expeditionaries. Within days, nearly all the exiles had been caught and executed. Only Ochoa and a handful of others—running for their lives, climbing hills, swimming rivers, and hiding in caves—were able to evade Trujillo's army.

Just over a month later, a young Dominican Army officer held a press conference to announce the apprehension of these last few insurrectionists. The night before, the rebels had been hunted down and surrounded. After a brief firefight, they surrendered to Trujillo's forces.

Time magazine reported the press conference: "Last night we caught the final six rebels," announced the army officer, Fernando Sanchez. "These rebels ran like guinea fowl. I've never seen anything like it. This Ochoa! Instead of coming to traipse about our mountains, he should go to the Olympic Games!"

Trujillo threw Ochoa in prison, sparing his life. Maybe he was impressed with the man's fortitude. Perhaps he was waiting for Fidel, who he expected might be willing to bargain for his compatriot's life. Whatever the case, Ochoa lived, and his fate would become, according to some, entangled with Morgan's.

Given the plot Morgan was involved in, the timing of the invasion seems a bit strange. Why would Castro sanction the action? Perhaps it signified fear of invasion from the Dominican Republic. With Rebels in the Dominican hills, Trujillo would have been forced to commit his troops internally, leaving him fewer men for an invasion of Cuba. If this was true, the mission failed because the invasion ended quickly. If, on the other hand, the invasion was meant to increase Trujillo's appetite for Castro's head, the plan worked. Rumors of an anti-Castro force forming in the Dominican Republic continued to grow.

≡ As the plot moved ahead, Morgan made the curious decision to contact the U.S. Embassy, attempting, it appears, to draw it into the scheme or at least to find out to what degree it was already involved. His decision may have had something to do with a piece that had appeared in the *Miami Herald* on May 23 and caused Morgan and Fidel to worry that their cover had been blown. Just days after the Agrarian Reform law was passed, Westbrook Pegler reported that William Morgan was one of "nine or 10 communists on the general staff" of Fidel Castro. Pegler, a Batista supporter, had been spreading the news that Castro was a Communist from the outset of the Rebel victory. He painted Morgan, by association and affiliation, with the same, red brush.

Referring to William as "Alex," Pegler provided more information about Morgan's past than had been reported by any journalist to this point. He knew that Morgan had joined the merchant marine at fifteen. He knew that the boy had been a "hoodlum" and that the young man was dishonorably discharged from the U.S. Army. All of these details were lifted directly from Morgan's classified FBI file and were trotted out by Pegler in what appeared to be a calculated attempt to destroy any sympathy the American people might have felt for the American Rebel.

Pegler's job as a journalist was a cover for his work as an FBI informant. Along with Manuel Benitez's, Pegler's name appears again and again as a source in the FBI files that track the activities of anti-Castro exiles in Miami.

A month later, on June 29, Morgan called up his acquaintance Paul Bethel in the U.S. Embassy. The CIA-agent-cum-press-attaché Bethel agreed to meet at 7:30 on June 30 at Morgan's house in Miramar.

That morning, after he was checked by the armed guards watching Morgan's door, Bethel suggested they move into the garden "the size of a football field," behind the house, to talk more privately.

There Morgan said to the press attaché, "I have five thousand men, willing and able to fight against Communism."

"What did you say?" asked Bethel.

"Castro is a Communist, see," said Morgan, "and we don't like Communists. I told you this before," he continued, referring to his earlier meeting with Bethel. "Well, we've been working to get our people into strategic spots."

Bethel asked Morgan what he wanted the Americans to do about it, and Morgan responded, "Plenty, if you don't want Communism here." Morgan said he "had been told" that the

U.S. government was interested in removing Castro, so Morgan outlined the counterrevolutionary plot for Bethel. The agent, however, appeared noncommittal. In a letter to his superior, Jim Noel, he reported that Morgan also worried about getting a visa for Olga to go to the United States. "He had taken no oath of fealty or done anything (including joining the new Rebel Army) which would endanger his citizenship. His desire for a visa for his wife is second only to his anxiety over his own citizenship," wrote Bethel in his report to Noel. "To put it bluntly, Morgan feels he may have to leave the country fast if the counter-revolution fails. . . ."

"My guess," concluded Bethel, "is that Morgan is attempting to trade information for a clean bill of health on his citizenship and help in paving the way for his wife to enter the United States."

Bethel's guess was wrong. Morgan was really just trying to convince him of the sincerity of the counterrevolutionary plot, and expressing worry about his citizenship was simply a way to make his story more believable.

While Bethel gave Morgan no indication of how he felt about the information the American was divulging, he believed that Morgan was, indeed, conspiring against Castro. The fact that he parked his car several blocks away from Morgan's house and chose to approach on foot, in addition to his passing reference to the counterrevolution in his letter to Noel, suggest that he was not naïve to the plot before he arrived.

Morgan was out on a limb, deep in the role of double agent, fooling men who would be embarrassed and angry when they realized what he'd done to them.

MIAMI

By July, tracking Morgan's movements was like trying to pin down the precise location of an electron. One could state with a degree of probability, however, that if he wasn't in Cuba or Miami, he was somewhere en route between the two. And if he was in Cuba but wasn't in Havana, he most likely was in the Escambray, working with his "counterrevolutionary" army to build an airstrip where the Dominican Foreign Legion would land.

Father Velazco flew to Cuba to meet with Morgan a second time, and Morgan drove him from the airport in Havana to the ranch in the Escambray. Morgan didn't talk much, but Velazco felt he bonded with the American and by the end of the visit would say that he considered him both a friend and a "good Catholic." Morgan gave Velazco a tour of his ranch, and Velazco estimated that approximately three hundred men worked there. These men, Trujillo's priest concluded, were less farmers than members of Morgan's personal army—part of the force that would be used to junk the four-month-old Revolutionary regime.

Velazco flew to Miami to inform Ferrando of what he'd seen and then went on to the Dominican Republic, where he delivered a written report to Trujillo, informing his boss that his trust in Morgan continued to be "100 percent."

Manuel Benitez, on the other hand, was getting cold feet. By the middle of July, he told the FBI that Morgan had taken $100,000 from Pedraza, but that he, Benitez, felt certain that the American did not intend to carry out the plan to overthrow Castro. It's unclear what precipitated Benitez's change of heart.

Regardless of Benitez's worries, on July 27, 1959, the legal attaché in the U.S. Embassy, James Haverty, reported that Morgan and his accomplices in the counterrevolution would act whether or not they received the million dollars promised them.

The day Haverty filed his report, Morgan and Olga flew to Miami. Morgan took his wife, who was only a month away from giving birth to their first child, as a cover, aware that the U.S. authorities were tracking his activities, though he couldn't be sure what they knew. However, he needed to collect one more arms shipment and cash drop before the counterrevolutionary trap was sprung.

As he stepped into the Miami airport, two FBI special agents stopped him. Leman L. Stafford Jr., who'd been involved in tracking Morgan for months, and his partner, Thomas Errion, invited the American to an interview room at the airport. It was the first time either agent had met Morgan in person. They estimated that the thirty-one-year-old comandante was six feet tall and weighed about two hundred pounds. His eyes were blue, his hair brown and beginning to go white at the sides. They assured Morgan that they just wanted to ask him a few questions and he was not being arrested, but he had the right to have a lawyer present.

Morgan told the men he was aware of his rights and spoke with them at some length. The purpose of the visit, he said, was recreational. He and Olga planned to visit friends and shop for baby clothes.

The conversation covered general points about Morgan's time in the Escambray with Menoyo. Morgan told them he held no official position or rank in the new Cuban government or army. He also mentioned that Westbrook Pegler's article in May had upset him. There were many things he'd done he was not proud of, he said, but he'd never considered becoming a Communist.

When asked about the rumors of a revolt brewing within Cuba, Morgan stated that he was aware of them and commented rather vaguely that he expected *something* to happen before the middle of August. However, he said, any successful attempt to overthrow Castro would have to come from outside the country.

Morgan ended the interview saying that he wanted to rejoin his wife and take her to their hotel. The couple was staying at the Eden Roc on Miami Beach, a hotel that, along with the Fontainebleau, defined the designer Morris Lapidus's concept of the resort—a place where guests could sleep, eat, shop, swim, play, and drink without need to leave the premises. Frank Sinatra and the Rat Pack favored the Lapidus creations as places to party and play. The vast marble lobbies, the chandeliers hanging like small suns from the ceilings, the staircases that swept to the floor like perfectly tailored wedding dresses, could make anyone feel like a millionaire. Morgan, a couple of weeks from becoming an internationally recognized figure, kept a low profile in the glamorous setting.

On July 30 Stafford and Errion called Morgan for another interview, this time in their Miami offices. As they pressed him further for details about the counterrevolution, he told the gumshoes that he and the men of the Second Front would never unite behind José Pedraza nor any other pro-Batista elements.

Contradicting what he'd told Paul Bethel, Morgan assured the agents that Fidel Castro was not a Communist, that he talked often with Fidel and admired him. Fidel, he explained to the FBI men, would not remove Communist Party members from the government just because the U.S. told him to do so, but this did not make Fidel a Communist; Fidel believed that if the Communists operated in the open, they would be easier to control than if repressive policies forced them underground. He admitted that Che Guevara was a Communist but claimed that the Argentine's star was fading in Cuba.

Morgan said that all he wanted was for the United States to give Fidel a chance. Anyway, he told Stafford and Errion, Fidel Castro's popularity was so great that no counterrevolution could succeed. Then he said he would refuse to be interviewed in the future and left.

To prevent being detained in the U.S. for conspiring to overthrow a foreign government, Morgan had told Stafford and Errion a great deal of truth, of course leaving out the part about being Fidel's agent. Even so, the FBI clearly did not believe him. All hard evidence suggested that a counterrevolution was imminent.

A day later, on July 31, Haverty reported from the U.S. Embassy in Havana that Morgan would kill Fidel Castro and that immediately thereafter "forces from the Dominican Republic will invade Cuba." In the same bulletin, Haverty wrote that he had overheard someone tell Menoyo at a Fourth of July party at the embassy, "anytime he wanted the men . . . [they] were ready." Haverty interpreted this to mean that the forces from the Dominican Republic were ready to invade. He also referred to a CIA source who had visited Morgan's house in Havana and described the place as "an armed camp," noting that Morgan and his assistants were "studying maps of Cuba and discussing revolutionary plans." Among those recognized in the house was one Blanco, the very same Batista soldier Morgan had sprung from prison.

The following day J. Edgar Hoover sent a memo to the Miami office: "CIA August one advised [William Morgan] in contact with CIA source in Miami. Subject described by CIA as 'Wild Gangster type.' Morgan advised he and his organization to assassinate Fidel Castro between now and Monday. He requested money from CIA source, but none was given him. Stated he had forty to fifty men in Cuba to carry out this operation. Once Castro killed, five thousand men will be ready to overthrow government. . . . Immediately determine if Morgan in Miami and interview him concerning allegation. Keep Bureau and State Department locally advised. Be certain State Department locally aware CIA Data. . . . Advise [the State Department] locally and Bureau if indication received Morgan leaving U.S." Hoover sent a copy of the letter to Haverty, as well, asking him to let the bureau know if Morgan turned up in Cuba.

The FBI staked out the Eden Roc Hotel, but after Olga left for Havana, Morgan gave the men the slip. He called the bureau on the morning of July 31 to let them know that Olga was gone and said he'd be leaving on a Pan-American flight on August 2. However, Morgan never returned to his hotel room, abandoning a suitcase full of clothes, and did not board the plane he said he was going to catch.

Instead, Morgan went to Tampa, St. Augustine, and Jacksonville. He stayed in motels and registered under an assumed name as he waited for Augusto Ferrando to come through with the last shipment of arms.

On August 3, 1959, Phillip Bonsal, the American ambassador to Cuba, caught wind of the trouble brewing with Morgan at its center. A political officer in the U.S. Embassy had informed Bonsal that José Pedraza was definitely planning an invasion of Cuba, but he astutely predicted that such an invasion would be a failure and would "merely unite anti-Batista and pro-Castro groups." Bonsal, who held out hope for smooth diplomatic relations between Cuba and the United States, decided to inform the Cuban foreign secretary, Raúl Roa García, of unconfirmed reports that Morgan was planning to assassinate Castro. Roa expressed his gratitude.

Bonsal then told the State Department he felt obligated to do this, worrying that if the plot were successful there might be violent reprisals against Americans living in Cuba. "Morgan," wrote Bonsal, "appears to be thoroughly irresponsible and unprincipled. If he should succeed in assassinating Castro or even carrying out unsuccessful attempt to do so, impact on Cuban-American relations and threat to safety of Americans resident here would be very great."

Still in Florida on August 4, anxiously awaiting the arms and cash from Ferrando, Morgan telephoned the FBI again and told them he would return to Cuba on a 5:00 P.M. flight on the next day. He again didn't turn up on the appointed plane. Was Ferrando getting cold feet? Had Benitez convinced him that Morgan was a fake?

Finally, on August 6, Ferrando came through. Morgan chartered a fishing boat and loaded it with the arms and cash he'd collected. Dominick Bartone was the middleman in the transaction, sourcing the arms for Morgan. Manuel Benitez reported to the FBI that Morgan took five hundred thousand dollars' worth of arms to Cuba.

Morgan left Miami for the last time. He rendezvoused at sea with a yacht provided by Ferrando and crewed by two foreign mercenaries who transferred the cargo from the fishing boat. The plan was to land on the northern coast of Las Villas and make for the city of Trinidad, on Cuba's southern coast, all the while maintaining the appearance of the counterrevolution. However, the boat ran low on gas, giving the men no choice but to steer toward the closer port: Havana.

Morgan radioed ahead to let Menoyo know that there was a problem. In Havana Harbor he would have to go through customs. If anyone discovered he was working with Cuban authorities, his cover would be blown and the possibility of trapping the enemies of the Revolution would be squandered. Morgan arrested the two conspirators on board; surprising them with a machine gun, he disarmed them and forced them to dock the boat in the capital. When the boat arrived in Havana late on August 8, Cuban authorities seized it, the cargo, and the two mercenaries. Morgan handed the customs officials seventy-eight thousand dollars in cash he'd been given by Ferrando, announcing that it was for Agrarian Reform in the Escambray.

While Morgan was in Miami, the government-in-waiting ensconced in his Havana living room was working out the final plans for the coup. After he radioed Menoyo from the boat, Menoyo called Fidel.

Less than an hour later, as Roger Redondo and Ramirito were standing guard outside Morgan's house, a car pulled up and parked down the block. A man got out. With a rifle slung over his shoulder, he started jogging toward the house. The man wore a Rebel uniform. Suddenly they realized that it was Fidel emerging through the patchy light of the street lamps. When he came upon the guards, the leader of the Cuban Revolution said, "How are things going, boys?" They nodded in response. Then he said, "Let's go inside."

The two soldiers followed Fidel into Morgan's house, and from behind him they witnessed the reactions of the conspirators as the man they were trying to depose suddenly appeared among them. Fidel entered the living room, and one of Menoyo's men turned to the plotters and said, "A new comandante has joined up." Menoyo grabbed a machine gun, pointed it at the members of the shadow government, and yelled, "Don't move or I'll fry you all." Jesús Carreras ran to the door and screamed, "Ya!" Men of the Second Front hurried into the room to secure the house and arrest the helpless men, who were shocked, bewildered, furious, and, finally, resigned.

Only one man panicked, racing up the flying staircase. Roger Redondo gave chase and as the man reached for his pocket, Redondo fired one shot that struck the man in the hand. He stopped running and started to cry.

Fleites, Carreras, Menoyo, and Artola stared down the barrels of their guns at their supposed allies.

Now that the leadership was detained and the conspirators' plans were foiled, all others involved had to be intercepted to prevent chaos. Around the country, Revolutionaries arrested thousands of potential conspirators as quietly as possible, but leaks to reporters led to stories in the Miami papers the next day.

By the time Morgan set foot on the docks in Havana, the national roundup of actual and potential conspirators was well under way.

Given Benitez's concerns and problem with the boat, Morgan worried that his true allegiance might be discovered and at any moment, someone at the FBI or in the Dominican Republic might blow the whistle on the counterrevolution. He had to work fast if there was to be any chance of capturing Pedraza and Trujillo's foreign legion.

Morgan went straight from the port to the military airport and, very late on the night of the eighth, flew by military plane from Havana to Las Villas.

TRICK

As soon as he arrived in Las Villas, Morgan radioed Pedraza and Trujillo to tell them that any reports of arrests they might be receiving were lies placed by the Cuban government to dishearten and discourage the counterrevolutionaries. In Las Villas, he reported, the fighting had begun. "It's intense, but we are winning the war." To heighten the realism and sense of urgency, Morgan had his men fire guns and shout military orders in the background as he talked over the radio. We have taken one casualty, he told the Dominicans, but now control a significant portion of the middle of the country. We need arms and reinforcements immediately!

Following Morgan's report, the Dominicans beamed a radio broadcast to Cuba with the "news" that cities were being taken and that the Cuban Army had been seized by panic. Cubans sitting in their homes heard these reports and wondered what was happening. Fidel ordered all communication severed with the center of the island and the electricity cut around Trinidad, lending credence to the Dominican radio reports.

Trujillo himself came on the radio, shouting "Attention, Peasants! Look for the arms that will be delivered to you today! This is a fight for life or death! Fire, fire, fire to that demon Fidel Castro and his brother Raúl!"

As night fell on August 9, Morgan radioed Santo Domingo

again, to say he and his men had taken Trinidad and airplanes from the Dominican Republic could use Trinidad's airport.

"*Alo, alo, alo,*" he said, raising Johnny Abbes on the radio. "*Hablar Henry . . . Tener Trinidad, Manicaragua . . . Avanzar para Cienfuegos. Mandar hombres y técnicos.*—Speak Henry . . . To have Trinidad, Manicaragua . . . To advance for Cienfuegos. Send men and technicians."

Abbes responded, "Okay . . . okay . . . William. . . . You will receive all the help promised and more . . . you will receive help. . . . Tonight the 'truck' will arrive at the agreed point. . . . This is Johnny Abbes speaking with you. . . ."

On August 10 James Haverty reported that Morgan and Menoyo had betrayed the counterrevolution. He advised that conspirators were being apprehended all over the country and the Cuban Air Force was decimated by arrests that "almost paralyzed the efficiency of the group." The next day, in a telex to FBI headquarters, Haverty wrote, "Now publicly known that both Eloy Gutierrez Menoyo and William Alexander Morgan were ones who divulged plot to Cuban Authorities. Plot leaders arrested in house in Miramar, Havana Suburb, which had been set up by Gutierrez and Morgan and in which microphones and motion picture cameras were placed by authorities. Arturo Hernandez Tellachea was to be president and Morgan received money from the Dominican Republic for part in affair. Morgan reportedly has turned over to Cuban agrarian reform part of money he received from plotters and from Dominicans." In a later telex that day, Haverty informed Hoover that "Morgan is definitely on side of Castro but sending radio messages for Pedraza to come to aid him hoping thereby to entrap Pedraza."

Oddly, on the same day, J. Edgar Hoover informed the Department of State that "information from an unidentified source [indicates] that Havana Harbor will be bombed at 4:00 am August 12, 1959, immediately preceding an invasion of Cuba by land forces led by William Alexander Morgan. Morgan is an American soldier of fortune who fought with the Castro forces against Batista and allegedly is now involved in anti-Castro activities." Hoover's memo makes no mention of the information received from Haverty, which by this time was explicitly stating that Morgan was working for, not against, Fidel.

Meanwhile, on both the 10th and 11th, C-47 airplanes took off from the Dominican Republic and dropped arms near Cienfuegos. Pedraza and Trujillo continued to hold out hope for an assault on Cuba.

On the night of the 12th, Trujillo again sent Padre Velazco to assess the situation. As the priest disembarked from the plane, Morgan's men chanted, "Down with Fidel Castro! Long live Trujillo! Down with Communism!"

Gunshots could be heard from the hills. When the priest asked what the noise was, Morgan told him a few men loyal to Castro were persisting. This, however, would not keep them from moving on Manicaragua and Cienfuegos. Thrilled with the progress, the priest embraced Morgan.

Ramiro Lorenzo walked up to the priest with a pair of scissors, and with a dramatic flourish, Ramiro cut off a lock of his own hair and held it out to the priest. "Father, I want you to take this lock of hair to the generalissimo as a souvenir of his concern for our country and the great help he is lending us."

"Thank you, son," replied Velazco. "Tomorrow your priceless lock will be in the hands of the generalissimo."

As Velazco's plane took off, laughter floated into the air above the landing strip. Fidel, who had arrived moments before, walked into the airport: "This is fantastic, incredible. It could make a film. Trujillo is crazy!" As time passed, however, the ruse was becoming more difficult to maintain, and more costly.

All the next day, Morgan sent radio messages to the Dominican Republic announcing progress in the counterrevolutionary efforts, encouraging Trujillo to send in his foreign legion. At the last minute, Trujillo balked and decided one more exploratory trip was necessary. As the plane was being loaded, the dictator dispatched a man to fetch Padre Velazco. He found the old priest in bed, passed out from drink and unable to summon the coherence to make the trip. Nine men flew to Cuba that night without the priest. Among them was the son of the former mayor of Havana, a young man named Luís Pozo. Though their politics differed, Pozo was a close friend of Menoyo's, and he had used his influence to help keep the Rebel out of prison after the 1957 attack on the Presidential Palace. Trujillo thought Pozo, being Menoyo's friend, might be well placed to assess the situation.

Ramirito stood next to Eloy as the plane taxied to a halt along the dirt airstrip at Trinidad. Behind Menoyo, under a mango tree and obscured by the shadows, stood Fidel Castro and Camilo Cienfuegos. As the propellers slowed, the men waiting for the plane, including Castro, began to shout "Down with Communism! Death to Fidel Castro!"

The first passenger popped out onto the disembarkation ladder and waved in Menoyo's direction.

"What is *he* doing here?" Menoyo said to Ramirito. As he said this a look of panic flashed across his face. It was Luisito Pozo, his friend from Havana.

Morgan, Bibe, and others walked Pozo and a few others to the airport building, casually chatting about the counterrevolution, while the pilot and another group stayed behind to unload the plane. Once Pozo had disappeared into the building, Menoyo turned to Ramirito, "Go tell them 'Now.' It's over."

Ramirito ran to the administrative building and yelled "Now!" Morgan, Bibe, and the others pulled their guns and quickly subdued the conspirators.

Shots sounded from outside, and Ramirito ran back out to see a gunfight erupt around the plane. The pilot, who'd been Batista's personal pilot in Cuba, had become suspicious and opened fire. As Ramirito ran forward, his close friend Elio Paz was shot dead.

The game was up, though the victory had not come without a price. Two of Cuba's defenders, Elio P. Paz and Frank Hidalgo Gato, died in the final firefight on the airstrip. Though they didn't capture Trujillo's foreign legion or the bulk of Pedraza's exile army, they had thwarted the internal threat of a major counterrevolution. And the Revolutionaries had a much clearer picture of who their enemies were.

Ramirito ran back inside, tears streaming down his face.

"What happened to you?" asked Camilo Cienfuegos.

"Go to hell," said Ramirito, distraught at the loss of his friend, incredulous that the others could celebrate under the circumstances.

Camilo walked over to Morgan and patted him on the back. "Nice job, *comevaca*," he said.

Morgan grinned. "You rob it and I'll eat it."

It was a teasing moment of camaraderie, an inside joke from the time the Rebels spent in the mountains that suggested mild competition between the 26th of July and the Second Front. A *comevaca* was a Rebel who didn't fight Batista's army, and instead passed his time stealing cows from peasants and eating them.

For his efforts, Morgan had made dangerous enemies who wouldn't soon forget what he'd done.

CELEBRATION

If one were listening for the true death rattle of the Batista regime, one might hear it in the Trujillo Conspiracy. From then on, Cuba's Revolution would march more surely forward into the future.

"Morgan and Menoyo got you good! You gave them money and arms and they caught you!" Cuba's musical-comedy duo Pototo and Filomeno pranced around the stage performing their song about how Morgan and Menoyo had fooled "Chapita." The Cuban people hummed along, full of pride for their Rebels and especially for the clever American who'd pulled Trujillo's tail for the whole world to see.

The editors of *Bohemia*, Cuba's most important weekly magazine, drew two lessons from the events of the conspiracy. First, they noted that the enemies of the Revolution, though many were still at large in the United States and the Dominican Republic, had learned that they couldn't succeed in a fight against "the people." In contrast, the Revolutionaries—without political experience, but with the support of the population at large—were able to anticipate and dismantle the conspiracy with a minimum of military force. The time in Cuba for a military coup was over, announced the editors, because the people and the military apparatus were not divided. "Today a tangible link exists between the civilian and the soldier, for within each uniform of a rebel soldier lives a citizen like any other, without privileges of any sort, and in the same way within each civilian there is a potential soldier, ready to give his life for the cause of the Revolution."

Second, *Bohemia* declared Trujillo the most dangerous menace to peace in the Western Hemisphere. "The hour has arrived, without doubt, in which Trujillo . . . will be unmasked in an international scenario. History will dictate his sentence." In fact, Trujillo received his sentence less than two years later when, in May of 1961, a small group of Dominicans supported by the CIA assassinated the generalissimo. By then, things inside Cuba were dramatically different and *Bohemia*'s editor, Miguel Angel Quevedo, was publishing his magazine from Venezuela.

In any case, the Trujillo episode renewed the Revolutionary energy and the sense of national unity. In the face of adversity from abroad, Cubans were proving their patriotic mettle.

Fidel played the drama to the hilt, reminding the people that winning the fight against Batista did not mean they could let down their guard. On August 14 Castro appeared on national television to explain the whole affair. He spoke about José Pedraza and Dominican Consul Ferrando, about Trujillo's building a foreign legion to launch an attack against Cuba, and he told how Morgan had officially been named commander in chief of the whole operation by Trujillo, so much did the Dominican trust the young American. Morgan had convinced men in three countries that he was on their side. The theatrical details, such as Trujillo's promise to deliver a bicorne for Menoyo to wear on his victory ride into Havana, and Morgan's code name, "Henry," after the English rogue, enchanted the audience.

When Fidel interrogated some of the conspirators in front of the television audience, Morgan got into the act, standing up to comment on a taciturn Spanish mercenary who'd come on the last plane: "I want to say one thing. I don't throw the towel at anybody, but this is the most unhappy counterrevolutionary in all of Cuba. This one doesn't know why he's a counterrevolutionary." Morgan, with his deficient Spanish and irreverent tone, sent the whole studio into laughter. Fidel looked up at the American with pleasure and admiration as he began to clap. When he complimented Morgan on a role well played, Fidel called the American "a Cuban." It was a generous compliment from a man who only nine months earlier had wished Morgan gone.

While it was easy to play up the farcical aspects of the events, Fidel did not limit his television presentation to the superficial facts about the conspiracy: "All this forms part of a great plot of which Trujillo is merely an episode. It speaks to a giant conspiracy against the Revolution, supported more or less directly by national and international interests, economic and political. . . . It's manifested in the campaigns against us in the United States . . . , in the aggression toward Cuba, in the campaign that accuses us of Communism. . . . These foreign interests have influence in the political life of other countries, in the delivery of information, in the press, and they employ these to discredit us. . . . They have sworn to be enemies to the death of the Revolution and try to isolate us from other peoples."

There were people, Fidel warned, who would wipe out the island completely. This apocalyptic imagery from the post–World War II nuclear age was something people understood.

It *was* possible to wipe out everything—look at Hiroshima and Nagasaki. Three years later, this possibility came to the brink of reality when American reconnaissance planes spotted Soviet nuclear missiles in Cuba. The choice Fidel presented in August of 1959 was to stand against corrupt foreign interests or be destroyed by them. It was a fight between existence and nonexistence. It is the same choice he presents to the Cuban people today.

For most Cubans, Fidel's big picture caused some anxiety, but the celebration was more real at the moment than abstract notions of world power dynamics. Cubans sang along with Pototo and Filomeno and hungered for more details about the trick, while reporters scurried about to deliver the inside scoop.

≡ When a reporter interviewed Menoyo in the small bar above his club in Vedado, nearly one hundred of the Second Front's men had packed into the room, including Ramiro Lorenzo and Roger Redondo, Armando Fleites, Lázaro Artola, and Max Lesnik. They were in a festive mood. Menoyo told the reporter, "I wouldn't want to be in the shoes of the Dominican consul in Miami," referring to Augusto Ferrando. "His last act was to give William Morgan seventy-eight thousand dollars for Agrarian Reform."

"For the reform?" asked the reporter.

"Yes. He gave it for the counterrevolution, but William changed its route."

A roar of laughter filled the room, and the reporter's subsequent questions were drowned out by the din.

≡ In the thick of the conspiracy, Trujillo had requested that the liberal editor of *Bohemia*, who'd invented the mocking nickname "Chapita," be sent to him as war booty. The dictator had hoped to make the newsman pay for his ridicule. Miguel Ángel Quevedo, relieved to be safe from Trujillo's gruesome revenge fantasies, threw a party to recognize the "biggest leg pull in American history," as his magazine was calling the affair. The smell of cigar smoke and rum filled Quevedo's house as the men of the Second Front milled around with *Bohemia*'s reporters, honing the event into perfect anecdotes. Each guest was handed a paper bicorne, and soon a fleet of small white ships bobbed over the festive sea of revelers, who felt free and virtuous and invincible.

Fidel did not attend the festivities, sending his brother Raúl in his stead. Raúl stood to the side, aloof to the joyful mood. Enticed by Communist ideas since his youth, perhaps Morgan's and Menoyo's growing popularity and their anti-Communist views caused him concern.

Morgan arrived at the party with a little monkey he'd named Chapita in honor of Trujillo. He hung a medal around the monkey's neck and, as he tried to coax a plumed hat onto its head, people laughingly scolded the monkey: "Listen up, Chapita! Obey Morgan." The monkey became a constant companion of Morgan's in his house and in his car, and for the Cuban people, a symbol of Morgan's loyalty to and affection for their country.

Morgan told reporters, "[Trujillo's men] will probably try to kill me, if they have the opportunity, but I'm not going to be a sitting duck. To the man they rent to kill me, I recommend he think three or four times about it before he tries it. . . . It's important that the American people understand this type: . . . he doesn't *deserve* jail. He's an assassin that doesn't respect borders and for the first time in thirty years ran up against people who weren't afraid of him. . . . Tricking Trujillo is dangerous. Perhaps, I'll be his next corpse."

The *Bohemia* reporter marveled at Morgan's poise in the face of danger. "Those who visit the American Morgan . . . will find him always in good humor. He knows that Trujillo has long claws. He knows how much pain can be caused by the underworld of international lowlifes. But Morgan doesn't fear. Morgan laughs."

Morgan's laughter buoyed people who had lived too long in fear. If before the Trujillo Conspiracy Morgan had been popular, he was now a celebrity. Crowds gathered wherever he went. People wanted to talk with him and to touch him. Children asked for his autograph.

≡ In the United States, American reporters didn't seem quite sure what to make of the Trujillo Conspiracy. With a hint of incredulity and suspicion of the Revolutionary government's trajectory, *Time* magazine reported that the "tool of Fidel Castro's battlefield victory last week was a crafty, U.S.-born double agent who worked so smoothly that he lured Castro's enemies into the open at home and conned a Dominican invasion plane into a trap in central Cuba, nipping the first major rebellion against the seven-month-old regime."

≡ By August 17 the CIA had filed its interpretation of what had transpired. The agency accurately suggested that the whole event had bolstered Castro's standing in the country and given him a chance to "show himself as savior of Cuba in the face of aggressive action by 'capitalist imperialists.'" The report also pointed out that the conspiracy revealed the extent of the opposition to Castro, though it also demonstrated that an overwhelming majority of Cubans supported Castro over Batista.

Morgan, feeling justified in what he'd done but worried about the repercussions of some of his actions—particularly how they might affect his citizenship—called the FBI during the afternoon of August 20 to apologize to Leman Stafford Jr. He acknowledged that when Stafford had interviewed him twice at the end of July, he had not told the truth. According to Stafford's notes, Morgan explained that he didn't think he'd broken any laws, but he might have "bent" a few. He went on to say that he would never "sell out Cuba," where he had many loyal friends.

The call to the FBI, however, was too little too late as far as J. Edgar Hoover and other American authorities were concerned.

On August 29, 1959, Olga gave birth to a baby girl. The baby was christened Loretta, after William's mother. Eloy was the godfather, Blanquita the godmother. Five days later, Morgan received word that the U.S. Passport Office was reviewing his American citizenship. Though he'd known that was a possibility, considering his crossing of the FBI and his run-ins with Paul Bethel, it was still a shock. It also limited his options for protecting himself and his family. Trujillo wanted him dead, and now the United States might turn its back on him. While Trujillo might balk at assassinating a high-profile American citizen, he wouldn't think twice about killing a Cuban.

On September 3, 1959, in an interview with Representative Francis Walter of Pennsylvania, one of J. Edgar Hoover's closest allies in the Congress, the Washington *Evening Star* broke the story that Morgan's citizenship was being revoked. The message was simple: If you're going to go play in Latin American revolutions, you might not be allowed to come home again.

Morgan responded in the next day's *Revolución*, appearing with Olga in the lead photograph. As the two look at each other, Morgan wears an expression of affectionate bemusement, a slight smile on his lips that seems to say, "Well, here we are." Olga returns Morgan's gaze with a look of adoration. "I don't know why," Morgan told the *Revolución* reporter, "they [the United States] condemn me for doing what they taught me to do."

Soon it became clear that the U.S. government would not review his case. On September 24 Morgan went to a broadcasting station in Havana and recorded a renunciation of his American citizenship. He told an Associated Press reporter the following day, "I married a Cuban. My daughter is a Cuban and I am tied up completely in this Revolution. I believe in what they are fighting for."

Fighting as a Rebel did not merit loss of U.S. citizenship. However, joining a foreign state's army or taking an oath of loyalty to a foreign government could be interpreted as renouncing one's citizenship. The "[c]rux of this analysis," concluded an FBI summary of a State Department meeting called to review Morgan's case, "is that it does not clearly delineate where initiative lies for ruling on or starting expatriation." Given the inexact nature of expatriation, the FBI report advocated an active role on the part of the bureau, suggesting that it work to find the proper means for expatriating Americans who participated in foreign revolutions. "While expatriation is not within our jurisdiction we . . . can properly disseminate data we develop . . . in order to make certain [that] data which might warrant expatriation gets to those in a position to act on it."

An internal FBI document, dated September 10, 1959, laid out the case against Morgan in the clearest terms. Therein, the U.S. Department of State requested the "US Embassy in Havana to rush action to remove the citizenship of William Alexander Morgan. . . ." The letter went on to explain why, precisely, this action was to be taken: "Expatriation," the letter stated, "is a powerful weapon in contending with U.S. nationals active in Caribbean revolutions and properly applied can be an effective deterrent."

Seven months later, J. Edgar Hoover no longer worried about alluding to the on-the-books reason—allegiance to a foreign army or country—behind Morgan's loss of citizenship. Instead, he bluntly referred to him as "a soldier of fortune who has lost his U.S. citizenship because of his pro-Castro activities."

It was no secret that the men behind Morgan's loss of citizenship were Pennsylvania Representative Francis Walter, Senators James Oliver Eastland of Mississippi and George Armstead Smathers of Florida, and FBI Director Hoover. Morgan singled them out, making reference to a recent scandal in which they'd encouraged a broadcast network to accept payment to produce positive propaganda for Trujillo. Morgan gave an impassioned interview to *Revolución*, saying "members of Congress bribed by Trujillo gold who have caused the temporary loss of my citizenship are no better citizens than I. Our country knows them well. Public opinion will be on my side. I will utilize [in the United States] the same direct methods of Fidel. I will go on television and [the American people] will have to listen to me. The trouble is that I am the man that Trujillo hates most. We have seen how his money poisons the United States, buying the press in the recent scandal of the Mutual Broadcasting Company, which accepted $750,000 to defend his rotten regime. Those same dollars penetrate into the Congress and many of his men, like Eastland, Smathers, and Francis Walter, have influence in the Department of State. So if I am murdered [by Trujillo], it cannot be said that an American citizen was killed."

Some in the U.S. Embassy in Havana warned of the negative consequences revoking Morgan's citizenship might have on the United States's image in Cuba. Daniel Braddock wrote, "[Morgan] has become a local celebrity and something of a hero as a result of . . . the part he played in the abortive conspiracy and invasion. A number of people can be expected to object to an action which will be interpreted by them as hostile to Morgan, intended to punish him for actions of which they approve."

Indeed, the Cuban press was outraged. A reporter for *Revolución* stated that there was "no convincing explanation" for the act, and that Morgan's participation in the Trujillo conspiracy was "one of the most extraordinary events in our contemporary history."

An editorial in a Cienfuegos newspaper, *Liberación*, condemned the State Department's action against Morgan. "The initiative was that of a Congressional Committee, this time presided over by Francis E. Walter and, following our understanding, forms part of a block of measures imposed by the U.S. Government to stop conflicts in the Caribbean. . . . We cannot but mention the fact that the moment chosen for this action compromises the State Department's position, in that the condemnation can be seen as punishing Morgan for his loyal action to destroy the Trujillo conspiracy against our revolution and our country, and that it proclaims a certain support for the tyranny in Santo Domingo. . . . Fortunately, William Morgan has in Cuba a second country. The Fundamental Law of the Republic confers, for a notable combatant, the right to our citizenship. If, disgracefully, they [the U.S.] don't review his case, the valiant combatant of Las Villas, who has a heroic, Cuban wife, will stay among us. . . . We are not giving you this, loyal companion! You earned it!"

≡ With all the acclaim and the press attention, also came immediate reprisals from those who had been fooled by Morgan. Threats began coming in daily. The Domincan Consul in Miami, Augusto Ferrando—himself in the hot seat for falling for Morgan's con—told the FBI that Trujillo was "extremely angry and upset over the trickery of William Alexander Morgan." It was Ferrando's opinion that Trujillo would "take steps in the future to eradicate Morgan." On September 3, the day the announcement questioning Morgan's citizenship appeared in the *Evening Star*, shots from a car were fired at the American comandante's house, but no one was injured.

In the United States, hit men were planning to collect Trujillo's bounty. The FBI was aware of at least one of these plots. Immediately following the Trujillo episode, two former FBI agents tried to recruit an officer from the Miami sheriff's office to travel to Cuba to "assess" William Morgan's status there. The man's identity is redacted and protected in FBI documents that have never been made public. An urgent teletype from Hoover to the Miami field office on August 21 states, the "decision as to whether X should accept proposed assignment is entirely his to make and he should not be influenced in this regard. However, while not encouraging him to take the assignment you should not discourage him and it should be pointed out to him, that if he accepts assignment, he will possibly be in position to furnish valuable information to FBI and U.S. Government." That was an implicit sanction for an assassination attempt on Morgan.

It appears that the unidentified man eventually declined

the assignment, and it remains unclear whether anything ever came of this plot.

The attempts on Morgan's life persisted. One man was picked up as he landed on the Cuban coast, attempting to sneak into the country to kidnap or kill Morgan. More shots were fired at Morgan's house. However, getting to El Americano was no easy feat. The Cuban government protected him with eleven armed guards, who patrolled the streets around his house and demanded identification from anyone coming to visit the comandante.

Cuba was, perhaps, the only place in the world that would, or could, keep Morgan safe.

Part III

REVELATION

INTERVIEW

Morgan's exploits and the rather convoluted story surrounding his citizenship drew several American journalists to Havana. Among them was Clete Roberts, a square-jawed, slick-haired, metallic-voiced NBC television journalist. Roberts was in Cuba looking for subjects who might help the American people stop worrying that the Cuban Revolution was Communist. What he found was Morgan—an American and an insider in Cuba, who would tell anyone who listened that the Cuban people would never allow Communists to take over.

Late one evening, at the end of September, Roberts visited Morgan's home. In the black-and-white footage of the interview, Roberts, a minor celebrity who occasionally played the part of a reporter in movies, makes his way past several bodyguards and into Morgan's big house in Havana. Morgan meets Roberts at the door, offering his hand with a big smile. The Comandante wears a long, dark bathrobe over a white dress shirt, and his military flattop is a little disheveled. Together he and Roberts examine some machine guns on a table. Roberts fingers them gingerly, whereas Morgan handles them with the nonchalance of a gardener holding a trowel.

This interview represents Morgan's most comprehensive statement of his feelings about Cuba.

Seated on a couch in the living room, Roberts begins by telling his viewing audience, "I think I ought to tell you back in the United States that Mr. Morgan and I are sitting in what you might call an armed camp. I can hear voices just outside the window here of guards, the men who are guarding him. There are more machine guns lying on a table here just in back of . . . the camera. . . . There must be a price on your head, Bill."

Morgan smiles, "Well . . ." You can hear a touch of the round vowels and clipped consonants of the upper Midwest. "Half a million dollars at the moment if they can deliver me alive to Santo Domingo." Morgan answers Roberts's questions carefully, pausing to choose the proper words. He exudes calm confidence and practical smarts. The lines in his face make him look older than his thirty-one years.

CR: That's what Trujillo is offering for you?

WM: That's the going price in Miami right now. I imagine it will go up over a period of time.

CR: How does it feel to have a half-million-dollar price on your head?

WM: Well, it isn't too bad. (He smiles.) They are going to have to collect it. And that's going to be hard.

CR: Bill, you look pretty tired. I want to apologize for coming in this late at night and routing you out of bed, and I want to thank you for taking the trouble to see me. What have you been doing?

WM: I went down to Las Villas to see some farmers and to find out about a cooperative that we are trying to get started and what they wanted. I had to drive down into the southern coast of Cuba and then up into the mountains and then drive all the way back. So, I just got in about an hour ago and I'm kinda beat.

CR: You are organizing this cooperative?

WM: Well, when we got the money from Trujillo—the seventy-eight thousand dollars—it was agreed that it would be turned over to the land reform and I asked that it be used in the Escambray, which was where I fought. And I asked that it be used to start a canning plant or start a cooperative for the farmers, something with which they could earn money all year 'round over and above their normal crops. Fidel agreed to it and I've been down there trying to check around and find out what they wanted.

CR: What are you going to can down there? What have they got?

WM: Well, over and above their normal products of coffee, which is their biggest industry down there, we've got freshwater shrimp, fish, a lot of fruits. They grow oranges, they grow *guayaba* [guava], peanuts, all of these things, which can be made into candy, jellies and jams, and so forth and can be sold here in the country or exported. I think on an all-around basis if we can set it up so for a while we'll can chicken and for a while tomatoes and then we'll can fish and we can keep the thing going all year 'round.

CR: I imagine that part of the country has changed quite a bit from when you were fighting down there, hasn't it?

WM: Well, it's changing every day. They are opening up new two-lane highways where we used to go up by horses and mules and go up by foot on cow trails. Bulldozers are coming up and opening up roads in the mountains for the first time in the history of Cuba so the farmers can get out. And they are building schools, and they are going on a public-works project putting in houses, putting in stores, and little cities trying to get electric lights up there for the first time. In our particular zone they are completing a power dam, which will light up all this part of the mountain country and also furnish a beautiful freshwater lake. I forget how many square miles this thing will be—a couple of hundred, I guess. Takes up all the valleys in the mountains. They are going to stock this with fish and turn it into a tourist's paradise. So, all around it's changing. The next time we have a revolution we will have to use boats.

CR: Now you are convinced? Enlightened?

WM: Should Mr. Trujillo or any of his people come here and try to stop the Revolution, as far as the Rebels are concerned, as far as about the seven or eight thousand men who were actually in the mountains, the people in the cities, they are going to have to kill every damn one of us.

CR: I don't mind telling you, you are a very disappointing man. I came down here looking for a soldier of fortune standing around in a uniform with a machine gun in one hand and his other hand up waiting for someone to throw a lot of money at him. And here I find someone who has taken seventy-eight thousand dollars off of Trujillo and has turned around and contributed it to the nation of which you are about to become a citizen. You aren't fitting the pattern at all, boy. You're very disappointing!

WM: It all depends on what you believe in. I don't know about soldier of fortune because there isn't any fortune. People who fought here in Cuba fought for an ideal, fought for a reason. I think it's about time the little guy got a break. He never had one before. As far as money goes, I don't think you need it. I don't think I could starve to death in Cuba. I don't think I could go hungry in Cuba. I have a tremendous amount of family. I have a tremendous amount of friends. I have people who have faith in me and I have faith in them. And I understand them. And as far as clipping Trujillo for seventy-eight thousand dollars, I probably clipped him for four hundred thousand dollars. I didn't get the million dollars he promised me. Over and above that, money isn't everything.

CR: I think another question my viewers might like to put to you, if they had the privilege of sitting here and talking with you as I have, is about surrendering your U.S. citizenship. Do you mind talking about that?

WM: (He sits back and crosses his arms, sighs.) Well, I was born an American. I was brought up on American principles. I'm a funny kind of a fella. I don't believe it's important what country you live in or what piece of land you happen to occupy. A lot depends on what you think. In order for me to help these people, in order for me to complete certain moral promises that I made over the time in the mountains—that I was going to help them with the problem of land and with schools and so forth which we made all these promises in the mountains—I would have to violate American law, the neutrality law to be exact. . . . After the problem with Trujillo it was bounced back and forth between the State Department whether I was going be kicked out or I was going to be in. I'm married to a Cuban girl. I have a baby that is thirty-two days old. It's completely impossible for me to return to the United States; I wouldn't live twenty-four hours in Miami.

CR: You mean Trujillo would kill you?

wm: Well, he kidnapped Galindez and Murphy [the Spanish academic and the American pilot who flew Galindez from New York to the Dominican Republic]. In fact, he's done just about anything he's ever wanted to do over about thirty years. At least here I am allowed to carry a gun. I have my own gun, I have my own people. And it's going to be a little harder. In Miami I wouldn't have that kind of protection. I wouldn't depend upon the local police to protect me. [Trujillo's people] pretty well know what they are doing.

I believe in what [the Cuban] people are doing. I wanna help 'em. I feel that the best way I can do it is as a Cuban. They offered me Cuban citizenship as a native-born Cuban, which to me is an honor. These are people who never saw me before in their lives. They never knew me. They just know me by what I've done or how I've been with them. I feel very deeply for them, and I'm very happy to be a Cuban. When you are an American you think and act and work to help the United States or to work for the United States. Now I'm a Cuban, I'm working and doing everything I can possibly do to help the Cubans.

cr: Let's get one thing straight. The United States government did not take your citizenship away from you.

wm: No. In fact, the moment I was renouncing my American citizenship a cable came out from D.C. that they had suspended the action, that they were still going to investigate and so forth. But no, they did not take my citizenship away from me.

I was born an American. I was brought up on American principles. . . . I believe in what these people are doing. I want to help them. I feel very deeply for them. I'm very happy to be a Cuban.

[Clearly Morgan did not present the details of his loss of citizenship entirely accurately, but it is understandable that he wanted to appear as though he were choosing his own future, that becoming a Cuban was a positive action, not a reaction.]

CR: Seems to me I detected a sense of loyalty on the part of these guards around here. These are not mercenaries, are they?

WM: No. For the most part, [the guards] I have here in the house with me are farmers. I have two or three boys who can't read and write who fought in the mountains. They are going to school now. In fact, my wife is a school-teacher, she's teaching these fellas. . . . Most of these kids are students. The average age of the Rebel here was seven-teen or eighteen years old. We had 'em from fourteen up. And these kids, sometimes they get paid, sometimes they don't. Some of 'em haven't even been worried about going to go sign for the paycheck. They made up their minds they are going to clean up a country where everybody's been kicked around by a favored few for a good many years. And this time of Batista cost about twenty thou-sand lives. A lot of innocent people. And they made up their minds they are going to clean it up. They are doing a pretty good job. They are doing as best as anyone could expect 'em.

CR: The airline pilot said to me the other night when I landed, he said, "Are you going to do any work there?" And I said, "Yes. I'm going to try." And he said, "That's the one thing you're gonna find out about Cuba, these people are trying."

WM: That's right. You have to understand something when people talk about they can't possibly do it, they can't possibly change a country the way they are doing. As you know, I didn't fight with Castro—I fought with another group. He went into the mountains with twelve men. And at this time, his odds were seventy thousand [the number of soldiers in Batista's army] against twelve that he wouldn't make it. We won the Revolution the first of the year. Now it's probably five and a half million against, probably, forty-fifty-sixty thousand of the old people that we can succeed in building a country, in building up the economy and the standard of life. They will get a chance to go to school . . . , a chance to work all year 'round, a chance to own something. It's a drive in everybody. A lot of people don't understand the situation because they don't understand the language, they don't understand the people. But these people have a faith, and when you have faith and you have the willpower you'll succeed.

CR: I met a young man here the other day . . . who described this as a spiritual revolution. Do you think that's a good phrase?

WM: Well, you see, let me say something in this way. When the first of the year came, everybody thought after the first of February, the first of March, the Revolution's all over. The shooting's all over and done with, so we'll just change jobs. The funny thing was, the Revolution just started the first of the year. The only thing we won the first of the year was the chance to prove that what we wanted to do was the right thing and we wanted to give these people a break. We wanted to do the things that should have been done. And the Cuban government and the Rebels aren't the most experienced people in the world. They are all young. And they make mistakes diplomatically, government wise, and every other way. But as they make them, they correct them and keep going. They don't let it stop them.

CR: I'm not going to pull any punches on some of my questions. But you said, "Be my guest," when I walked in. I get the feeling that there is some disorganization, you picked up some people who were probably pretty good back up in the hills but they are not too sharp in the administrative field right now. Do you think that's a fair evaluation?

WM: Well, we picked up all kinds of people. Well, we have comandantes who can't read and write but we are sending them to school. We have the opportunists that you pick up in one of these things.

There's a saying in Spanish that literally translates in English as "A revolution is like a river that floods." When it floods it picks up all kinds of trash. The trash clogs up the river and makes it muddy. As the river runs out it throws the trash out to the sides and the rocks stay and the water runs clear. That's what's happening to the Revolution, it's still in the process of elimination. It isn't important what political party a person belongs to. What's important is that he's a Cuban first and a member of a political party second. Or, whether he's really based on the Revolution, that he's ready to go to work, ready for the hard knocks instead of looking around for a soft spot or a soft job. It's working out.

CR: Bill, as an American citizen, I think you are pretty much accustomed to rearing back on your heels and expressing an opinion, a dissident opinion or an unapproving one. I think that the folks back in the States and—if this is translated into German, which I think it may be—the folks over in Germany might want this question asked about freedom of expression down here, the ability to criticize or the freedom to criticize. As you and I know, in the last two or three days there've been a couple of newspapers here who've spoken out somewhat critically of the Revolution or the administrative policies of Mr. Castro. Mr. Castro has been on the television and has answered them. And the newspapers have cracked back again, apparently to the surprise of a lot of people, to say that he was a little unfair in taking a personal attack upon the writers. Do you think that a year from today that freedom of expression that was exercised here will still be exercised?

WM: Let's take some basic facts. These kids just finished kicking out a dictator. The Cuban people just finished kicking out a dictator. They fought for the freedom of their country. They know how to fight. They're not a bit afraid of anybody. You have the right in Cuba today—and I believe you'll have it for the next ten years or the next fifty years—to say anything that you want to say. I can criticize Fidel Castro or anyone else can. But you have to have reason and you have to have the moral strength behind you. In other words, the newspaper came out and they criticized certain aspects of the government. Castro came back and he defended his stand on these certain points of the government. The newspaper's free to criticize. Anybody can buy it. Nobody restricts them printing it or restricts the sale of it. He just defends himself. When they come out and take a crack at him, he's always gone on the basis that he goes out and tells the people the truth.

In Trinidad, when this thing came up about Trujillo, a little false propaganda . . . would have helped us tremendously and we probably would have trapped all of Trujillo's legion. But Fidel wouldn't give out false information. He said, "Once you lie to the people they lose faith in you." And he said, "I won't lie to them under any circumstances, no matter what the cost is." I respect that in him. As I said, I didn't fight with him. And I've told him I'm not a Fidelist [term for a Fidel Castro loyalist]. I don't belong to anybody. I'm a Cuban now. And I believe in Cuba, and I believe in the Revolution, and I have a tremendous admiration—a tremendous respect—for the man. I respect his moral courage and I respect his honesty above anything else.

CR: You believe he has integrity.

WM: Definitely.

CR: I think another question that would be asked up in the States would be about the political complexion of this government. Now, I'm the first to admit that there's a lot of nonsense that gets published and broadcast. There's a lot of misinformation that gets out. We are beginning to hear—and you know what's coming—we are beginning to hear that there's Communist influence around here. Now I must say that I met one of the important secretaries over in the Castro echelon the other day who's the greatest anti-Communist that I've ever come up against. She says to me, "I've sworn to myself that I will never give my right hand to anyone who's a Communist." And she's pretty close to Fidel. Is this typical?

WM: Well, I belong to an organization that numbers—in fighting men—between three and four thousand people and we don't have one Communist and we never made a pact with them. I don't know of any place the Communists

fought in Cuba, any particular front where they did anything to contribute to the Revolution. You always have a
few of them sneak in when there's a little bit of turmoil.

As you can see, I have fish tanks out here in the back
room. I like to raise fish. And I feed these fish tadpoles.
Now a tadpole and a baby fish look an awful lot alike. But
a tadpole grows up a whole lot faster. And instead of trying
to drain out the tank and clean out all the tanks to get out
all the tadpoles, I just let 'em grow up. And when they get
big enough I just take 'em out and feed 'em to the big fish.

The Cuban people are not Communists. They would
never go along with a Communist government under any
circumstances. Their history shows that over a period of
time, they have always been pro democratic very strongly.
They are individualists. They are very political minded.
Each fellow likes to get out and talk on the corner and talk
on his own soap box for his own candidate. The basic aims
of the Revolution are strictly against Communism. Communism breeds on ignorance and poverty. And the first
thing that the Revolution is doing is creating schools and
creating jobs and creating homes and giving people land in
which they can increase their income. The average income
of the farmer was about two hundred dollars per year and
now it will be increased about ten or fifteen times. So, the
basic aims, the completion of the Revolution alone, eliminate the possibility of Communism itself.

CR: I think that what we hear in the States on the other side
is that Castro is no Communist. I've heard no one say that
he's a Communist. But that there may be economic chaos
and that the Communists may take over down here. Do
you think there's any chance of that?

WM: They say that Batista may come back also, but the chances are about equal. If he came, the army wouldn't have to fight him—the people would get him.

CR: Just a moment ago, Mr. Morgan introduced me to his lady, Mrs. Morgan, who was, when I met her, dressed in a uniform—a green gabardine uniform—and she was very military in her bearing. And she had a small and very efficient-looking gun on her left hip. Right?

WM: I was the head of the general headquarters of the Second Front at that time and she worked as my secretary and also taught school and fought. The uniform was because we went up into the hills and it's a lot more comfortable for her. But the pistol, she knows how to use it.

CR: I can believe that. You know, Bill, what you've just told me—the meeting with Mrs. Morgan, the romance, the kind of a life you live—sounds to me like all of the movie scripts that were ever dreamt about in Hollywood. How has it happened that you haven't offered a diary for sale? It's been done, I understand, out on the West Coast.

WM: Well, I happen to know the person you are talking about. He went on television the other day and called me—"Fidel's gangster" I think were his words. Manuel Pesetas. Well, let me tell you why I didn't do it and then we'll get back to him. I don't believe that you should cash in on your ideals. I don't believe I was an idealist when I went up into the mountains, but I feel that I'm an idealist now, at least I have an awful strong faith in an awful lotta people, in what they want to do.

This other gentleman that you were talking about with the diary is a fellow who went up into the mountains and was there thirty days or sixty days, one of these things.

He came down from the mountains and the first thing he did was try to sell the diary for a movie. And he came out with a big publicity campaign and so forth and as he came out with the publicity campaign the newspaper *Revolución* came out and told his life story, who he was and what he was — a would-be rebel. And he came back with a lawyer and was going to sue the Revolution. And about that time one of the heads of the Revolution called him in and talked to him and said, "Are you trying to make money with your beard?" And handed him a razor and a shaving brush. And he shaved off his whiskers. So, since then Mr. Pesetas has been in the United States and he's cracked at Fidel and he's cracked at Raúl and he's cracked at the Revolution and the other day he took a very pointed crack at me, and he said, "This William Morgan he's an American soldier of fortune, he's Fidel's gangster." Which is alright because I don't know what kind of book he could have, but if anybody actually reads it and bases it on actual fact they're gonna find out it's awful phony.

CR: Well, Bill Morgan, I want to thank you. It's very kind of you to get out of bed to give up of your sleep, but I think this is just about the first time the story has been told in detail for the people of the United States and I'm deeply appreciative as a reporter.

WM: I'm very happy to be able to talk to you and now I just hope that now a few people realize that the people here aren't looking for money and they aren't looking for position. Actually, they just want to set this country up and give the people the same kind of a break they've already got in the States. They've never had it. That's basically what they want, to raise the standard of living and give the little guy a chance. And they're going to do it.

Not long after the interview, Morgan and Olga moved from the Vadia house to a penthouse in a new apartment building on the corner of Seventh Avenue and Sixteenth Street in Vedado. The building stood across the street from the Malecón and looked out at the water. The apartment was easier to guard than the house in Miramar. The only access was by stairs or elevator. An armed guard stood watch at the door to the building. Several members of Morgan's bodyguard stayed in the apartment with the family around the clock. When Morgan went out, he went with guards. His blue 1958 Oldsmobile was equipped with three car phones and enough guns to take on a small army.

Now that the Trujillo Conspiracy had ended and he'd accepted the loss of his U.S. citizenship, Morgan wasn't sure what he would do next or what role, exactly, he would play in the next phase of the Revolution.

At home Morgan had installed huge aquaria and filled them with tropical fish. He relaxed by spending hours tending to the fish, separating the young ones out so that the bigger ones would not eat them. "He talks to the fish," said Olga.

FROGS

The new government was making changes all over Cuba. It built housing for Cubans who had previously lived in squalid shacks. It built schools in poor neighborhoods and ran electric wires into hamlets and shantytowns where people still used candles and kerosene for light. Street urchins were gathered up and placed in boarding schools where they were taught the skills necessary to reenter society. The excitement of reform and promise was palpable.

In May 1959, when the new government had begun its land redistribution program, the implementation of the First Agrarian Reform Law had not gone smoothly in the Escambray. Though the law was intended to provide opportunity for poor, rural Cubans, in some cases the intended beneficiaries of the program found themselves with less work rather than more.

The primary coffee-growing region had its own socioeconomic composition, which included a significant population of middle-class tenant farmers, who leased land from large landowners. The tenant farmers grew the coffee, harvested it with the help of numerous laborers, and then sold it, sharing a small percentage of the profits with the wealthy proprietors. When the government instituted Agrarian Reform, the land of the large landowners was confiscated and divided among the tenant farmers. However, it was difficult for the farmers to hire the coffee pickers because they lacked the cash, which in the past had been loaned to them by the landowners. The poorest people, who relied on seasonal work and day wages, suffered immediately. The unintended consequence of the reform was that the little guy, rather than catching a break, found himself out of a job and people at all levels of society were unhappy.

It was problems like these that inspired the First Peasant Congress. During the second week of October 1959, the men of the Second Front went back into the mountains en masse for the first time in ten months. This time, however, with the money that Morgan had clipped from Trujillo, they hoped to start projects that would improve the lives of the people.

Peasants from all over the region made their way to the First Peasant Congress. Some took buses to the end of the line and then walked, others went in wagons usually used for hauling coffee beans, others by horseback or mule. They all came to the Congress to express their views, their fears, and their hopes and, moreover, to work out solutions. The Rebels arrived by Jeep, taking with them bankers and agronomists. Peasants, Rebels, businessmen, and scientists convened at El Nicho, a small community of coffee growers high in the Escambray. In all, nearly five thousand people were in attendance.

Fidel sent the popular Camilo Cienfuegos as his representative. The lanky Rebel—perhaps the most loved of all the Verdes, still sporting his long beard—showed up to keep an eye on things. As the conference was inaugurated, he embraced Menoyo, thereby offering government sanction for the event. Camilo was the man who could communicate with everyone. No one knew much about his political beliefs, but he was Fidel's diplomat.

Eloy Gutiérrez Menoyo opened the event with an impassioned speech, calling on memories of the battle against Batista that had torn through the Escambray. "We have returned," said Menoyo, "to these unforgettable hills of Las Villas where together we fought for the liberty of Cuba and where the bones of our brother combatants rest. . . . This time we do not come, as yesterday, to ask for your help. We come here to fulfill our promises that were sealed with a blood pact before the bullets and the fire of the Dictatorship. The hour has come for those leaders of the Revolution who fought in these mountains to . . . make good on our words and promises of yesterday.

"This first Revolutionary Peasant Congress, organized by the Second Front, is not nor can it be in any way a sectarian act of our organization . . . because when Batista's soldiers fired their rifles and the despot's planes dropped their bombs, they did not distinguish between the different militias, they did not look to see what amulet a guerrilla wore, nor which flag he fought under. . . .

"We want to know from your mouths, peasants of the Escambray, how many schools you need in these hills so that your children will not be illiterate. We want to know how many roads and highways to construct so that the agricultural produce of the region can be transported to markets, thereby creating a higher standard of living in your homes. We want to know what assistance you need so that children in these hills do not fall victim to epidemics. We want to know how the Revolution can help you men and women so that we put an end to the 'forgotten corners' of this country. For these reasons, we have convened this Congress, so that our partners from the cities who are here with us, standing for the first time on the generous and free land of the Escambray, understand that here, as in the Sierra Maestra, we must take revolutionary steps to cancel the effect of tyranny. We will gather your messages and deliver them to the Revolutionary Government that embodies all our longings and hopes, our honor as combatants and our destiny as a free country. . . ."

Meetings during the Congress addressed myriad regional problems, which included infrastructure, utilities, education, and health care. The Second Front's major accomplishment—an inspiration of Max Lesnik's—was to organize a system of microloans from a local bank, which made it possible for the mid-level landowner to hire laborers to harvest the coffee crop. This solution averted a major economic crisis in the region and was intended to solve the problem of joblessness, a problem that had led many to question the Revolution.

The energy generated by a shared purpose was palpable. There was a sense that this congress exemplified the ideal revolutionary process: Engage people concerning what they want and need, and help them to help themselves.

Morgan was more interested in the people than the speeches. Like an older version of the impulsive kid who never liked school, he borrowed a mule to ride into the mountains to visit the farmers and peasants he'd come to know there. He ascended the steep slopes, sweating in the outdoors rather than suffocating indoors through speeches and meetings. He wanted to get on with the work of building businesses that would exploit the area's resources and create steady, year-round employment for the people. In fact, Morgan was tired of the talking and planning; he was itching to roll up his sleeves and get to work himself.

≣ Shortly after the Escambray Congress, Antonio Núñez Jiménez, the first president of the Instituto Nacional de Reforma Agrario—National Institute of Agrarian Reform (INRA)—appointed Morgan to head the River Repopulation program. It was an experimental post created to test the feasibility of freshwater aquaculture as a means to produce jobs and food. It was also the perfect position for a man who loved Cuba's rural denizens, raised tropical fish as a hobby, and wanted a nonpolitical job. "I've never been a politician—I'm a soldier," Morgan said.

Perhaps thinking about the tadpoles he fed to the fish in his tanks at home, Morgan decided his first project would be bullfrogs. Frogs, he believed, created the opportunity for a diversified business: The legs would be sold to restaurants; the skins would serve as material for high-end accessories such as wallets, purses, and ladies' shoes; and what remained could be used to make high-protein cattle feed.

Morgan selected three swampy sites to build frog nurseries: one just west of Havana; one on the eastern outskirts of the capital; and one in the Escambray, on the banks of the Hanabanilla River. He hired teams of Cubans to scour marshes and riverbanks for bullfrogs. Others he set to work digging the long, damp trenches in which the frogs would be raised. Morgan wasn't afraid to get his uniform dirty, and he joined the men and women at the messy work, catching the slippery frogs and digging the muddy trenches.

With the landscaping preparations under way, Morgan contacted a friend in Toledo, Frank Emmick, to be the importer on the U.S. side. Emmick would purchase the frog legs from Morgan and distribute them to restaurants in the United States.

Within months, Morgan had achieved what some called a miracle in the swamps. He employed nearly six hundred workers, shipped fifty thousand pounds of frozen frog legs to the U.S. every month, and produced fashionable products from the skins. According to *Look* writer Laura Bergquist, Castro gave bullfrog handbags and shoes to the women of the Peiping (Beijing) Opera when the company visited Cuba from China.

To help with PR, Morgan hired Michael Colin, an American living in Havana, as his director of public relations. Colin's being from Toledo appears to be coincidental. When Colin came to Cuba in January, just after the Rebel victory, he was trying to make a splash in the Hollywood film business. It was Colin who had optioned the film rights to the diary of Manuel Pesetas, the would-be Rebel who had called Morgan "Fidel's gangster." When the Revolutionary government shut down the movie project, the whole Hollywood team Colin had assembled returned to the United States. That is, except for Colin himself. During his few weeks in Havana, Colin, forty-one and married, with a child in California, had begun wooing a seventeen-year-old Cuban model and dancer named Olga Calero. When he went back to his wife and child in the United States, he took the young lady with him, announcing that he'd brought a nanny for the couple's son. It didn't take long for Mrs. Colin to figure out the real situation, and she sent her husband packing back to Cuba with his Latin lover. Colin and Olga Calero married and lived in a small apartment in Havana until they met Morgan. When Colin started working for the frog business, they moved into a large house with an ocean view and swimming pool.

Another of Morgan's assistants on the project was a strapping six-foot four-inch former U.S. Marine named Gerry Patrick Hemming. Hemming, who referred to himself as a technical adviser to Morgan, had earned a place in the Cuban Revolution by smuggling stolen guns into the Sierra Maestra. Afterward he'd done some freelance work for the Revolutionary Air Force. Hemming, it seems, was also providing information to

U.S. Army Intelligence about military and counterrevolutionary activities in Cuba, including the sympathies and inclinations of William Morgan.

Later, Hemming would spend years planning covert operations against Castro and has even been implicated by some scholars in the Kennedy assassination. But in Havana in 1959, he liked to roughhouse with his buddy Morgan. The two would grapple wildly around Morgan's house, and though he was smaller than Hemming, Morgan could wrestle the bigger man to a draw. Sometimes the horsing around escalated, such as the time Morgan pulled out a sword and slashed the air around Hemming, who defended himself with a wooden chair until the two men collapsed in laughter.

It remained a boisterous time in Cuba. To most people it seemed that things were getting on track, that the river was beginning to run clear, and that what remained to be done was the day-to-day work of creating an efficient and equitable economy.

However, small problems continued to fester. Huber Matos, the military chief of the eastern province, Camagüey, wrote a letter of resignation to Fidel, claiming that too many Communists were finding their way into the provincial and national governments. Matos challenged Castro to take an ideological stand, to come out once and for all as either for or against Communism. Several of the men under Matos's military command joined in his resignation.

At the end of the third week in October, Fidel dispatched Camilo Cienfuegos to try to avert a political crisis in Camagüey. Camilo spoke with Matos, but as he flew back toward Havana to report on his meeting, the weather turned stormy and his plane disappeared. According to official records, the remains of Camilo's plane and body were never found. While the Revolutionary Army and volunteer citizen brigades scoured the coast for evidence of the aircraft, the Cuban people began mourning the loss of their most beloved comandante. Camilo had been a symbol of the Revolution's humanity, serving as a calming force and a trusted mediator.

Bohemia published the last photograph ever taken of Camilo in an issue commemorating the man's life; it shows him inside the Presidential Palace in Havana, turning to smile at the camera as his left hand rests easily on the shoulder of William Morgan.

☰ As the Agrarian Reform program in Las Villas continued to appropriate and redistribute land, it became clear that the implementation problems in the Escambray—despite the efforts and advocacy of the Second Front—were beginning to spawn violence. By November out-of-work laborers had formed small guerrilla bands to fight the Revolution that, despite its promises, had not provided them with work. On November 19 thirty-three people were detained in Cienfuegos for planning an armed campaign against the Revolution.

Beside such apparently minor, if irritating and sad, setbacks, the general optimism continued. After an extended absence from his favorite home, Ernest Hemingway returned to Cuba, shook hands with Fidel, and announced that he considered himself just one more Cuban.

Morgan, meanwhile, pressed ahead with the frog business, filling pools and trenches with the amphibians. He hired more workers and paid living wages. Men who had never before worn shoes could now afford them. Women who had worn only clothes they'd made by hand purchased dresses for the first time. Morgan's frog farm was changing the lives of the people who worked for him.

Morgan himself worked day and night. When he finished surveying the frog nurseries, he would go home for a nightly dinner meeting with Michael Colin to discuss the business. Eloy Gutiérrez Menoyo and Jesús Carreras often joined them. Hemming attended most nights. Other members of the Second Front, including Ramirito and Roger Redondo, drifted in and out of Morgan's house and these meetings.

Colin always brought along his young wife. Olga Calero remembers, "I would ask Mike, 'Why do we always have to eat in Morgan's house?' There was a long table where everyone would eat hamburgers with ketchup. We ate like Americans there. I said to Mike, 'I want to stay home and eat chicken.' Morgan was a bit tiresome, but I got along very well with his wife, Olga. She was very loving. If we didn't eat at Morgan's, Mike would go to the Capri Hotel to meet with other friends and I would stay home."

Calero also said that shortly after her husband began working for Morgan, the couple found themselves with plenty of cash. Mike's "other friends," possibly the ones he met at the Capri Hotel, came by the house with briefcases and left stacks of money on the desk in his office. Colin would tell her to take what she needed. Once, he told her he was working for the CIA. As Morgan began doing the work of the Revolution to improve the lives of poor Cubans, it appears that Hemming and Colin, two of the men closest to him, had ulterior motives. They stuck close to the new Cuban citizen in hopes of gleaning valuable information about the Revolution's course.

≣ After Camilo's death, Fidel flew to Camagüey and arrested Huber Matos for conspiring against the government, also accusing him of a number of lesser crimes, which were never proved. In December 1959 Matos was tried and sentenced to twenty years in prison for treason and traitorous activities. Moderates and reformists around the country took notice, unsure what to make of the Matos situation. Was it an isolated event? Or would it mark the beginning of widespread intolerance for dissenting views, for opinions that ran counter to Fidel's own? Even worse, did it mean, since Matos had denounced Communism, that Fidel supported Communism? Even to vigilant anti-Communists like Morgan and Menoyo, the latter possibility seemed improbable and extreme. Rebuilding a country was no easy task, and the last thing the Revolutionaries needed was people crying "Communism" when they were just trying to figure out the best way to implement a fair economic and political system.

LA COUBRE

"I was alone in the house when it happened. Mike was not in the house. He said that he was going to the Capri. I was watching television, and all of a sudden I felt the house trembling. The house was beside the sea. And I heard the sound. Everywhere dogs barked. After a few moments, it was on television. Morgan was there on television right after *La Coubre* blew up. He was there with the army." Olga Calero remembers clearly the moment on March 4, 1960, when a ship with a hold full of weapons, recently purchased from Belgium by the Cuban government, exploded in Havana Harbor. Seventy-five men were killed, more than two hundred injured.

By January 1960, there were three basic sticking points between the United States and Cuba. One was that the U.S. government refused to accept the manner in which Cuba was offering to pay for the American-owned land it was expropriating as part of the Agrarian Reform laws. The Americans insisted that cash be paid to the owners, whereas the Cubans said they would issue notes and pay off the debts over time. Another was Castro's constant public attacks on the U.S. government. Philip Bonsal requested that Castro tone them down as a gesture of goodwill and openness to the possibility of improved relations. For about a month, until the explosion of *La Coubre*, Castro did scale back his critiques of the "imperialists" to the north. Finally, the Cuban government requested that the United States intervene to stop the airplane raids originating from the United States, which were sponsored by Cuban exiles and the CIA and were setting fire to sugarcane fields on the island.

Meanwhile, the changes taking place in Cuba began to make Morgan's predictions during his discussion with Clete Roberts seem naïve. On January 11, 1960, Fidel gave the order that government-sponsored "clarifications" be printed below newspaper articles. Shortly thereafter, the government began to expropriate the newspapers. By severely curtailing freedom of the press, the government pushed a great deal of information to the level of rumor and speculation. In October Morgan had believed that freedom of speech would continue in Cuba, and yet less than four months later it was being curtailed.

President Eisenhower gave a conciliatory speech at the end of January, a half-hearted attempt to preserve relations between the two countries.

Castro received a visit a week or so later from Soviet Deputy Prime Minister Anastas Mikoyan, which the United States interpreted as a pointed provocation. During the trip, Mikoyan agreed to purchase sugar from Cuba and to loan the country one hundred million a year over twelve years. This was not necessarily a sign that Cuba was moving toward Communism, but it disturbed both the American government and moderates in Cuba, including the men of the Second Front.

≡ Also in mid-January of 1960, the men and women accused of planning the Trujillo Conspiracy against Fidel Castro and the Cuban government went to trial. Behind-the-scenes negotiating by Menoyo and Morgan had led the government to declare that it would not seek the death penalty. The sentences were delivered in early February and 104 people, including Menoyo's friend Luís Pozo, were sentenced to prison terms that ranged from three to thirty years.

Amid the political tension, on February 28, Eloy Gutiérrez Menoyo announced the dissolution of the Second National Front of the Escambray, declaring that the disbandment was in the interest of national unity. While this may have been true, the decision also had to do with disagreement within the group, between those who believed that Fidel would steer the country properly and those who believed the time had come to actively oppose the Revolutionary government.

≡ On March 4, seventy-six tons of military equipment ignited inside *La Coubre*. The first explosion rocked Havana at 3:10 in the afternoon, followed a few minutes later by a second, larger blast.

After the first explosion, Ramirito sped toward the dock in his Jeep. When the second explosion shook the ground, he stopped and dove beneath the Jeep, hoping for protection from falling debris and possibly more explosions.

All military personnel, along with police, firefighters, and medical workers, raced to the horrific scene.

Menoyo and Morgan arrived separately. Morgan walked around the docks investigating the destruction and doing what he could to help.

As Che Guevara watched the dead and injured dockworkers and longshoremen being carried from the wreckage, a young Cuban photographer named Alberto Díaz Gutiérrez (now better known as Alberto Korda) focused and snapped. In the photo,

Che looks like a lion with a man's face, simultaneously wild haired and compassionate, fierce and beautiful, his face framed by a chic beret. From this moment he emerges—through a complex combination of deeds, propaganda, rage against U.S. foreign policy, and a photographer's luck—as an icon.

One could argue that this moment and this legendary photograph would mark the ascendancy of Che's influence in Cuba and, in turn, the diminution of Morgan's.

As with the explosion of the U.S.S. *Maine*, which conveniently drew the United States into Cuba's fight for independence from Spain, it has never been conclusively determined whether or not the destruction of *La Coubre* was caused by a careless accident or by sabotage. Castro, however, immediately indicated that sabotage was a possibility and pointed his finger at the United States; the vitriolic attacks in the Cuban press against the American government resumed and escalated.

Historian Hugh Thomas refers to this event as the point of no return in Cuban–American relations, suggesting that the explosion and its immediate aftermath rendered a rapprochement between the two countries impossible.

To honor the dead, Fidel organized a funeral march through Havana the day following the explosion. It was headed by the Revolution's most prominent leaders, including Fidel, Che, Morgan, Menoyo, and the president of Cuba, Osvaldo Dorticós Torrado. A photograph captures Morgan and the rest of the somber Rebel leaders walking arm in arm through Havana. In the face of the disaster, they showed unity of purpose and mission; this unity, however, was beginning to crumble.

For several weeks prior to the explosion, a blond, blue-eyed young man from Oklahoma named Jack Lee Evans had been a guest in Michael Colin's house. Evans, ostensibly a cotton expert from Oklahoma, had been consulting with the Cuban government on the best ways to grow cotton. However, according to Colin's wife, Evans rarely left the premises, spending his days swimming in the pool and sunning himself beside it.

Immediately following the *La Coubre* explosion, Evans left for Miami. There he gave an exclusive interview in the *Miami Herald* in which he suggested that William Morgan might have been involved in the sabotage, saying that the comandante had visited the cargo ship that morning. The reporter interviewed Morgan, who refuted Evans's implications.

Shortly afterward, Morgan fired Michael Colin, saying that his PR man had been talking to the wrong people and was going crazy. Colin, in turn, accused Morgan of taking a five-thousand-dollar kickback on a business deal. Was the CIA, through Colin and Evans, trying to set Morgan up, to sow misinformation that would cost him the trust of the Cuban government?

After he fired Colin, Morgan sent Gerry Hemming to Colin's home to check on his former employee. According to Hemming, Colin appeared morose and despondent, and he told Hemming that Morgan would be killed by members of his own bodyguard. Hemming reported the conversation to both Morgan and an army contact in the U.S. Embassy, concluding that Colin was, indeed, crazy.

Nevertheless, Fidel's bodyguard received special instructions to keep an eye on Morgan and Menoyo whenever they were in the presence of the prime minister.

≣According to Herbert Matthews, after the *La Coubre* explosion, the U.S. government stopped making a distinction between Cuba and Communism; and on March 17 President Eisenhower gave orders to arm and train Cuban refugees for a possible invasion of their homeland, an act that would lead to the Bay of Pigs invasion in April of 1961. In the six months since Morgan's interview with Clete Roberts, the political reality in Cuba had changed dramatically: The Revolutionary government was beginning to limit individual freedoms, loyalties were no longer clear, and the United States government had concluded that working with Castro would be impossible.

Everything was changing in Morgan's adopted country—alliances were in question, and Fidel's political intentions were unclear. Was there still a place for Morgan in Fidel's new Cuba?

CHOICE

Throughout the political turmoil and the firing of Michael Colin, Morgan kept hard at work at the frog business. American journalists continued to be intrigued by the American-born Cuban citizen who still worked for the Cuban government and continued to insist with confidence that Cuba would be a democracy.

Time reported on Morgan's current work, calling him "Frogman." Although Morgan had stocked lakes and streams with sunfish, perch, and black bass, the big business was still frogs. He announced plans to ship more than two million dollars' worth of frog legs to restaurants in the United States during 1960. By late spring his operation was slaughtering about thirteen thousand frogs a day for export.

The *Miami Daily News* picked up Morgan's story in April and presented it with a cynical slant, stating that the comandante was "one of some two dozen Americans who, having cast their lot with Castro in more glorious days, now find themselves playing outcast roles stripped of glamour." The journalist emphasized what he saw as a vast disjunction between the first days of the Rebel victory and the current state of affairs: "Those were the days when Castro was portrayed as Latin America's Robin Hood, and newspaper stories of Morgan's exploits were enough to make schoolboys drool. He seemed headed for big things in the Castro regime. . . . This time I met him beside a sun-scorched frog tank at one of Cuba's new collective farms on confiscated land outside Havana. . . . He rides in a blue Oldsmobile hardtop outfitted with three radio telephones, two submachine guns and a glove compartment full of hand grenades. He boasts that 'enemies of Cuba have offered $500,000 for me dead or alive.' . . . The trappings do not disguise the fact that Morgan has been relegated to a civil servant's job of minor consequence."

Despite the journalist's interpretation, Morgan expressed nothing but enthusiasm for his new line of work. "Cuban frog legs are tops. We will dominate the world market when we get the breeding ponds going. . . . They couldn't have given me a job I'd like better. . . . I'll stay with the Revolution as long as they need me and then go into business here in Cuba. . . . We couldn't be happier."

To a *Miami Herald* reporter, he catalogued the Revolution's successes: "The poor man in the country is living better. Cuban people in the country lived like pigs before. We are building roads, schools and trying to create new industry. Batista built hotels, but no industry."

For a man who, three years earlier, could not hold down a job, who had moved with his American wife and two children back into his parents' home, his place in Cuba seemed pretty good. A friend of Morgan's from Toledo visited him in Havana and remarked that Morgan was "exceedingly popular with the Cuban people." Despite the shifting political winds, Morgan remained an admired figure. When he walked down the street, children still shouted excited "*Hola!*—Hello!'s" to their Revolutionary hero.

Confident, perhaps overconfident, of his place in the hearts of the Cuban people, Morgan refused to tone down his anti-Communist rhetoric or to adjust his analysis of Cuba's political direction. Moreover, he continued to defend Castro. "Americans don't understand the Cubans," he bluntly opined in a *Miami Herald* article, "and they are scared of the word *revolution*. There are a lot of people in the United States and in Latin America who are trying to create ill feelings between the United States and Cuba. There has been way too much talk about communism. I am no communist and never have been. Fidel is not a communist. The revolution is not communistic and the Cuban people will never accept communism. . . . Castro is between the frying pan and the fire. The communists and the people of Cuba support him. He is getting no support from the people or the press of the United States."

To *Time* magazine, Morgan boasted that "Fidel and Raúl know that I'm against the Communists. The Reds tried to hold a meeting on the frog farm, and I threw them out."

In all his public statements, Morgan attempted to walk the line between energetic support of the Revolution and his strong anti-Communist opinions. On neither point did he mince words. Morgan found himself fighting for a middle ground in the escalating ideological conflict, pressing the United States to give the Revolution a chance and insisting that Cuba was not turning to Communism.

After *La Coubre*, however, Morgan had privately begun to worry that his optimism for Cuba's future might be misplaced. In March, as he passed through Trinidad, he encountered Manuelito, the friend and fellow Rebel from the Second Front who had come to Morgan's aid the night Edmundo Amado was shot in the mountains. Manuelito, who was working as a city police officer, took Morgan aside to deliver a message.

"Edel Montiel wants to talk with you," said Manuelito.

Though they didn't speak of it, both men knew that Montiel, a Second Front Rebel, had gone back into the Escambray to organize a counterrevolution. To deliver messages for Montiel was dangerous; to meet with him would carry tremendous risk. Castro's government was sweeping up anyone suspected of conspiracy and holding him—or her—in prison.

Manuelito felt little sympathy for the Revolutionary government, but he wasn't ready to commit to more months in the mountains, let alone decades in Cuban prison. Out of the loyalty forged when they fought together, Manuelito felt obliged to facilitate the communication between the two former members of the Second Front. As far as anyone else was concerned, the conversation, Manuelito told Morgan, had never happened.

Morgan had a decision to make. He had often mentioned having commanded up to five thousand men who looked to him for direction. Edel Montiel and his counterrevolutionary band were counted in this number. If he didn't meet with Montiel, he might lose standing with those men. They would think Morgan was afraid to talk with them, that he was trying to protect himself, or that he was letting go of the democratic ideals he'd been articulating since his arrival in the Escambray.

Morgan knew that he couldn't let down one of his own men, especially at a time when Fidel's tolerance for dissent had diminished in the face of threats from both inside and outside Cuba. If he met with Montiel, Morgan would place his life and his family at risk. Still, he believed that as long as he stayed loyal to Fidel, the Cuban leader would take care of him.

Days later, Morgan went to the cemetery at the southern edge of Trinidad and passed through the gate and under the high, mustard-colored arch to stand among neat rows of family crypts. Edel Montiel had stolen down from the mountains to wait for the American in the evening half-light. The two men talked. Montiel told Morgan that he and eighty men were preparing to fight to put the Revolution back on the path of democracy. He asked Morgan if he would help arm his growing band of counterrevolutionaries.

Morgan told Montiel that he would keep an eye on the situation in Havana, that he still hoped Fidel would reject the Communists, and that he would also do what he could to help a friend. Montiel melted back into the night, convinced of Castro's totalitarian tendencies, Morgan returned to his life as a father and a frog farmer.

When Frank Nelson had arrived in Cuba, dangling a million dollars in exchange for Fidel's head, Morgan had gone straight to Castro with the news. Morgan kept this meeting to himself.

Everything was changing quickly. Morgan found himself unable to turn away from his hopes for this island where he had made his home, nor could he break the promises he'd made to the peasants, to Menoyo's father, and to the men with whom he'd fought. Morgan had taken a real first step toward subverting the man whose integrity he had publicly lauded time and time again.

CONSPIRACY

Throughout the spring and summer of 1960, tensions escalated between Cuba and the United States. In May the Cuban government asked the American-owned oil refineries on the Island to process Russian oil. When the plant managers refused, Fidel Castro kicked them out of the country and nationalized operation of the refineries.

During the first week of July, President Eisenhower halved the U.S. commitment to purchase Cuban sugar, severely threatening an economy that relied on the premium prices the Americans paid in order to protect their own sugar farmers and to curry political goodwill with the island. Philip Bonsal said of Eisenhower's decision: "With this action I contend that the United States turned its back on thirty years of statesmanship in Latin America." He also believed that "the Cuban government was doomed by its own disorganization and incompetence."

Challenges to Castro's power were mushrooming. In Miami the CIA, which had long since abandoned its wait-and-see attitude, was working hard to unify the Cuban exiles and hoped to fortify their activities against the Castro regime. At the same time, inside Cuba, former Minister of Public Works Manuel Ray began to organize clandestinely against the government but refused U.S. support. The left-leaning Ray operated under the slogan "Fidelism Without Fidel," attempting to communicate that he was for the Revolution but against the direction in which it had turned.

In the middle of June, Morgan, Menoyo, and a handful of trusted men from the Second Front met at Morgan's penthouse in Havana. They discussed the current situation and decided, finally, that their worst fears had been confirmed: The Revolution had turned Communist. They'd worried about this possibility since the first of the year, and the evidence could no longer be denied: The deteriorating freedom of the press, the ongoing expropriation of private lands, and the continued creation of state-run cooperative farms indicated, at the very least, the consolidation of power in the hands of only one man and his most trusted advisers. While Morgan and Menoyo had no problem with the concept of cooperative farming, the degree to which the Cuban government was expropriating people's land—as though the very concept of private property no longer had a place in Cuba—bothered them, as did the erosion of personal freedoms they'd fought to preserve.

Since the inception of the Second Front, these men had spoken repeatedly and publicly against Communism. Even Morgan's bodyguards had been overheard criticizing Castro. One could argue that the leaders of the Second Front had been backed into a corner by their own rhetoric. To change their opinion on Communism at this point would not be credible either to the government or to the men who looked to them for direction.

With the acknowledgment of the Communist problem came responsibility. They had to do something to protect the Revolution and themselves. Over the course of the meeting, the men began planning an anti-Castro uprising, which, given the number of counterrevolutionaries already in the mountains, they believed could occur within twelve weeks.

Notes from this meeting were passed on to U.S. Army Intelligence by an unknown source. The most likely candidate was Morgan's technical adviser, Gerry Patrick Hemming; in any case, it was certainly not Morgan. Army intelligence had requested a background check of Morgan from the CIA, and the agency had warned against trying to cultivate him as an asset. Following his role in the Trujillo affair, the CIA considered him unreliable. In fact, the activities of Michael Colin and Jack Lee Evans suggest that the CIA might even have been actively trying to undermine Morgan's position in Cuba. The army, however, decided to follow Morgan's counterrevolutionary activity and wait for the proper moment to cultivate it.

In his public life, Morgan behaved as though nothing at all had changed. Olga gave birth to the couple's second child in July, another daughter, whom they named Teresa—the pet name Morgan had given his first wife, Ellen.

By August the American press was obsessed with the idea of Communism in Cuba. Morgan continued to address questions directly, but his tone shifted ever so slightly from the "it will never happen" position of earlier interviews. "If anything happens to me," he said, "you'll know the Commies have really taken over." Morgan reiterated his earlier assertions, echoing Menoyo's father, that he believed Fidel to be creating a "third force," by which he meant a system that was not Communist, but neither was it completely capitalist. Fidel might use the Russians or Cuban Marxists to "achieve his own revolutionary aims," Morgan speculated, but his heart was really with the non-Communists, people like Menoyo and himself.

≡In August 1960 Miguel Ángel Quevedo had announced that he'd witnessed a "revolution betrayed" and left for Venezuela, where he started *Bohemia Libre*, a magazine that would relentlessly criticize Castro's Cuban regime.

That month more members of the now defunct Second Front joined the counterrevolution, including a young student and former member of Morgan's column, Siniseo Walsh, who went into the mountains north of Cumanayagua to establish a presence near El Nicho. The Escambray was becoming infested with small groups of counterrevolutionaries who hid in caves, worked to turn peasants into collaborators, and did their best to threaten the Revolution's program for the entire area.

Plinio Prieto, former captain of the SNFE, established a guerrilla group in the area of Guanayara. Using the old Rebel propaganda technique, Prieto broadcast radio messages to win people to the counterrevolutionary side. "We return anew to the Escambray, not to overthrow Fidel, but rather to keep Communism from achieving power."

Cienfuegos became the urban center for the counterrevolution. An underground formed, or re-formed, one might say, which gathered supplies and raised money for its compadres in the hills. Members of the Catholic clergy once again entered the fray; they began to sell war bonds, one of which read "With God and with Cuba, again on our feet to fight the red revolution of Communism. Voluntary Bond. One Peso." In a church in Cumanayagua, government security forces discovered a stash of dynamite.

As multiple groups and bands of guerrillas appeared on the landscape, many of them led by former members of Menoyo and Morgan's Rebel group, the question arose as to whether or not they could be brought together to form a unified front.

The only people deemed capable of creating this cohesion were Menoyo and Morgan. No one else commanded such respect or had their abilities.

The government had to take the problem seriously. It began referring to the counterrevolutionaries as "bandits," people who wanted to steal the hard-won Revolution away from the Cuban people. Castro sent one hundred members of the Revolutionary Army to the Escambray in August. The force was not sufficient to address the problem and ended up simply trailing the guerrillas around the hills, just as Batista's soldiers once had. One of these militiamen said, "In reality we didn't encounter a single bandit, although we arrived at a few houses where there were few people and a lot of food. Anyone could tell that they were surely nearby."

On September 5, 1960, Fidel Castro organized a meeting in Cienfuegos, in the Jagua Hotel. There he convened military and government leaders from Las Villas to adopt a plan to rid the mountains of the counterrevolutionaries. He knew that if he weren't careful, if he underestimated the counterrevolutionaries, the Revolution might be in real trouble. The only choice was to challenge the insurrectionists with overwhelming force. So a force made up of Revolutionary Army soldiers and volunteers from citizen militias, numbering as many as seventy thousand, would be mobilized to comb the hills, meter by meter, for "bandits."

Morgan was still waiting, biding his time, hoping against hope that Fidel would come out against Communism and thinking about how to challenge the Cuban government if it came to that.

Shortly after Fidel went to Cienfuegos, however, Morgan told an army source that when the counterrevolution started, he and his wife, Olga, would travel into the Escambray, while Olga's sister would take the couple's two children and seek asylum in a Latin American embassy. From the safety of the embassy, the sister and the children would request permission to travel to Toledo, Ohio, apparently with the intent of residing with his parents. His intentions were no longer in question. Morgan was working out the details of an insurrection.

Around the middle of September, Morgan was having little luck finding a safe haven for his daughters. The Army Intelligence source described Morgan as "anxious" to figure out what to do with them. By the end of the month, Morgan said that if he couldn't make official plans for his children, he would consider dropping them off at the U.S. Embassy before heading off to fight the counterrevolution in the Escambray.

It seems that the pressure began to get to Morgan just as Castro was stepping up his campaign against the disaffected Revolutionaries. Over coffee at a café near Menoyo's bar, Morgan told Max Lesnik that if Fidel didn't steer the Revolution right, he would "pay for it." Lesnik quickly leaned in and whispered, "Don't ever threaten Fidel physically." Statements like that, Lesnik said, would be considered the equivalent of actual physical violence. The wrong people might overhear and Fidel would retaliate quickly and brutally.

≣ The leaders of the counterrevolution were to be Morgan, Menoyo, Armando Fleites, and Lázaro Ascencio. The men expected that once they established a base camp, five thousand sympathizers would join them within thirty days.

The emerging counterrevolutionary group sent a representative to the United States to garner support from American authorities and to request aid. However, the representative was to decline all aid from Cuban exile groups who might be, if not pro Batista, in favor of the old, corrupt ways. They employed a slogan not unlike that of Manuel Ray: "Not anti-Castro but anti-Communist." Apparently Morgan and his followers still held a slim hope that Castro might reject Communism.

By mid to late September, Morgan had begun moving arms into the Escambray. He used the Jeeps issued to him for his river repopulation work for INRA. The weapons, for the most part, had been secreted away by the men of the Second Front after the fight against Batista. Others were left over from the Trujillo affair and had been shipped to Cuba a year earlier from the United States and the Dominican Republic. Now Morgan and his men packed the guns into fifty-gallon metal drums, drove them into the mountains, and buried them near his frog farm on the Hanabanilla River for later use.

As the plan expanded, Morgan brought in more men. Menoyo counseled the American to choose only the men he trusted most, but Morgan allowed the government to provide him with bodyguards, perhaps thinking that by using state bodyguards he would appear to be fully supportive of the government. Maybe he even thought that he could convince the men that his way was the better way. One of his bodyguards was a young man named Cecilio Castro (no relation of Fidel's), a new member of the nascent Cuban Intelligence Service, or G-2.

Almost immediately, Cecilio began witnessing what he considered suspicious activity. He heard Morgan counsel his employees on the dangers of Communism. Close to the American Rebel, he realized how dangerous the man could be to Fidel's vision of Revolution. Morgan was smarter than he'd expected, charismatic, and was believed by the people of Cuba to have their best interests at heart. Morgan was persuasive. And Cecilio could tell that the man who liked to laugh and joke was as tough as all the stories from his time in the Escambray suggested. If Morgan weren't stopped, Cecilio decided, he might very well establish a massive force in the Escambray . . . and quickly.

≣ During the fall of 1960, the Cuban government first became aware that a significant number of exiles were undergoing military training in Florida and Guatemala, preparing for an invasion. The island nation bristled with anticipation. Soldiers were on constant alert, and Fidel called upon the vigilance and patriotism of citizens to help protect the country. Many of the six and a half million inhabitants joined citizen brigades and scanned the horizons for signs of attack by water or by air. In this way, some minor attempts to destabilize the government were noticed and apprehended, as when a small boatload of men put ashore west of Havana in Pinar del Río and were caught trying to scramble into the countryside.

Morgan was still waiting for the proper moment to go into the mountains. He wanted to move more arms but still hadn't found a safe haven for his children. Prieto and Walsh had been apprehended by the Revolutionary Army force, which was sweeping the Escambray. The challenge of building a front was increasing.

Meanwhile the business of frog skins was burgeoning. The beautiful wallets, shoes, and handbags that his employees were turning out made Morgan proud. When the head of the Cuban Armed Forces, 26th of July veteran Juan Almeida, was to be married, Morgan picked out a handbag and planned to deliver it to Almeida personally as a wedding gift for the comandante's bride.

Morgan drove to the military headquarters on October 21. As he entered Almeida's office, the police arrested the American comandante. He had waited too long. The Revolutionary government, operating on the information of Cecilio Castro, decided its future would be safer with Morgan behind bars.

At the same time, police were also apprehending Morgan's friend and fellow member of the SNFE Jesús Carreras and taking several members of Morgan's bodyguard into custody.

Philip Bonsal was recalled to the United States that same day, for what was described as a "long consultation"—a trip from which he never returned to Cuba.

The Cuban government soon expropriated all the remaining U.S. businesses in the country, including the Coca-Cola plant. On October 30 it announced an intensive development plan in the Escambray, designed to win over peasants and to increase its presence in the troubled region, which had suffered, according to the Revolutionary analysis, "under poor government, large landowners, and opportunists."

In addition to that development plan, Fidel's military operation continued. Seventy thousand soldiers and militiamen combed the peaks, valleys, and caves of the Escambray for counterrevolutionaries. They were still looking for the "bandits" who, the *Revolución* reported, "abused the peasant women, killed the peasant men, took up arms against the Revolutionary Army and militias, with no goal but to drive the country back into the gloomy past . . . of exploitation, injustice, crime, and pillage."

In Cienfuegos, *La Correspondencia* reported Morgan's arrest: "Yesterday, during the afternoon an official note was distributed by the Ministry of the Revolutionary Armed Forces, announcing the arrest of William Morgan and Jesús Carreras. . . . Both men were put at the disposition of the Revolutionary Tribunals, which ordered a broad investigation of the allegations."

Two days after the arrest, Manuel Ray, the leader of the

Movimiento Revolucionario Popular—People's Revolutionary Movement (MRP)—who was advocating "Fidelism without Fidel," told a U.S. intelligence source that Morgan had been instrumental in providing arms to his group and that everything should be done to spring him from prison. Without Morgan, he argued, the chance to create a unified, moderate counterrevolution inside Cuba all but disappeared.

The police took Morgan to the jail of G-2, the national intelligence agency, where they interrogated him for a month before moving him to La Cabaña, an eighteenth-century Spanish fort that had been converted to a prison.

PRISON

A small peninsula juts into the ocean opposite Havana, forming the northern edge of the city's broad harbor. The Cabaña fortress hunches along the top of this peninsula, its walls undulating slightly as they follow the topography of the ridge. They look as though they have been draped over the landscape, like a rope laid out on the grass. The Spanish built the sprawling structure in the mid-1700s to keep the English from entering Havana harbor. Despite the massive fortification, the English took the city a few years later, bargained for trading rights, and returned the city to the Spaniards when their demands were met.

Under Fulgencio Batista's rule, La Cabaña served as a barracks, jail, and torture chamber. Once Batista fled Cuba and Che Guevara took control of La Cabaña, the fort served as jail, courthouse, and execution site. One passes through the outer walls and across a stone bridge that spans a deep, dry moat. Inside, one immediately sees the resemblance to a small medieval city—cobbled streets, a chapel, open courtyards, meeting rooms, warehouses, and row upon row of cloistered barracks-rooms-cum-cells that can hold scores of prisoners. It's easy to see that the site, originally designed to keep the enemy out, could be used, and perhaps more effectively, to keep the enemy in.

Prisoners were jammed like sardines into the galleries. The beds were stacked in vertical columns of three, each column about three feet from the next. A prisoner's bed—about six feet long by three feet wide—represented the full extent of his personal space. Morgan slept in a lower bunk.

Guards served the prisoners ground shark meat, noodles in broth, a piece of bread. In the morning there was a meager cup of coffee. Twice, Morgan discovered ground glass in his food. Had he eaten this, it may well have killed him.

Once a week, on a rotating schedule, every man was provided a bucket of water for bathing. A hole in the floor of the gallery was the latrine.

A visitor brought Morgan a sheet, and every morning when he arose, he tucked the sheet neatly around the corners of the thin mattress, arranged his few possessions under the bed, and dressed in the prison uniform—an old khaki Cuban Army uniform from the time of Batista.

When his small space was orderly, he exercised—sit-ups, pushups, toe touches, stretches—and then marched around the courtyard outside the gallery, clicking his heels on the stone, turning the corners sharply, perhaps more precisely than he ever had as a soldier in the U.S. Army or as a guerrilla in the Escambray.

The order of his routine, the precision of his marching, and the tidiness may not have given him hope, exactly, but it surely offered a sense of control, some small way to exercise his will in a world where freedom had been taken from him.

Ten years before, Morgan had been a prisoner, often locked in a solitary cell, in the United States. There he raged at his plight. In Cuba he behaved differently, always affable, upbeat, quick with a joke.

César Fuentes, caught conspiring to assassinate Castro, landed in La Cabaña two months after Morgan. The day before he was arrested, Fuentes had a vision that he would be caught. The next day it happened, exactly as he'd seen it in his mind.

Fuentes was held in the same "galleria" as Jesús Carreras. The two men struck up a friendship and talked guerrilla strategy. "We always left the Cuban Army a way out when we attacked them," said Carreras. "We didn't have the numbers to defeat them as a group, but we could surprise them, inflict casualties, and capture supplies and sometimes prisoners when they fled."

It was easier to talk about less complicated times. They did not speak of the current situation, afraid they might be overheard and always assuming that some of the prisoners were spies for the government.

The prisoners lay down every night to the sounds of executions in the dry moat beyond their walls. They heard sobs, screams, groans, and defiant shouts of *"Viva Cuba Libre!*—Long Live Free Cuba!" After the volley from the executioners' rifles, there was another shot or two—the coup de grâce—to make sure the business was finished.

When Cesar was allowed to cross the courtyard to visit his friend Joaquín Martínez Saenz in another galleria, he sometimes saw Comandante Morgan. He came to know him as a popular man who revealed very little of himself.

One day when he went to visit Saenz, the heat of the day was particularly oppressive, radiating off the stone walls and floors. The gallerias were sweltering, and inmates in various states of undress had draped themselves about the cell and over the bunk beds. Morgan was sitting on his bunk in his underwear, his legs dangling in a desultory way over the edge of the bed. It was unusual, César recalled, to see the comandante in a moment of repose. What struck César, however, wasn't Morgan's attitude, but how red his chest was in the flush of heat. César read Morgan's skin as a premonition. As he'd foreseen his own arrest, he now envisioned Morgan's execution. Later he would foresee his own release from prison before it happened, but now he thought of the firing squad. As far as César Fuentes was concerned, Morgan's chest had already been riddled with bullets.

≡ When Morgan was arrested, the remaining leaders of the Second Front established contact with the Argentine ambassador to Cuba, Julió Amoedo, and requested asylum. They thought their own arrests might be imminent. Amoeda agreed to take three of the men, and, through his efforts, the Brazilian embassy also agreed to take three. However, there were twelve of them, and none would accept asylum until arrangements had been made for all.

In late December Menoyo and his men were still in Cuba and still free. He and Ramirito went to visit Morgan. They found their friend as calm as always. Morgan joked with Ramirito, asking if he was going to return a book he'd borrowed. Then he sent Ramirito away so he could talk with Menoyo alone. Menoyo told Morgan that he thought he should leave Cuba, but worried that his departure might jeopardize Morgan's chance for a fair trial. Morgan told his friend not to worry, that there was no point in both of them being in jail. From the United States, Morgan argued, Menoyo might be able to do more to save the Revolution for which they'd fought. The two men said good-bye, calling each other "my brother."

A few days later, in early January 1961, the remaining leaders of the Second National Front of the Escambray met at their usual spot, the café at F and Línea streets, kitty-corner from Eloy's Club and the Gutiérrez Menoyo home. The café was below street level, in a terrace that held a few tables. Stools affixed to the cement floor edged the counter. Men tossed back shots of coffee, smoked, talked baseball and politics, ate a croquette or two, and passed the time, gathering information, feeling for Vedado's, for Havana's, for Cuba's pulse. Pronouncements were made in this place, grudges bred and settled, lives changed. It was the café where Morgan had told Max Lesnik that Fidel Castro would "pay" for turning to Communism.

A group of SNFE men huddled at a table, among them Max Lesnik, Armando Fleites, and Ramirito Lorenzo. Eloy commanded the table, talking about the only subject: What were these men to do? They had lost any favor they might have held with the Revolutionary government. Two of their high-profile companions, Morgan and Carreras, were in jail. The Revolution that Fidel commanded allowed no room for dissent. As the Maximum Leader had said, you were either with it or against it. If you were against it, what were your choices? You could swallow your disagreements and get on with your life. Or you could try to hide and fight, create a counterrevolution. This debate was a constant in all their lives whether they were awake or asleep, eating or making love.

"We have to leave," announced Menoyo. "We will take a boat from Alamar. Everyone here is invited to come."

Some discussion followed as the men quietly aired the difficulty of making such a complex decision. On the one hand, it felt like a betrayal of friends, family, lovers, of the dream for which they had all risked their lives. On the other hand, perhaps in the United States they could regroup, make a plan, and return to steer Cuba toward a more tolerant, open government. What good would they be to anyone—their families or their country—if they were locked up?

In the end, everyone but Ramirito decided to leave. The handsome young soldier had a wife now, a baby, and a way of life in small-town Cuba that he understood. He would take his risks at home. He would try to keep a low profile and work hard without dissembling too much. Rather than attempting to sail over the horizon to Key West, he would make the longer trip east from Havana to the dusty little town of Camajuani.

The men stood up to leave. Ramirito faced Menoyo and snapped a stiff hand to his forehead, offering his comandante a crisp, and perhaps final, salute.

Within days of the meeting, Eloy and his followers pushed off the Cuban coast in a small boat. A couple of days after that, they made Key West.

TRIAL

It seems that Ché has won the fight.
Jesús Carreras, in his last letter
smuggled out of La Cabaña

On January 3, 1961, Fidel Castro, aware of the possible invasion by Cuban exiles, demanded that the U.S. Embassy staff be cut to eleven persons. In response, President Eisenhower severed diplomatic relations completely. The slender thread that had connected the two countries had finally been cut.

The public trial of William Morgan began early in 1961. In late January, while Morgan marched in squares around his galleria, Fidel Castro initiated a vigorous propaganda campaign to discredit the Cuban "hero" and others who had been members of the Second National Front of the Escambray. In a speech he delivered in Olga Morgan's hometown of Santa Clara, Fidel said, "Not only was the Second Front of the Escambray bad, but they were a poor and deficient and negative part of the leadership. . . ." He went on to describe them as "ambitious and pseudorevolutionary elements" who were "opportunists" and who had not even fought against Batista but claimed credit on January 2, the day after Batista had left, for deposing the dictator. "It was necessary to say this one time," Fidel warned his audience in the clean, upright town. "It was necessary to say this, because a little thorn, or maybe a big spine, has been stuck in the province of Las Villas. . . . There is no reason to be tolerant of this country's traitors."

Ten days later, Che Guevara published an article entitled "The Escambray: A Sin of the Revolution," which attempted a more reasoned, though no less merciless, critique of the leaders of the Second Front. Speaking of the postvictory allotment of responsibility, he wrote of the SNFE, "We did not permit them to rob nor did we give key posts to those who aspired to be traitors: but we didn't eliminate them, we compromised, all for the good of a unity that was not completely understood. This was a sin of the revolution." Like Fidel, he marked a line between the "pure revolutionaries" and the "pseudorevolutionaries." The truth was, he had never liked the men he was describing. And they did not like him.

This effort by Fidel and Che was not merely to identify differences between the 26th of July Movement and the SNFE, but to retroactively erase traces of the SNFE from Revolutionary history. By denouncing the character of these men, they avoided an ideological confrontation. "Pseudorevolutionary" is not an ideological category, after all. It signifies someone false and weak in character.

Morgan's court trial was held five months after his arrest and fell during a particularly tense time. On the last day of February 1961, a bomb exploded in a private girls' school in Havana. One girl lost an eye and nine others suffered lesser injuries. *Revolución* blared, "Criminal hands, at the service of Yankee imperialism, provoke a tragic toll of more than nine injured." A headline reported, "The people reject all attacks by the mercenaries." In response to the bombing, crowds gathered wielding signs that called for peace, executions of the guilty, and an end to imperialist—meaning U.S.-sponsored or -endorsed—attacks. A day later, the incident would be blamed on Falangist priests, suggesting that the terrorists were supported by both the Fascist Spanish dictator, Francisco Franco, and the United States. Anti-American rhetoric was reaching fever pitch as signs increased that the United States might act to remove Fidel Castro from power.

Fear of an invasion from the United States had been building for months. People were worried that the isolated bombings and the handfuls of counterrevolutionaries who'd been captured were only hints of what was to come. They were right. On March 3 *Revolución* published photographs of men in a jungle, dressed in camouflage, holding automatic weapons. The photographs had first appeared in the *Miami News* the day before and were said to reveal the activity in a secret camp in Guatemala where U.S. military advisers and C.I.A. officers were training Cuban exiles for a big operation. A Russian newspaper warned that Cuba should expect an invasion of at least fifteen thousand men.

Those training in Guatemala were mercenaries, freedom fighters, sore losers, or terrorists, depending on the point of view. Their sponsors were exiled Cubans in Miami and the CIA, both of whom were doing their best to create havoc, dissension, and fear while they anxiously awaited the day when Fidel might be toppled. Their moment was fast approaching.

In advance of this threat, Cuban soldiers and police continued combing the country for bandits. They didn't want the invaders to find any able sympathizers when they landed. They captured whole bands of counterrevolutionaries and came across stashes of arms, which appeared to have been airdropped by the CIA.

As pressure from the outside rolled like storm clouds across the narrow stretch of water that separated Miami and Cuba, the margin for dissent, past or present, under Castro diminished even further.

On March 9, 1961, Morgan and ten of his men were tried by a military tribunal. Olga Morgan, who had sought asylum in the Brazilian embassy, was tried in absentia, as her husband's accomplice. The trial began at 8:15 P.M. Morgan arrived first in the courtroom, followed by Jesús Carreras and then the others. The prosecuting attorney, Fernando Luís Flores Ibarra, announced that he sought the death penalty for Morgan and Carreras. He stated that "one day, during the month of September 1960, the accused William A. Morgan met in a room of his house with members of his personal escort, and told them sharply that he had decided to rebel against the Revolutionary Government and that he was sure that all of them would follow him, threatening that he would kill anyone who did not follow. All accepted. . . ." Following that meeting, Flores Ibarra (known to some people as *Charco de Sangre* — Puddle of Blood) continued, Morgan used vehicles provided by the government for use on the frog farm to transport arms to counterrevolutionaries in the mountains. In addition, strategic maps of the Escambray region were found in Morgan's house.

"These men are adventurers," he concluded, "who fought against the tyrant [Batista] not because they were [R]evolutionaries but because they aspired to his position and when they realized that the Revolution had no place for opportunists, they betrayed the Revolution, committing all the acts mentioned to promote an armed rebellion against the Revolutionary Government, to topple it and to establish a regime in the previous style that would permit them to satisfy their bastard ambitions."

Morgan's defense attorney was Jorge Luís Carro. Not until they appeared in the courtroom did either Carro or Morgan know the charges that were being leveled against Morgan. There was no time to contact any witnesses.

Ramirito walked in and someone said to him, "We don't want any Mau-Mau defending these people," meaning that no Revolutionaries were to offer any support of the defendants. When Morgan saw Ramirito, he gave his friend a big smile and a wink. Morgan and Carreras were completely calm throughout the trial, Ramirito remembers.

Morgan denied all charges, saying that he had always supported the Revolution. "I stand here innocent," he said, "and I guarantee this court that if I am found guilty I will walk to the execution wall with no escort, with moral strength, and with a clear conscience."

All ten defendants were found guilty of conspiracy and treason. Morgan and Jesús Carreras were sentenced to death by firing squad, and the others, including Morgan's twenty-three-year-old wife, were condemned to thirty years in prison.

Morgan's request for an appeal was not granted. He then asked to speak with three people: his mother, his wife, and Fidel Castro. Once again his requests were denied. Finally, he asked to be executed immediately. That request was granted.

EXECUTION

Ya ves que es una tristeza sin final, un paraíso que no termina. No cambio uno de estos días por toda mi vida anterior.

Now you see that it is a sadness without conclusion, a paradise that doesn't end. I wouldn't change one of those days for all my life that came before.

Cuban poet Rafael Alcides Pérez,
from his 1970 poem "Temporal"

After the trial, Jorge Carro's wife, Edy, called Morgan's mother in Toledo to tell her that her son would be executed. Loretta Morgan had occasionally communicated with Morgan during his months in jail, but she'd been unable to reach him for several days. She fainted when she heard the news. Once she revived, she acted without delay. From Toledo she contacted the FBI's Cleveland office and sent a telegram to the U.S. State Department informing it of her son's imminent death, imploring it to help.

In the FBI's Washington office, Special Agent Kenneth Haser received word of Loretta Morgan's telegram. He contacted Robert Johnson, general counsel in the Passport Office of the State Department. The Passport Office and Morgan had had a history since his U.S. citizenship was revoked in 1959. Johnson informed Haser that because the "subject had expatriated himself," no formal action could be taken by the department.

Unwilling to let the matter rest, Haser looked for an alternative avenue by which to make an appeal. The United States maintained a diplomatic channel with Cuba through the Swiss Embassy. Loretta Morgan's appeal was sent there with a note of introduction from the State Department that stated, ". . . while we [the U.S. government] have no legal responsibility [for William Morgan] we have humanitarian concern."

On March 11 Robert Williams, a leader of the National Association for the Advancement of Colored People (NAACP) in North Carolina and a member of the Fair Play for Cuba Committee (FPCC), sent a telegram to Fidel Castro on behalf of the FPCC requesting that he commute Morgan's death sentence to a prison term. Williams, as a member of the FPCC, which worked to promote the positive aspects of the Cuban Revolution in the United States and to shift the policy on Cuba, was worried that Morgan's execution would make the job of the FPCC—namely, to improve Cuba's image in the minds of the American people—harder.

≡Morgan and Jesús Carreras were to be executed on what was the last day of carnival. Revelers came out to celebrate, whirling late into the night down the raised marble boulevard toward the sea and along the Malecón. The torches of the revelers flashed in the water between the long seawall and the old fort. Dancers thrust and spun and drank warm rum. The rhythms of the drumming and the ecstatic whoops carried across the narrow entrance to Havana Harbor, where William Morgan could hear them.

Martin Houseman, writing for United Press International, quoted an "official observer" who saw Morgan's last moments:

Just before 10 P.M. he was led into the grassy moat of La Cabaña. Floodlights bathed the bullet-pocked wall for the army marksmen holding high-powered Belgian rifles. The sounds of Havana's Saturday night carnival could be heard drifting over the walls of La Cabaña. The cheers of other prisoners were in Morgan's ears as he walked from the cell block, into the moat and to the wall. Morgan, who received spiritual succor and the last rights of the Roman Catholic Church from two priests, embraced the captain of the firing squad who approached him. To the end, he swore allegiance to the Castro regime which accused him of feeding supplies to anti-Castro rebels in the Escambray Mountains. He maintained innocence to the end. As he awaited the firing squad Saturday night, his words to Attorney Carro were:

"I am a believing Catholic and not afraid. Now I'll find what's on the other side." "He died with extraordinary valor," said the official witness.

Observers predict Morgan's execution will backfire and that, dead, he will become a symbol of martyrdom for the rebels in the Escambray Mountains—whom he steadfastly denied ever helping.

≡ By the time the "personal appeal" from Morgan's mother was forwarded via the Swiss Embassy to the Cuban government, William Morgan had been shot. It wouldn't have mattered. Morgan had lived like the point of land he died on, jutting away from the mainland toward powerful and dangerous forces.

William Morgan, a little man in his hometown, a failure in the U.S. Army, a lousy janitor at the Rosary Cathedral in

Toledo, a poor example as a father, and for a brief moment a big man, a good husband and father, an innovative business-man, and a success and a hero in Cuba, was dead. He ended his life in a way that those who knew him and those who had fol-lowed his time in Cuba would always remember. He marched and whistled to his date with the firing squad and showed no regret, accepting what awaited him with courage. No matter who tells his story, in Cuba or in the United States, against him or with him, it ends with courage.

He and Jesús Carreras were buried together in an unmarked, traitors' grave in Havana's beautiful Cementario Colón.

There's a version of Morgan's last moments that one will hear told in hushed tones by old Rebels in both Cuba and Mi-ami. As a comandante, he outranked the men who would shoot him and so was allowed to command the firing squad himself. After his embrace of the squad captain, he asked for a final cig-arette. Shoot me, he told them, when I toss away the cigarette. One can imagine that final flick of thumb and middle finger, the arc of that butt, a small, hot fire burning out.

Epilogue

I have noticed that when a man dies, no matter at what age or by what cause, his life then has a beginning and a middle and an end, and sometimes his death explains his youth.

Shelby Foote, historian

Morgan's life had a long, searching beginning, an extraordinary middle, and a quick and violent end. Throughout the three acts of his life, he has struck me as completely, incorrigibly human; he led with his heart and with his dreams, and sometimes these carried him into dark and frightening corners of the human experience. But always, when he was presented with choices, right or wrong, he made them. He was a man of action. And yet he always remained the boy who "wanted to be accepted" by his schoolmates.

Over the time I have lived with Morgan inside my head, the aspect of his character that perhaps has touched me most deeply is his constant yearning to be part of something significant, to do things that would give his life meaning. He fought, he wrote, "to once and for all . . . be sure that men will never again have to fight and die to be free." Morgan was not a humble man; he was not cut out to wear a gray suit, to carry a briefcase, to measure out his life with coffee spoons. Rather, Morgan dared to eat a peach, or a guava or a papaya or a piece of boiled malanga. By daring to choose something difficult, by daring to hurt the people he left behind in Toledo and the people he came to call enemies, Morgan gave an extra dose of meaning to the lives of others, to Olga, to Menoyo, to Ramirito, to Redondo, even to Fidel Castro and Raúl Nieves.

By following Morgan's story and the history of the Second National Front of the Escambray, I found myself in the murky, in-between world of the Cuban Revolution, where the questions are painfully fresh and the answers given are often not completely true or clear. Was there one thing that made Morgan decide to go to Cuba? Who was responsible for the *La Coubre* disaster? Could the Cuban Revolution have turned out differently? Why didn't Fidel Castro just throw Morgan in jail and leave him there for twenty or thirty years as he would later do with Menoyo and so many others? After all, the American hadn't actually killed any of the loyal Revolutionaries; he had only threatened and plotted.

Many of the former members of the Second National Front of the Escambray have wondered why Morgan was executed. He had no blood on his hands. Menoyo, for example, returned to Cuba near the end of 1964 with four other men and the intention of starting a counterrevolution. One of the four was a Cuban intelligence officer. After forty-five days, Menoyo was apprehended. He spent twenty-two years in a Cuban prison before the Spanish government convinced Fidel to set him free. Ramirito, who stayed in Cuba, ended up spending thirteen years in prison for organizing in rather unspecified ways against the government.

Though he doesn't seem to recall the details today, Max Lesnik offered a theory about Morgan's demise to FBI agents who interviewed him in the INS Detention Center in McAllen, Texas, in 1961. During the first three months of that year, Castro and Trujillo began to normalize the relationship between their two countries. Fidel Castro, said Lesnik, wanted two things from the Dominican Republic: He wanted Trujillo to return the Rebel Delio Gómez Ochoa, who'd been in a Dominican prison since the disastrous invasion in 1959; and he wanted to buy rice cheaply. Trujillo wanted one thing in return: He wanted William Morgan dead. Gómez Ochoa returned to Cuba. Cuba got rice. Morgan was executed.

According to CIA sources, Trujillo sold Cuba one million bags of rice at four cents a pound, one quarter of the going rate for rice in the Dominican Republic. A CIA document dated May 11, 1961, reported such a sale and went on to state: "Trujillo made an arrangement with Castro whereby Castro would execute Major William Morgan on trumped up charges, and Trujillo would deliver Captain Delio Gómez Ochoa to Castro. Gómez was captured along with other Cubans and pro-Castro Dominican exiles who attempted to invade the Dominican Republic at Constanza in June 1959. Apparently the bargain was kept: Morgan was executed a short time ago, and Gómez has been released from prison." It's unclear whether the CIA's source was the FBI report generated by the interview with Lesnik or an independent source.

It could also be that Morgan truly posed too great a risk to Castro's government. Should Morgan escape and make his way into the mountains . . . It was better to eliminate the possibility entirely, as far as Fidel and his fellow Revolutionaries were concerned.

On April 16, 1961, just one month after Morgan was executed, Fidel Castro, for the first time, defined the Cuban

Revolution as socialist. Two days later, on April 17, 1961, Cuban exiles clambered onto Playa Girón—Giron Beach—and were killed by the Cuban Revolutionary Army when President Kennedy refused to supply U.S. military air cover. This is the battle Americans call the Bay of Pigs. No organized counterrevolutionary force inside Cuba rose up to support the exile force.

Morgan's comrades Menoyo, Lesnik, Fleites, and the others who had left by boat in January heard about the Bay of Pigs from inside an INS detention center in McAllen, Texas. When their boat landed in the Florida Keys, Cubans in Miami—Batistianos, who couldn't believe Castro was still in power—called the men Communists. From Havana, Fidel declared that they were CIA agents. They were men without a country, men in limbo between the Scylla and Charybdis of the political Left and the Right. The U.S. government, unsure of who they were or what to do with them, shipped them to Texas, where they spent six months in the immigration holding pen.

After they had been in McAllen for more than a month, a government official visited Menoyo to ask if the comandante and his men would be interested in participating in a significant action against Castro. Menoyo declined. He wanted nothing to do with the Batistianos, who were hell-bent on retrieving their illegitimate power, and he predicted with uncanny accuracy that the operation would be defeated within seventy-two hours.

Despite this, Morgan's influence and the influence of the SNFE lasted well beyond the American Rebel's death. Max Lesnik later said, "We told Morgan he might be infiltrated by Castro's spies—and he was. He was operating against Castro in the same manner as against Batista. He was the mastermind of the uprising in the Escambray Mountains before the Bay of Pigs, something he has never received credit for. All the Escambray rebels were in some way connected with him."

When I toured the Escambray in 2002, my guide told me that people had moved out of those mountains following the Revolution. He didn't explain why. The Escambray was the most problematic region for Castro's government and continued to be so for years after Morgan's death. Despite the massive sweep that Castro organized in 1960, counterrevolutionary guerrillas ran throughout the hills until 1965. At least two hundred of them were killed in battles with the Cuban Revolutionary Army. Even more dramatic, however, between 1961 and 1964, nearly eight thousand people were forcibly "re populated" from the Escambray region of Las Villas Province to towns in Pinar del Río, at the western tip of the island. The government moved these people—exiles within their own country—into apartment buildings far from the land they knew—and away from the counterrevolutionaries they had supported in the Escambray.

Raúl Castro said of that time, "After we got rid of Batista, we had to win a civil war." This statement has been hidden from the Cuban public, locked up in Communist Party archives. Fidel and his Communist-style government have always claimed that they represent "the people." That is, *all* the Cuban people, not merely a single political party. Therefore, such active and widespread dissent from within (dissent that would qualify as a *civil war*, as was found in the Escambray) challenges the government's self-justification.

A museum in Trinidad preserves the memory of the period when these counterrevolutionaries were wiped from the hills. It is called the Museum of the Fight Against the Bandits, but not a single "bandit" is represented in the exhibit. Only those are portrayed who defended the Revolution against the counterrevolutionaries, heroes who defeated a few vicious agents of the imperialists set on stealing the Revolution away from the people.

▤ Curiously, Olga Fariñas Morgan ended up in Toledo, Ohio. Charged with being her husband's accomplice, she spent years in a Cuban prison. Later she lived with nuns in a convent in Havana. She was at last allowed to leave Cuba with the Mariel boatlift in 1980. She met and married a man in Morgan's hometown, where she advocates for the restoration of Morgan's U.S. citizenship and the return of his remains to the United States. William and Olga's daughters also live in the United States.

The U.S. government has shied away from Morgan's case. To date, it has not granted Olga her wish, though officials continue to say that they are reviewing the possibility of restoring Morgan's citizenship. The matter is complicated. The economic embargo that President Eisenhower set in place in 1960 is still in effect; in fact, it's much more comprehensive today than it was in 1960. The policy has not been effective, in that the goal is to remove Castro from power. Nor has it inspired Castro to change his internal policies. Yet the policy remains, due, it seems, to inertia, confusion, a desire on the part of the government to curry favor with the Cubans in south Florida, and ongoing uncertainty among foreign-policy makers about how to deal with leftist leaders.

Very little exists in the government's public record regarding Morgan. However, in March of 1962, an American woman by the name of Viola June Cobb, who'd worked for Fidel Castro in 1959 and 1960, was interviewed by a Senate Internal Security

Subcommittee. The Subcommittee's counsel, Jay Sourwine, asked her the questions.

Mr. Sourwine: Did you know William Morgan, an American on Castro's staff?

Miss Cobb: Very well, yes.

Mr. Sourwine: What can you tell us about him?

Miss Cobb: Oh, that he was a very loyal American in my opinion, that he was a boy with ideals. He had a tremendous desire to be helpful. The last time I saw him he was very happy with the progress of that little industry he had organized, using frogskins for pocketbooks and shoes and so forth, and frog meat for export, because there were a couple thousand very wretched campesinos employed—the ones I had seen in rags and barefoot now were wearing shoes and stockings, looking decent. He had even planted flower gardens around the buildings.

Mr. Sourwine: When was this?

Miss Cobb: This was about a month before he was arrested. In other words, he was delighted because he was doing something constructive. On the other hand, he was very proud of his role as being one of the few Americans who were trying to help in what he considered a good cause. And third, he had the idea that he was standing by and that when Fidel finally realized that the Communists were taking over—then he would blow the whistle and William Morgan and Gutierrez Menoya [*sic*] and some of the others would help him rescue the country from a Communist takeover. . . . I know his sentiments.

Mr. Sourwine: You think he was vigorously anti-Communist throughout?

Ms. Cobb: Vigorously. Sincerely.

Mr. Sourwine: Perhaps this is what cost him . . .

Ms. Cobb: This is absolutely what cost him. It could either have cost him because he was actually conspiring, or it could have cost him because just because they knew it so well. Whether he conspired or not, they wanted to get rid of him. I think he was not conspiring. He was standing by, doing a good job, and waiting.

Author's Note: In April 2007, as this book was going to press, the U.S. State Department restored William Morgan's citizenship, stating in a letter: "We cannot sustain the finding of loss of nationality in this case. Mr. Morgan shall be deemd never to have relinquished his U.S. nationality."

▤After he was released from Cuban prison in 1986, Eloy Gutiérrez Menoyo went to Spain. A couple of years later he moved to Miami and started a small nonprofit organization called Cambio Cubano—Cuban Change—which campaigns for nonviolent change in Cuba through negotiations with the Cuban government. This is a radical idea in Miami, where many Cubans say they will never go back to their native island until "the bearded one" is in his grave.

Menoyo and his organization have a simple political agenda advocating basic freedoms for Cubans and programs for economic opportunity that they think would put an end to poverty on the island. His basic ideas and principles haven't changed much over the years. His politics are probably what Morgan's would have been had he lived to keep working for the people of the Escambray.

In August 2003 the sixty-nine-year-old Menoyo moved back to Cuba to breathe life into the decimated dissident movement there. In its World Briefing section, the *New York Times* published a short paragraph about Menoyo on August 8, 2003:

Cuba—Exile Figure Says He's Returned

Eloy Gutierrez Menoyo, a revolutionary comrade of Fidel Castro who later fought against him, endured a 22-year prison sentence and has been living in exile in Miami since the 1980's, announced that he was settling in Cuba to join the island's beleaguered dissident movement. . . . The Cuban government has allowed him to visit in recent years, and it was during his current trip that he decided to remain while his family returned to Florida.

I believe that the minute Menoyo arrived in Cuba, he became one of the most important people in the country. A Cuban official admitted to me that he is "legitimate in the eyes of the Cuban people." Legitimate in this case means that he fought against Batista and risked his life for Cuba (ironically, this is the same thing the spy Cecilio Castro said when he described the danger presented to the Revolution by William Morgan). The Cuban people don't see Menoyo as a supporter of the pre-Castro regime. He fought for the people but not for Communism. Now he is once again making a play for the future, for a chance to be a leader in a post-Castro era.

Fidel Castro's health is deteriorating. Forces inside and outside the Cuban government are positioning themselves for what may come next. Jorge Dominguez, the Cuban scholar and Harvard professor, wrote in a *New York Times* op-ed that "the battle between succession and transition is the key to Cuba's politics." The Cuban government has been putting a succession plan in place since the spring of 2002. Raúl Castro, Fidel's brother and a hugely unpopular choice for Cubans, has been named Fidel's successor. Even less appealing than Raúl is a government-in-waiting, made up of reactionary Cubans from Miami and backed by the current U.S. administration, that sits in Puerto Rico awaiting the slightest chance to assert itself.

Menoyo has calculated that now is the time to show the Cuban people that a third choice may exist. At a time when the Cuban government was jailing and silencing dissidents, Menoyo made a bold, strategic move. Today he is in a far better position than most to gain the trust of the Cubans who are ready for a new government and terrified of what might come from Miami.

≣ Max Lesnik also favors a different relationship between Cuba and the United States. Whereas Menoyo focuses on change in Cuba, Max targets U.S. policy toward Cuba. For his work, Lesnik, who has lived in the United States since 1961, has been called both "anti-American" and an "agent of Fidel Castro."

Like Cubans on every side of the debate, Max Lesnik, Eloy Gutiérrez Menoyo, and Olga Morgan have been unable to let go of their cause. They keep fighting, day by day, for their particular Cuban dream.

≣ Eloy Gutiérrez Menoyo and Ramiro Lorenzo were reunited in Miami. Now that Menoyo is back in Cuba, the two talk regularly by phone. Ramiro lives in a comfortable house in a tidy Miami suburb; his wife is a nurse. His daughters grew up in the United States, attended college there, and have good jobs. He's proud of them. His house is full of dogs, cats, and birds. The animals give Ramiro comfort and a respite from human complexity when the memories become too much to take.

Ramiro is frail. His vision is weak and he walks with an unsteady and slightly erratic gait. His memory, however, is excellent. Talking about the time in the mountains is emotional, and when I interviewed him, we needed to take breaks. During the breaks, he would smoke and together we would drink shots of syrupy Cuban-style coffee. During my second visit to his home, I decided to read him the letter that Morgan wrote to Herbert Matthews from the Escambray shortly after he had arrived. I was translating from the English when suddenly I noticed that Ramiro's eyes had filled with tears. I looked at Ramiro's wife, who was sitting at the table with us. "He was the boy with the broken foot. Morgan saved his life." I almost fell off my chair. The letter that I had found in the Herbert Matthews Collection at Columbia University and had been carrying around for three years suddenly took on a life beyond what I had ever imagined.

The love Menoyo and Ramiro feel for William Morgan is as absolute and tangible as is the confusion and discomfort of Morgan's high-school classmates in Toledo.

Ramiro is fascinated by Cuba's history. He reads everything he can get his hands on. Like so many of the men of the Second Front, he wants to know the truth. What happened and why? Getting an answer to these questions is often impossible. When the world seems too much, Ramiro picks up his little dog and says in a serious voice, but with an ironic twinkle in his eye, "*Humanos malos. Animales buenos.* —Humans bad. Animals good."

There are times when that simplicity, in the face of so much that is unknowable, so much gray, so much conflict, offers some relief.

≡ Before he died, William Morgan wrote a letter to his daughter Anne. He gave the letter to his lawyer, Jorge Luís Carro, who made sure it was delivered to Toledo. It is handwritten in a penmanship that has become familiar to me after reading

Morgan's signature on the official documents of the Second National Front of the Escambray. In the letter he tries his best to explain himself to his young, American daughter. It was not easy for him to justify the choices he made. It's not easy for anyone, which is why each of us, in his or her own way, keeps trying, and it is why I wrote this book.

Dear Anne—

When I saw you last you were just a little tyke who was into everything all of the time. You used to sit at the window and when you saw my car drive in you would say—Daddy—Daddy—I think those are the first words you spoke.

And I know when I did not come home anymore, I know you missed me and looked out the window for your Dad. This was a long time ago baby. And possibly you don't remember but I do and always will. You are going to grow up to be a beautiful girl with a fine disposition. Stick close to your Mom, I don't think you can find anyone better. When the time comes for you to get married and have a family of your own, pick a good man Baby, one with his head high but both feet on the ground. And if your future husband wants to see the world or dream of castles in the sky—let him see the world, Baby, by himself. Possibly you may never see this letter. But if you do, remember your Dad was one of those people who saw the world and it's very hard for those who love such a man. I may not be alive when you read this Anne, but wherever I am I will be watching you and Billy and your mother and always wishing and praying for the best for you.

Your loving Dad,
William Morgan

Acknowledgments

There are more people to thank than is possible here. And there are some whom, for their safety, I will not acknowledge. There are people in Cuba and Miami who risked social ostracism or even political persecution for the sake of a more complete history, for the sake of the truth.

To all my friends in Cuba, thank you for your patience and your tolerance of a nosy American whose curiosity drew attention, not only to me, but to you. Thank you also to certain members and former members of the Cuban government who offered assistance even if it meant risking employment and hard-won privilege.

When I began this project, I found help in a place I did not expect. Just twenty miles away from the house where I grew up in Maine, I discovered Sherry Sullivan, who has worked tirelessly to unravel the mystery of what happened to her father. Geoffrey Sullivan flew covert missions over Cuba in the early 1960s, and on one of these flights, the plane he was flying disappeared along with Geoffrey and his passengers. Sherry opened her files to me, representing two decades of work to push the U.S. government to acknowledge its connection to her father and his fate. I'm happy to say that I was able to attend the ceremony where Sherry's father was recognized by a military color guard as a soldier of the Cold War. It was tacit acknowledgment that he had been working for the CIA.

Sherry started an organization called Forgotten Families of the Cold War, and through this organization I met Christy Hughes Cox, whose restless, searching mind kept me on my toes as she tries to solve the puzzle of her father's disappearance in or around Cuba in the early 1960s. Through Sherry and Christy, I met Howard K. Davis. Davis, like my subject, William Morgan, was a young American who was first a supporter of Fidel Castro and then turned against the young Cuban leader. Based in southern Florida, he spent years participating in efforts to unseat Castro.

Bernard Diederich, journalist, writer, entrepreneur, adventurer, raconteur, and friend of Graham Greene, inspired me in more ways than I can say. Diederich founded the *Haitian Sun* newspaper in 1950 and ran the English-language daily out of Port au Prince until 1963. He has lived a life of purpose and adventure that, quite frankly, turns me green with envy. Through the maze of politics and innuendo, Diederich helped me keep my eye on the essential story, believing that William Morgan's history could be told, that it should not slip away like sand through fingers because the complete truth was unknowable.

Diederich introduced me to Eloy Gutiérrez Menoyo, who invited me into his home and took the time to answer all my questions, however naïve or uninformed. He provided the scaffolding of events and analysis—as well as many wonderful anecdotes—around which I began to understand Morgan's time in Cuba. Eloy was a breath of fresh air as he told me his experiences as directly and honestly as he knew how.

Through Eloy I met Max Lesnik, Roger Redondo, Ramiro

Lorenzo, Bibe, and Miguelito, all in Miami, each of whom spent hours with me because they are committed to a more inclusive history of the Cuban Revolution, one that will include their stories and the history of the Second National Front of the Escambray. Ramiro has generously donated many of the photographs published in the book. Thank you also to César Fuentes, who talked to me at length about what it was like to be imprisoned in La Cabaña fortress.

Early on, Enrique Encinosa corroborated my feeling that Morgan's story was important, telling me that Morgan had been "like a rock star" in Cuba.

Thank you to Señora Lesvia Varona at the Cuban Heritage Collection at the University of Miami and to Holly Ackerman for guiding me to resources and encouraging my work. Sra. Varona worries with me about all the stories from the Cuban Revolution that are being lost, that need to be recorded and told.

Without the help of Jean and Bob Kreuze, Geri and Bob Brandon, and Jack O'Connell, I would have had little sense of Morgan's youth. These Toledans helped me to understand their city, their middle- to upper-middle-class Catholic milieu, and the complicated boy they knew as Billy.

Thank you to Edite Kroll, my rock-solid agent, who believed in me and the book and helped me make it better. My editor, Andra Olenik, has taught me the value of careful editing. From the beginning, the bad-boy Morgan appealed to her as he appealed to me, and she gave me the time, space, advice, and masterful comments that helped me make this book as good as I was capable of making it.

My friends and family gave me support and encouragement of all kinds as I left a stable job in New York to become an itinerant researcher, chasing down a story that I decided was important. I really cannot say enough. This book is as much theirs as it is mine. Among these are my incomparable friends, Sarah MacArthur, Jamie Rosen, and Oisin Curran, my trusted reader, who came with me to Cuba in support of my quest for Morgan. Over Cuban cigarettes and rum, we plotted the investigative approach. Julie Pecheur loaned me valuable materials that she had collected. Bill and Luz MacArthur and Daniela Kuper offered me their houses when I needed a place to live for months at a time. Jay, Mary, Daisy, and Katie Shetterly put me up whenever I was getting on or off a plane in Boston, listened to my stories, and asked great questions. The Reverand Colin Leitch spent hours hashing through ideas and theories about Cuban politics and the Cuban psyche.

My sister, Caitlin, inspires me with the important work she does, work that she dedicates to making the world a better, more understandable place. My father, Robert, and his partner, Gail, supported me tirelessly and constantly in my pursuit of Morgan's story, picking me up whenever my energy flagged, feeding me when I was hungry, and giving me shelter when I needed it. My mother, Susan, taught me all I know about writing and always reminds me that the important thing is to tell as true a story as I am able. I have far to go before I can match her skill.

Margot Lee Shetterly came into my life after I had begun this project. She embraced me and it together, and so doing, made my life better.

Bibliography

_____ INTERVIEWS WITH THE AUTHOR _____

Miami, Florida

Diederich, Bernard. December 2001.
Encinosa, Enrique. December 2001, via telephone conversation.
Fuentes, Cesár. 2004–05.
Gutiérrez Menoyo, Eloy. December 2001.
Gutiérrez, Orlando. December 2001.
Llado, Avelino. December 2001.
Lesnik, Max. 2004–05.
Lorenzo, Ramiro. 2004-05.
Miguelito de Camajuani. 2004–05.
Redondo, Roger. July 2004.
Sargent, Andrés Nosario. December 2001.
Vázquez Robles, Felix Rafael "Bibe." April 2005.
Winslow, Gordon. November 2001, via telephone.

Toledo, Ohio

Goodwin, Olga (Morgan). January 2002.
Harpen, John. December 14, 2001.
Kreuz, Jean, Bob Kreuz, Jack O'Connell, Geri Brandon, Bob Brandon.
    December 15, 2001.
Quinn, Cliff. December 14, 2001.
Sister Joachim. December 14, 2001.
Smith, Msgr. Bernard. December 14, 2001.

Cuba

Agee, Philip. Havana, May 2002.
Blanquita. Santa Clara, July 2002.
Bordón, Victor. Havana, August 2002.
Calero Mesa, Olga. Havana, June 2002.
Castro, Cecilio. Havana, August 2002.
Dreke, Victor. Havana, July 2002.
Farah, Levi. Havana, May 2002.
Fariñas, Lazaro. Santa Clara, June 2002.
García Marel, Gladys. Havana, June–August 2002.
González, Esteban. Cumanayagua, June 2002.
Machín, Ernesto. Cumanayagua, June 2002.
Nieves Mestre, Raúl. Havana, August 2002.
Rivera, Manuel. Trinidad, May 2002.
Soler, David. Cienfuegos, June 2002.
Tomás, Pedro, Gironda Muñoz Cruz, Jorge Livano Hernández,
    Gardenia Patiño Vasallo, Jorge Bolfe Rosado, José Cueto Sala,
    Manuel Matienzo Abuela. Cienfuegos, August 2002.

Other

Carro, Edie. Cincinnati, Ohio, January 2002, via telephone.
Hemming, G. Patrick. Wilmington, North Carolina, January 2002, via
    telephone.
Mallin, Jay. Washington, D.C., January 2002, via telephone.
Sullivan, Sherry. Stockton Springs, Maine, September 2001–present, via
    telephone.
Lesar, Jim. Washington, D.C., December 2001, via telephone.
Rynn, Jim. Boulder, Colorado, April 2003, via telephone.

PERIODICALS

Cuban

Bohemia (1958–1961).
La Correspondencia (1958–1961).
Hoy (1959–1961).
Liberación (1959–1961).
El Mundo (1959–1961).
Revolución (1959–1961).

Báez, Luis. "John Mac Meckples Spiritto: Nuestro hombre en La Ha-
bana." *Juventud Rebelde* (June 9, 2002): 6–7.
Velázquez, José Sergio. "Llevado W. Morgan a juicio: Para el y Jesús
Carreras piden pena de muerte." *El Mundo* (March 10, 1961): 1.

United States:

The Miami Herald, (1957–1963).
The Miami Times, (1958–1961).
The New York Times, (1957–1963).
The Toledo Blade, (1958–1963).

"Alexander Morgan: Former Edison Budget Director." *The Toledo Blade*
(June 12, 1965): 7, 18.
"Henry's Plot." *Time* (August 24, 1959): 29–30.
"Improbable Frogman." *Time* (May 30, 1960): 24.
"Loretta Morgan." *The Toledo Blade* (December 2, 1988).
"Plot, Plotters, 'Peacemakers.'" *Newsweek* (August 24, 1959): 42, 47.
"The Quiet Man." *Newsweek* (March 4, 1957): 75–76.
Armbrister, Trevor. "Olga's Dream." *Reader's Digest* (December 1981):
137–140.
Bergquist, Laura. "Epitaph for a Big Loser." *Look* (April 1961): 91–94.
Brinkley-Rogers, Paul. "America's Yanqui Fidelistas." *The Miami Herald*
(January 10, 1999).

ARCHIVES

Private Papers and Archives

Clete Roberts Collection. Executor: Peggy Roberts Macdonald, daugh-
ter. Interview with William Morgan, August or September 1959.
Herbert Matthews Collection. Archives. Columbia University. When
Matthews died in 1977, he left his papers to Columbia University.

Official Papers

"The Current Communist Threat: A Statement by J. Edgar Hoover."
Subcommittee to Investigate the Administration of the Internal
Security Act and Other Internal Security Laws of the Committee on
the Judiciary, United States Senate. Washington, D.C.: U.S. Government Printing Office, 1962.

National Archives and Records Administration, Washington, D.C. JFK
Assassination Archives. This archive includes about 1,000 pages of
FBI, CIA, State Department, and military intelligence files relating
to William Morgan.
"Testimony of Viola June Cobb." Hearing Before the Subcommittee to
Investigate the Administration of the Internal Security Laws of the
Committee on the Judiciary, United States Senate, Eighty-Ninth
Congress, Second Session, March 30, 1962. Washington, D.C.: U.S.
Government Printing Office, 1966.

BOOKS

Abella, Alex. *The Great American*. New York: Simon & Schuster, 1997.
Agee, Philip. *Inside the Company: CIA Diary*. New York: Farrar, Straus &
Giroux, 1975.
Album de la revolución cubana: 1952–1959. La Habana: Revista Cine-
grafico, 1959.
Arevalo, Juan José. *The Shark and the Sardines*. New York: Lyle Stuart,
1961.
Ayers, Bradley Earl. *The War That Never Was: An Insider's Account of
CIA Covert Operations Against Cuba*. New York: The Bobbs-Merrill
Company, Inc., 1976.
Baker, Christopher P. *Cuba*. Emeryville, CA: Avalon Travel Publishing,
2000.
Beruvides, Esteban M. *Cuba: Anuario historico* 1958, 1959, 1960, 1961,
1962. Miami: Colonial Press International, Inc, 1995–1998.
Castañeda, Jorge G. *Compañero: The Life and Death of Che Guevara*. New
York: Alfred A. Knopf, 1997.
Central Catholic High School "Fighting Irish" Year Book (Toledo),
1943: 44, 58.
Del Aguila, Juan M. *Cuba: Dilemmas of a Revolution*. Boulder, CO: West-
view Press, 1994.
Diederich, Bernard. *Trujillo: The Death of the Dictator*. Princeton: Markus
Wiener Publishers, 2000.
Dreke, Victor. *De la sierra del Escambray al Congo*. New York: Pathfinder,
2002.
Encinosa, Enrique. *Cuba en guerra*. Miami: Endowment for Cuban
American Studies, 1994.
Escalante, Fabian. *The Secret War: CIA Covert Operations Against Cuba
1959–1962*. New York: Ocean Press, 1995.

Fernández, Juan Carlos. *Todo es secreto hasta un dia.* La Habana: Editorial de Ciencias Sociales, 1979.

Franklin, Jane. *Cuba and the United States: A Chronological History.* New York: Ocean Press, 1999.

Furiati, Claudia. *ZR Rifle: The Plot to Kill Kennedy and Castro.* New York: Ocean Press, 1994.

García González, Ivette. *La Habana: Tiempo de conflictos.* La Habana: Ediciones Verde Olivo, 1998.

Gimbel, Wendy. *Havana Dreams: A Story of Cuba.* London: Virago, 1999.

Gómez Ochoa, Delio. *La victoria de los caidos.* Santo Domingo: Editora Alfa y Omega, 1998.

González de Cascorro, Raúl. *Aqui se habla de combatientes y de bandidos.* La Habana: Casa de las Americas, 1975.

Greene, Graham. *Our Man in Havana.* New York: Penguin Books, 1971.

Guevara, Che. *Guerrilla Warfare,* 3d ed, Wilmington, DE: Scholarly Resources, Inc., 1997.

Guevara, Che. *Reminiscences of the Cuban Revolutionary War.* New York: Monthly Review Press, 1968.

Gup, Ted. *The Book of Honor: The Secret Lives and Deaths of CIA Operatives.* New York: Anchor Books, 2001.

Harpen Wright, Mary Helen. *"S" Is for Susan.* Toledo: published by the Author, 1999.

Illman, Harry R. *Unholy Toledo.* San Francisco: Polemic Press Publications, 1985.

López-Fresquet, Rufo. *My Fourteen Months with Castro.* Cleveland: The World Publishing Co, 1966.

Mallin, Jay, and Robert K. Brown. *Merc: American Soldiers of Fortune.* New York: New American Library, 1980.

Martino, John, with Nathaniel Weyl. *I Was Castro's Prisoner.* New York: The Devin-Adair Company, 1963.

Matthews, Herbert. *Revolution in Cuba: An Essay in Understanding.* New York: Charles Scribner Sons, 1975.

——. *The Cuban Story.* New York: George Braziller Publishers, 1961.

Morán Arce, Lucas. *La revolución cubana: Una version rebelde.* Puerto Rico: printed by the author, 1980.

Navarro, Antonio. *Tocayo: A Cuban Resistance Leader's True Story.* Westport, CT: Sandown Books, 1981

Navarro, Osvaldo. *El caballo de Mayaguara.* La Habana: Editora Politica, 1990.

Orihuela, Roberto. *Nunca fui un traidor: Retrato de farsante.* La Habana: Editorial Capitán San Luis, 1991.

Perez-Stable, Marifeli. *The Cuban Revolution: Origins, Course, and Legacy.* New York: Oxford, 1994.

Porter, Tana Mosier. *Toledo Profile: A Sesquicentennial History.* Toledo: Toledo Sesquicentennial Commission, 1987.

Raffaele, Herbert, James Wiley, Orlando H. Garrido, Allan Keith, and Janis I. Raffaele. *A Guide to the Birds of the West Indies.* Princeton: Princeton University Press, 1998.

Rodríguez Cruz, Juan Carlos. *Hombres del Escambray.* La Habana: Editorial Capitán San Luis, 1990.

Rodríguez-Loeches, Enrique. *Bajando el Escambray.* La Habana: Union de Escritores y Artistas de Cuba, 1976.

Scott, Peter Dale. *Deep Politics and the Death of JFK.* Berkeley: University of California Press, 1996.

Sweig, Julia E. *Inside the Cuban Revolution.* Cambridge, MA: Harvard University Press, 2002.

Thomas, Hugh. *Cuba or the Pursuit of Freedom.* New York: Da Capo Press, 1998.

Valladares, Armando. *Against All Hope.* New York: Alfred A. Knopf, 1986.

White, E. B. "Homecoming," in *Essays of E. B. White.* New York: Harper & Row, 1977.